THE PRICE OF EXCELLENCE

THE PRICE OF EXCELLENCE

Universities in Conflict during the Cold War Era

Jacob Neusner
Noam M. M. Neusner

University Press of America,® Inc.
Dallas · Lanham · Boulder · New York · Oxford

Copyright © 1995 by
Jacob Neusner and Noam M. M. Neusner

Originally published by The Continuum Publishing Company
Reprinted by University Press of America,® Inc.
4501 Forbes Boulevard
Suite 200
Lanham, Maryland 20706
UPA Acquisitions Department (301) 459-3366

PO Box 317
Oxford
OX2 9RU, UK

Library of Congress Cataloging-in-Publication Data

Neusner, Jacob, 1932-
The price of excellence : universities in conflict during the
Cold War era/Jacob Neusner and Noam M. M. Neusner.
p.   cm.
Includes bibliographical references and index.
1. Higher education and state—United States.
2. Politics and education—United States. 3. Cold War.
I. Neusner, Noam M. M. (Noam Mordecai Menahem) II. Title.

LC173.N48 1995
379.73—dc20   95-16482 CIP

ISBN 0-7618-2733-1 (paperback : alk. ppr.)

⊖™ The paper used in this publication meets the minimum
requirements of American National Standard for Information
Sciences—Permanence of Paper for Printed Library Materials,
ANSI Z39.48—1984

CONTENTS

PREFACE

In our own day the academy in America has compromised the three principal freedoms that make critical learning possible: (1) freedom to appoint as a professor anyone whom the academy finds qualified to teach, (2) freedom to teach what the academy wants, (3) freedom to teach whomever the academy chooses as competent to learn. The political process now dictates these choices instructing universities on who enjoys preferential treatment in competition for professorships, what subjects will flourish, which ones will atrophy, and who may be admitted to study without regard to intellectual qualification in the competition for admission. These developments, abridging academic freedom in fundamental ways, attest to the entry of American colleges and universities into the political process. The Cold War enlisted the academy into national service and persuaded professors and students to turn the classroom and library into a political arena. No wonder then that, once admitted, politics never left. What was life like on the campus during the decades in which the academy entered the political process? Here we tell the story of great events and how they shaped one person's encounter with the American university world.

This is a book about two subjects. The first concerns how public policy in the Cold War dictated the answers to the five questions that universities and colleges, in order to do their work, must answer on their own terms and not in response to political intervention. These we represent in these five clauses, which form the mantra of this book: (1) who teaches (2) what (3) to whom, (4) how, and (5) why? When the academy mobilized for the Cold War, it not only accepted the political consensus but also joined the political process to change that consensus. That decision redefined the mission of universities and diverted them from their ancient vocation. When students rioted and faculties voted resolutions to tell the Government what to do or not do, learning languished in the competition with more exciting ventures.

The British say: Who takes the Queen's shilling becomes the Queen's man. We say: Who pays the piper calls the tune. No wonder then that, paid for by public funds and quasi-public funds through foundations, universities found themselves defined by forces other than those of rationality and intellect. Political considerations affected who would teach, what would be taught, and who would be granted admission and support to study. In entering the political arena, the universities, particularly those that claimed to lead and set the standard, lost sight of their unique mission, which is to nurture scholarship through research realized in both publication and engaged teaching. No other institution in society undertakes the tasks that universities carry out. Research institutes do not teach. Primary and secondary schools do not engage in original research or sift and criticize knowledge. Scholarship that takes the form of research and publication and also teaching finds its place only in the academy, and it is that unique mode of scholarship—joining learning to learner, veteran to beginner, personal communication in classroom dialogue to the medium of print and its analogues—that flourishes only in universities. So much for the precipitating topic that is addressed in these pages. It is a familiar subject, and by itself our treatment of it cannot lay a compelling claim for the reader's attention.

But what has happened to universities over four decades forms the setting for the second subject, which is particular to the senior writer of this book. That narrative takes up the academy in the Cold War in terms of how a specific career worked itself out in the times of expansion and contraction, high hope and deep frustration, and above all the disintegration of a once-firm consensus of purpose and calling, which all together mark the past four decades on campus. Although people may know that the Cold War made a profound impact on the academy, they may not fully grasp what that meant, for good and for ill, in a specific university career, one that is both exemplary and also quite particular. So we tell the story of how, in a time of change, when many new subjects and new disciplines were reshaping higher learning, that impact affected the life of a professor of a new subject in a new field—the study of Judaism within the study of religion.

The leitmotif of this story concerns how the senior author formed a vision of taking a special field of learning into the marketplace of free ideas, or, to shift the metaphor, to mainstream a backwater field. He grew up a Jew in an American society opening up to diversity, and he valued the learning of Judaism but wanted to share that learning with whomever it may concern—and did just that. In the process he found the university world restoring precisely what he worked to eliminate: the barriers to public and shared rationality that had been formed by origin, race, creed, color. This is not a book about a particularly Jewish subject as it made its way into the university, but about how the university dealt with difference over the decades of the Cold War—at first aiming to overcome it, later on preferring to underscore it. But through it all, this story of a career treats what is special as exemplary of what is general and accessible, a particular life on campus that tells what life was like on campus.

This is no jeremiad, and we do not look back in anger or in sorrow. Rather, we affirm the university and believe in its task and the way the academy goes about its work. So too, this is not an autobiography but more than a collection of episodes and anecdotes, the account of concrete experiences of a particular professor showing what the workaday campus was like when the academy went public—for good, but also for ill. This account also sets forth a viewpoint and a philosophy meant to influence the coming century of the American academy—although the details of that viewpoint and philosophy will be spelled out in a subsequent volume. The governing proposition is simple: the university faces a brilliant future in fulfilling its unique mission: joining scholarship in the form of research and publication to scholarship in the form of teaching to change minds, perhaps even conscience and character, through rigorous learning. Universities can do their job only through scholar-teachers, researchers who publish but also take to heart the intellectual development of those who come to study. Everyone else—researchers who do not teach, and teachers who do not pursue research and publish the results—belong somewhere else: the mere researchers in research institutes, the mere teachers in high school or community college, for instance.

But that deeply traditional and conservative position—which, if adopted, also would revolutionize campus life—while sometimes honored on ceremonial occasions, is not widely held. And scholar-teachers—a minority on any campus and especially on the elite campuses, which is particularly disturbing—face a difficult time in exercising the freedom to excel in their particular vocation. For some pursue research, and many teach without much concomitant work at learning, but only a few undertake to do both. And those who do pay for trying. The particular career in interesting times that is set forth in a few episodes here serves to highlight the university's loss of vocation. The exemplary stories we tell about specific events and actions serve to illustrate what it means when ancient institutions lose their way. This loss of vocation they suffered on several counts. First, they separated research from teaching, scholarship from the classroom. In doing so, the universities gave up their unique calling. Second, when they introduced a new commitment—to public policy—and laid claim on public support in unprecedented ways, universities transformed themselves into instruments of social amelioration. By substituting the practical enterprise of public policy for the intellectual tasks of independent thought and analysis, the elite colleges and universities abandoned the one task they alone could carry out in America's social order. That was not merely to transmit information, but to educate coming generations and to change their minds.

Why look back just now? The reason is that the Cold War, which carried the universities into the realm of public policy, has come to a successful conclusion. So we argue that universities ought to resume the task that they alone can realize, which is scholarship through the joined media of published research and effective teaching.

The joint authors of this book, son and father together, discern in the American academy the symptoms of a time of change. That is why we retrace the path that has led to the present impasse and outline the way that, we think, the universities should move ahead. We think that the history of the Cold War accounts for what has happened and is now taking place on the campus. But we discern in the past the sources of regeneration and foundations for hope. Our academic tradition draws from the German and the British—research from the one, teaching from the other. We have shaped a deeply native American amalgam: the teaching scholar, the publishing researcher who cares that students learn, the scholar who is an intellectual and wishes to learn from others beyond his area of specialization. These peculiarly American formulations of the academy and the character of the working professor have given our universities their many vital qualities. And they set the standard as well. So, we further maintain, the next century of the American university will find definition in the reunion of scholarship and teaching, the recovery of the rules of civil discourse and public rationality, and the representation of the curriculum as the occasion for solving urgent problems, that characterized, and today marks, our colleges and universities at their (alas! seldom-attained) best.

Two voices speak here, mostly in unison. The older of the two, the father (where necessary speaking through the "I" in what follows) walked that path, the younger, the son (the narrative voice throughout) peers over into the future that another generation will frame for itself. But here, the younger tells the story of whence we have come, and the older offers reflections on the future, the meaning and end of the academy. Working our way stage by stage in the formative past that now draws to a close, we lay out the path we think the academy should follow.

In practical terms the son tells the story of what has happened to the American university during the Cold War, 1946–89; the son also edited the whole. Then the father tells the story of what it was like to make a career and a living on the campus during those same years.

The son wrote the shank of the first four chapters; the father is the "I" at the start and finish of each chapter. But throughout we mean to speak in one voice. Working together, we hope we have captured how two generations of professors conducted the life of universities in concert with the larger issues of their age. We mean to place in perspective the current crisis in education and scholarship alike, marked by the failure of old ideals and the implausibility—not to say sheer vulgarity—of the special pleading introduced instead. We see universities as principal instruments of the national political process, primary media of expression of the political consensus by which this country forms public policy.

So our contribution to the debate consists in an account of how public policy defined the character of the American academy, its purpose and its position in the hierarchy of national priorities. We explain what has happened by trying to show the correlation between the stages of the Cold War and the chapters in the past half-century of university life in general—and the older of the two author's personal experience on the campus, in particular. What the "I" offers is the tale of how large and public events made their mark upon one man's path. Here is the story of the golden age of universities and a genuinely happy career lived from nearly the start to after the end of that golden age. If we do not know where we are going, we can at least understand where we are now by seeking from whence we have come; and, so the two authors conceive, we bear the responsibility, too, of peering beyond the furthest horizon. And to the campus today, this "I" wants to tell the story of how good things have been, are now, and can be again, if we assume once more the responsibilities that our tasks and our tenure impose upon us. Society confers upon us unique advantages, and these not only present opportunities but also exact commitments.

The son observes universities on the fringes, having been brought up in an academic home with other professors' children as friends and having chosen a career in writing and journalism. A certain cool, informed objectivity shapes his vision. He cannot be taken in by the rites and forms of professional and institutional self-celebration; he has seen too much from near at hand. But, too, he has not suffered. He chose a different path in life, and in the end, his heart lies somewhere else. With the father it is otherwise. His earliest destination in life was the campus; he got there; he never left. He could imagine no other life and wanted none. He saw the academy as the center of everything that truly mattered, to both him and the world. Recording the state of the academy and proposing to explain its salient features, the father, passionate about whatever matters this minute, professes no objectivity at all. Drawing upon the experience and reflection of a life lived wholly in higher education from nearly the beginning of the Cold War, he remembers starting in 1950 as a college freshman snatched from fighting alongside his high school classmates in Korea to spend time reading books at Harvard and Oxford and other places, until long after that war had come to an end. He remembers. He will always remember.

But reflecting upon a life of learning in interesting times, the father's remarks take an autobiographical form at the turning points of the several periods into which we divide the story, because in the fusion of the personal and the public, he has participated on the campus in all the great events of the Cold War. His has been a life lived wholly in learning in one particular place: from kindergarten at Beach Park School on Steele Road in West Hartford, Connecticut, through Alfred Plant Junior High school on Whiting Lane and Farmington Avenue, and onward through William H. Hall High School on South Main Street in that same West Hartford, then off to utopia—college and graduate studies, wherever the academy might call.

From then to now, the senior author never worked anywhere but in higher education and at the sole labor of learning; never wanted to, never did. He went where he conceived the action to take place: to Harvard College, Oxford University (following his chosen subject, the study of religion with focus on Judaism); to the Jewish Theological Seminary, the Hebrew University, Columbia University, and onward to research and teaching, for salary, at the University of Wisconsin–Milwaukee, Brandeis University, Dartmouth College, Brown University, the Institute for Advanced Study, and now at the University of South Florida, with summer semesters in visiting professorships at the University of Minnesota, Jewish Theological Seminary, the University of Frankfurt, Cambridge University, Åbo Akademi in Finland, the University of Canterbury in New Zealand, plus further teaching at Bard College and lectureships in many other academies. So he was there: much that happened in public took place also in the privacy of an individual career. Any exemplary academic life could serve to tell what things were like in private life during the interesting times that we have endured, but this one of mine will do. For what happened in one place happened, with variations in degree but none in character, everywhere else.

True, we point to universities in crisis and we highlight an academic bankruptcy. But that is not to suggest either that we are bringing straw to Tiberias, magic to Alexandria, coal to Newcastle—or that we are recapitulating the correct and familiar indictment against today's campus. Others have sounded the alarm. Everyone now knows—and most concur—that the universities cannot go on the way they have. Most reasonable people acknowledge that the academy has lost its way. But condemning a discredited past (still much in evidence to be sure) hardly suffices. The writers of this book believe in the academy and affirm the enduring truth of disciplined learning. That is why, in our judgment, it is time to abandon the work of composing indictments and to begin to think about the future, recognizing the past only to explain to ourselves how we have come to where we now are. So we offer a conservative program to ratify many of the radical changes of the past half-century—specifically, those that strike us as genuine improvements in the cultural and scholarly world of the campus. We speak of the increased enrollment of blacks, Latinos, Jews, Polish-, Italian-, and other Americans of later venue, including many formerly absent Catholics; the regularization of the role of women in the scholarly world and on the faculties and in administration; the broadening of the curriculum in the liberal arts; and the opening of the doors and windows to new currents of thought and unfamiliar perspectives. All of these sources of regeneration we welcome. But the new brings its excesses, too, and these, now fully exposed, require correction.

The issue of the academy proves urgent and immediate. For now that everyone recognizes society has ways of merely transmitting information that are better than the wildly expensive way taken by universities, and now that most people concede that the best teaching and the best learning do not necessarily take place within the academy at all, it is time to explain how to accomplish those tasks that we do uniquely well. Otherwise, the academy will recede in importance and cease to serve as the country's principal medium for higher education and research. Universities will atrophy and the country will lose what only they can provide. Only when we reestablish our claim to distinctive, indeed unique, capacity in our joining together the labor of learning and the enterprise of teaching will we show what makes our way the best among many paths in learning. So this book takes up a position in the vital center of the contemporary debate about the academy. In the spectrum of politics and everyday life, the father has always found a comfortable position in middle of the road—to the right of center to be sure. A long career in the academy and in public life has taught the lesson that the middle of the road is never crowded.

NOAM M. M. NEUSNER   JACOB NEUSNER
The son   *The father*
REPORTER   DISTINGUISHED RESEARCH PROFESSOR OF RELIGIOUS STUDIES
THE *TAMPA TRIBUNE*   UNIVERSITY OF SOUTH FLORIDA
TAMPA, FLORIDA

ACKNOWLEDGMENTS

The son, in everyday life a reporter for the *Tampa Tribune,* acknowledges especially the guidance of Harold Wechsler, who gave shape to the research of the subject. Since the collected research on the history of higher education would fill many shelves, Wechsler's collegial advice helped get the ball rolling, we hope, in the right direction. Most of the research was done through and at the libraries of the University of South Florida, where staffers gladly extended their assistance.

The editors at the *Tribune* indirectly aided this project: they believed in my skills, hired me, and taught me how to write cogently, intelligently, and accurately. C.T. Bowen, Lyle McBride, Lawrence McConnell, Bill Skutt, and Bayard Steele have, each in his own way, taken whatever skills I brought to them and shaped them for the better. Together with a host of other teachers, colleagues, and editors—too numerous to mention but few enough that they know who they are—made my career in journalism possible and, I hope, fruitful.

As this project took about a year's labor, mostly on weekends and vacations, I owe a special thanks to my wife, Andrea. The time devoted to the project came mostly at her expense, but she did not waver in her support, even when she spent her weekends wondering who and where her husband was. But she did not let my lazier instincts get the better of me, and more than anything, made this year as pleasant as any other in our still-young marriage. Our close friends, Mike Frankel and Laila Craveiro, supported the project with humor (the husband) and interest (the wife). They, like other friends and my brothers and sister spread throughout the country, never scoffed at the idea of my writing a book, an idea which might have made me laugh two years ago. Of course, working with the senior writer of this book, I soon got over that mental hurdle. He invited me into this project, set the scope, and, incredibly, made it seem relatively easy. To him, thanks and a promise that the next book will tax him less—although his influence on my thinking and writing will never cease.

The father did most of his work on this book at the University of South Florida as Distinguished Research Professor of Religious Studies. He expresses thanks not only for the advantage of a Distinguished Research Professorship in the Florida state university system, which for a scholar must be the best job in the world, but also for a substantial research expense fund, ample research time, and stimulating, straightforward, and cordial colleagues. Here as everywhere, while the debates on the purpose of higher education—its social vocation—go forward, the work goes on unimpeded, and we soldier on. For on the campus nothing waits; the future is upon us, the generation to come facing us in the classroom every day. That defines the urgency of our work, and the vocation to which this book means to respond.

DECEMBER 18, 1994
NOAM'S TWENTY-FIFTH BIRTHDAY

INTRODUCTION

Amerca now dismantles its once-great universities, placing limits on the subjects to be investigated and taught, restrictions on the use of professors' time according to professors' best judgment, dictating the admission of students possessing no qualifications for higher learning—unable, for example, to read and write—stressing academic credentials over academic achievement. And, as universities present themselves in practical terms as public welfare agencies and public policy research centers, public appreciation for universities declines.

I. THE LOSS OF VOCATION

That universities today suffer a loss of vocation explains why the rest of society loses confidence in academia. When toward the end of the nineteenth century universities found purpose and defined a calling for themselves within the public interest, everybody participated in celebrating them and supporting their work. Philanthropists competed in creating great foundations for universities: Rockefeller at Chicago, Vanderbilt and Duke by those families, respectively. Then, through the Cold War, universities gained prominence because they formed the nation's strongest line of defense. Science and technology, the humanities and the social sciences—all made their contribution to the cause. But now, at the end of the twentieth century, within the political consensus expressed by their own alumni, the intellectuals who alone form and pass opinions, universities find themselves confused and uncertain. And so the country loses confidence in them.

In an age of uncertainty, reliable guides prove rare; well-defined purpose seldom transcends the local setting. The various legislatures, foundations, personal philanthropists, and departments of the federal establishment, no longer invest in universities either heavy trust or vast sums of money as in the past. But we of the academy find ourselves equipped to address the crisis. We maintain that ideas still matter, insights reshape vision, and discoveries of intellect continue to change the world. So while we look backward, it is through wit, mind, and imagination that we seek the way ahead. With perspective on how the university has reached the present impasse, it can survive, surpass, renew. And, as we shall argue, the path to regeneration leads back to our original and uniquely American definition of the academy: places where scholars teach and care how students learn.

The defining moment, proclaiming the end of an era, struck when the billions for physical science, once routinely voted by Congress, ran out just when the great problems of physics appeared accessible to solution. The formerly great institutions of learning now can no longer take their preeminence for granted. In 1990, the Florida Legislature appropriated millions of dollars to lay the foundations for the National High Magnetic Field Laboratory for Florida State University, which brought to the South one of the country's twenty-eight national laboratories. The competing university was the Massachusetts Institute of Technology, which had held the contract for three decades. In excess of $300 million will go into the project. Now Congress has so radically shifted direction as to decline to carry through one of the great projects in pure science of our time. With $2 billion of an expected $11 billion spent, the Superconducting Super Collider was halted, by a consensus of congressmen and senators, who viewed the project as superfluous and overpriced. So we shall never know what the Texas project promised to tell us. Intellects who had brought us to the outer boundaries of the composition of the universe will now atrophy, relying on only the long known but still partial data. A nation prepared to pay any price to land on the moon—a project of only slender scientific promise, although considerable technological accomplishment—abandoned its long-standing conviction that learning, its own reward, was worth any price. Somehow the value of learning, so long embodied in physics, has lost its self-evident standing.

Harsh, well-credentialed, and persuasive critics have alerted the country to the failure and shame and scandal of the universities, which have translated political convictions into arguments resting on social utility and introduced debates on public policy into the academic context.[1] These critics have made their case. Briefly summarized, it is that, turned into instruments of

---

1. We refer here to a group of works, published in short succession in the late 1980s and early 1990s: Roger Kimball's *Tenured Radicals*; Charles Sykes' *Profscam* and *The Hollow Men*; E.D. Hirsch Jr.'s *Cultural Literacy*; Allan Bloom's *The Closing of the American Mind*, Dinesh D'Souza's *Illiberal Education*, and Lewis Perelman's *School's Out*. Each make ample reference to the trends which we identify, and serve

politics and power, the universities now teach the lessons that truth is negotiable, learning a function of self-interest, and academic fields—whether history or English or sociology or anthropology—mere instruments to be mediated by whoever is in charge that day. But leadership on the campus, vested in presidents, deans, and provosts, loses its way as well. If key academic fields in the humanities and social sciences have confessed they have nothing of worth to teach us, then we need hardly ask ourselves why deans, provosts, and presidents define their jobs from day to day and reinvent the university to suit their momentary requirement. Integrity has taken leave, and in its wake, anything goes.

That loss of vocation and purpose explains why the academy no longer enjoys self-evident status as the primary locus of research and scholarship and teaching. University-generated research proposals compete with those of industry, free-standing research institutes, and the like; the academy no longer sets forth a special claim. But at the same time that universities separated research from teaching, their unique union of research and teaching—scholarship in two media—comes under severe judgment. State legislatures and trustees respond when they demand teaching to the exclusion of research and take for granted that one competes with the other. Publishing scholars are assumed to be unable to teach, and the good teachers are assumed to possess no independent knowledge that they themselves have acquired through the exercise of sustained learning and critical judgment. So the authentic scholarship carried on in the union of research and dissemination in both teaching and publication no longer defines the work universities carry on. To trustees and regents, public opinion has dictated that teaching is everything, research a luxury—as though professors work only when they stand in front of a classroom. But with the intellectual bankruptcy of critical academic fields, that is hardly surprising. With classroom teaching defined as teaching without scholarship (beyond the Ph.D.) and scholarship in published form denied to a broad public, which once followed academic debates with interest and profit, what is left? Teaching becomes the mere transmission of information to whom it may concern, not the active engagement of intellect with intellect, teachers' and students'. That itself confirms the end of rigorous learning in the academic mode, carried on by teachers who are scholars, researchers who care to communicate their

---

as a far better source of information about some of the most recent failings of American higher education. We agree with many of them, but we choose not to dwell only on those failings, and hope to set them into the context of what happened before and what can happen now.

findings in important ways and through public media, in both print and the classroom. When universities respond to their vocation, it is precisely that mode of learning that they alone aspire to carry forward.

But the heritage of teaching scholars, the ideal of generations, finds no willing heirs except in small liberal arts colleges. These claim few noteworthy scholars among their professors, only erudites. Their professors commonly teach because they have nothing else to do and rarely contribute to learning. And elsewhere, mere teaching prevails as well, for most professors publish little beyond the dissertation, if that. Most books come from the tiniest minority of publishing scholars. When scholarship—sustained, demanding, self-critical learning in quest of solutions to problems and answers to questions—is removed from the classroom, what is left is the mere transmission of not so much information as opinion. Scholarship in literature, history, philosophy, and the study of religion trivializes even opinion and now denies itself the power to make responsible judgments or form compelling arguments for one thing and against some other. Everything goes. No wonder students emerge persuaded that "I think" or "well, that's my opinion" form primary data in the analysis of all manner of subjects.

If academic fields refuse to say why knowing what they teach makes a difference, claiming everything depends upon the exercise of mindless caprice, called hegemony, then all that is left are facts, and one person's interpretation of those facts is no better than anyone else's. If there is nothing to learn and no criterion of truth or falsity, then, in consequence, powers of intellect decide nothing, and that other function of universities—to bestow credentials for jobs—takes control. That is why today, in the mass universities, the boundary-line from high school to community college to university blurs; the difference now is measured in quantity, not quality. For when credentials form the issue, why make distinctions? Everyone is equally entitled.

II. THE MODERN HISTORY OF THE AMERICAN UNIVERSITY: WHEN IT BEGAN

Where is the "in the beginning" of this story of ours about creation and deconstruction and the architectonics of the reconstruction to come? We look backward to 1945, with attention to the dramatic, if limited, impact of the migration of the cream of Middle European universities in the 1930s. For from the end of World War II through the twilight of the Cold War, the American academy flourished. It was a golden age of intellect on campus, from which the academic institutions of the day for their part also acquired a glow; it was a time of remarkable achievement for the humanities as much as mathematics, the social sciences as much as engineering, medicine, and the natural sciences. In those days, it is not too much to claim, entire fields of learning were invented in this country, and in discipline after discipline, American professors mastered the world's intellectual achievements and made them their own. Heirs of the academic riches of Middle Europe, which, in the decade before World War II, had divested itself of the world's greatest intangible treasures of mind in philosophy, social science, physics and other sciences of nature, American universities remade themselves.

American disciples then transcended their Middle European masters, the men and women of reason revolted by Germany's descent into racism and irrationality, who, *en masse,* formed the first large body of great scholarship to root itself on our shores, then enriching an already lavish but deeply local intellectual heritage of our own. Possessed of distinguished natural science, we Americans found the surpassing masters now among us. Einstein stands for many. With a native tradition of social science, we confronted intellects of remarkable acumen. The Frankfurt school represents them all. In literature, history, art, music, and classics, we had attained a certain standard. Newly arrived on our shores before World War II, many of Europe's greatest masters in the humanities, possessed, to us, unfathomable erudition. They redefined the dimensions and imparted a new vision of these subjects. Whether in art or in music or in dance or in drama, whether in language and literature or in history or in political science or in economics, they brought their learning and imagination to us. For a time, to be a great professor meant to speak with a foreign accent. But we—the native academicians of that time, before and after World War II—showed a capacity beyond Europe's. For we humbly accepted the harvests of alien fields, making our own what outsiders had to contribute. But then, with dignity, we proceeded to frame our own vision of what we wanted to do.

It was, and is, America's greatness to learn from everybody, not dismissing what is foreign either in origin or in presentation. That power forms the gift of our history. A country of immigrants, we took for granted that anyone might belong by accepting a place among us. And it would follow, we would learn from everybody. That political and cultural judgment took form in the academy as well. For we learn with humility from everyone, and in those days, when it came to scholarship, we knew no pride; that was the peculiarly American virtue. And we found nothing alien. With humble dignity we crossed the oceans to learn from others, welcoming the gifts of foreigners too. And, also with dignity, we formed our own judgments.

When, within a brief interval, in 1945, we found ourselves in the continuation-war that would last another four decades, these traits of mind and attitudes of culture served us well. For now our country led the coalition of disparate nations facing Communism, and our academicians would have to learn how to understand both allies and enemies. Their experience within the academy prepared them for leadership beyond its bounds. Used to learning from foreigners, they undertook to form a vision of one world in social science and in humanistic learning to complement the political will of national unity and international cooperation.

Here we propose to tell the story of the American moment in the life of the ancient university of the West, to explain, in particular, why, for a brief moment, a nation determined to lavish its scarce resources upon the higher learning in its distinctive academic form. What did these billions buy? It was money well spent. Everyone knows how much mathematicians, economists, sociologists, physicists, and others in the sciences accomplished. Science, mathematics, and technology renewed, the universities also imposed upon the humanities and social sciences standards of achievement that beforehand few conceived; excellence was known, greatness not imagined. Few realize that the humanities and social scientists created that record of remarkable invention and imagination. For, across the curriculum of academic learning, America became not only best in most areas, but second best in precisely those areas that lay beyond its immediate grasp.

III. The Special, American Excellence

That is to say, those subjects that proved accessible without an act of cultural mediation, such as biology or chemistry or physics, would find in America their formative intellects. But those areas of learning by nature attached to foreign soil—French literature, Italian art, for instance—would make their way to these shores so that here too, our universities would attain real distinction. That is why in those areas in which others, by the nature of things, would excel, Americans would be second best. So—to take an obvious case—the best place to study French literature would always be in France or Quebec, but the second best place would be any of a dozen U.S. universities. Master Hebrew literature in Jerusalem, but in California come home to the regnant non-Israeli experts, at UCLA for instance. British history was done best in Britain, second best here. These typify the rest. And in not a few areas of humanistic learning and many in the social sciences, American scholarship took first place for achievement and influence. Only in Marxist ideology did the French excel, only in specific areas of military technology did the Soviets outshine U.S. accomplishment.

This brings us back to the question: why the rebirth of the social sciences and the humanistic subjects engaged in comparative study? It was not only that the refugee scholars and intellectuals re-founded learning. It was also that the Cold War required us to understand the faith and life of strangers. Taking second place to native speakers, our anthropologists and ethnographers learned how to learn from the cultures of other people, teaching the rest of us how to appreciate and work with exotic and alien folk. The field of the academic study of religion was reinvented in the United States, the first naturally, authentically multicultural field America would produce. That field adopted as its generative problem how to learn to understand and appreciate the other at that point at which the other was most particular and most bizarre to us, which is, in the rites and myths of the supernatural—and in the social and political order flowing therefrom.

It is easier to understand why in physics and chemistry and the other natural sciences and mathematics and engineering, medicine, and the social sciences, the American academy formed that distant light to which people looked for illumination. These remarkable academic accomplishments did not take place by accident or indirection. The Manhattan Project, yielding final victory in World War II, tells the reason why. The massive national investment in academic learning represented a chapter in the political history of a country that, as we shall see, had chosen to take up intellectual arms in a long, twilight struggle, meeting on battlefields of the mind, soul, and heart with the ammunition of ideas, attitudes, and deeply held convictions. As vast sums of money flowed into these subjects, the best minds found a welcome, equipment, and fine laboratories for research; and all the necessities of scientific greatness came together. Talent follows money.

IV. THE COLD WAR AND HIGHER EDUCATION

That is why we wonder how these mighty universities have fallen, with no special interest left to defend them and to explain what in times past required only the display of accomplishments? No institution in American life in its days of glory has ever enjoyed so high a position in the public estimation of the American people as has the academy, nor has any fallen so far so quickly. Neither the armed forces after Vietnam, nor Congress, nor the clergy—none competes with the academy's sudden and rapid fall from national appreciation. Our theory is that what explains the rise of the academy also has to account for its decline. So we define the tale of the university by referring to the story of Cold War America. That is because we think that the chapters in the Cold War correspond to the phases in the unfolding tale of the university from 1945 through 1989, and that the events in national politics find their counterpart in what happened on the campus.

We take as our convenience dates the following:

• 1946–57, for Chapter One; that is, from the Communist takeover of Poland, Hungary, Czechoslovakia, the Baltic States, Rumania, and much else, through the siege of Berlin and the Korean War, to Sputnik;

• 1957–69, for Chapter Two; that is, Sputnik to the Moon Landing;

• 1969–81, for Chapter Three; the retreat from Vietnam, the loss of Iran, the Soviet invasion of Afghanistan; the transformation of the national consensus by President Reagan;

• finally, 1981–95, for Chapter Four; the Reagan revolution, disintegration of the "Evil Empire," and the confusion brought on by the winding down of the Cold War.

These four periods, roughly a decade each, find their match in great and coherent periods of development on the campus: the reformation of the universities; the moment of truth; the onset of doubt; and the parting of company of the academy from the national will, with the unraveling of the alliance of the national consensus and the dominant voices on campus. But we need not tell the whole story all at once.

As noted above, we move in these pages from the narrators' "we" to the autobiographical "I." For the father of the team lived through the decades in which the academy rose to glory and declined to inconsequentiality. To impart immediacy and personality to the story, there is the report of this "I." That is, to convey a sense of how things were in the everyday world of the university in those four decades, I tell what it was like to be an undergraduate, then a graduate student, then a young professor; later, an academic player on the losing side of the university debates of the 1970s; and, finally, a contra on the campus.

What of the future? Having arrived in September, 1950, I now work my way through my fifth decade on the campus; there cannot be many more. But optimism costs no more than pessimism, but provides a surer guide to American realities. Ours is a country that knows how to achieve its goals. This country has solved its problems before. Therefore we do not doubt that the academy will renew itself in its service to the nation and to learning. For while what now impends we do not know, the future need not prove so bleak as some now anticipate. As we said at the outset, presently it appears that the country dismantles its universities as centers of higher learning. We refer not only to the specific, awful tragedy of the how national treasure of the California system of higher education is cut back and taken down. We have in mind the much more general shift in the universities' fundamental mission, with legislatures and trustees now asking them to teach the facts, not critically to reexamine them. The threat to the long-term utility of the university in America comes from those who imagine they can remove scholarship from the university classroom and define the principal task of universities as one of teaching—as though teaching without scholarship conveyed knowledge. But all that the teacher who is not a scholar too does is transmit information, either wrong or evanescent and ephemeral.

For fifty years, nothing cost too much, and everyone knew the value of scholarship. Now, teaching established and familiar truths, for a prescribed number of hours weekly, defines the academic task. Professors work—so people now imagine—only when they are standing in front of a classroom and talking at the students, but not otherwise. But the criticism and rational testing that scholarship undertakes find themselves priced out of the political market. These are political decisions, and, we maintain, the entire story forms a chapter in the politics of the nation, which, for its hour of peril, required the imagination and wit and intellect of intelligent men and women, and now that the time of trouble has passed, no longer values their services. So, to recapitulate our problem:

(1) People no longer find self-evident the claim of the academy to high priority in the use of public funds, and private foundations find their urgent causes elsewhere. The national consensus that bestowed upon higher education a reward commensurate to the risk of life and limb in the nation's service has shifted, and other means of compensation compete with academic education. Legislatures no longer find self-evident the value of learning of the academic kind, now treating the universities as a burden to be lightened. Why all this scholarship? Who cares for the results? What difference does learning make anyhow?

(2) In the 1950s and 1960s, the national consensus assumed these questions had permanently found their answers, even though few could have spelled out what they were. In the 1990s, many assume no plausible answers come forth, and academic ideals supply no compelling reason to employ in state universities scholars of accomplishment but only teachers with appropriate credentials. In 1945 college formed an extension of high school. For half a century, the academy aimed at something more. Many universities and colleges attained that goal.

(3) Today, many suppose all people are supposed to do in college is to learn more, the goals of the transformation of intellect and even character of thinking having lost all currency. The work of learning, conducted in libraries and laboratories, now is valued principally when translated into the

facts to be transmitted to masses of undifferentiated undergraduate students. The agenda of social amelioration has taken over, with courses aimed at indoctrination replacing instruction intending to provoke discovery.

(4) What are we to do now? The answer comes only when we understand the remarkable shift, over two or three generations, from rags to riches to rags, from poverty to wealth to poverty, which this book examines.

Since we correlate the academy and national politics, by this point readers may wonder why we insist that to make sense of the academy we must turn to its historical context. Admittedly, what we take as premise is not demonstrated: that what happens on the campus mainly finds its generative causes beyond the academy. It follows that we see universities not as detached from the social order but as a critical component of that order. They do not arise as unchanging relics of a distant past, bearing their own definition and imposing a lien upon coming ages, but find renewal in each generation that sustains them. They always serve the purpose of those who pay, send their children, and accept their judgments on personal qualification and public truth and value. Their professors live not in isolated communities but participate in the everyday life of the communities that universities are sustained to serve. Universities in the end do not decide even who will teach what to whom—unless society assigns to them the power to make that decision. For decades through the Cold War they exercised that power, but now they do not. That is why what universities have been is not what they now are, and what they will become will find its definition in the mind and imagination of people whom just now we can scarcely imagine, and whose problems we cannot envisage. All that stands firm are the buildings. And, without constant tending, these collapse.

That is why we propose to explain what has happened and what ought to take place now by appeal to the interests of this country's social order. From generation to generation in the nature of things, new people come along to determine answers to these questions of definition of higher education:

(1) who will teach
(2) what
(3) to whom
(4) how
(5) and why

These form the components of the higher learning. And when universities make those decisions, the nurturing order of society will define the setting in which matters are sorted out. The very conception of an autonomous, value-free, ancient, and enduring refuge from the world, where people freely and rationally reach determinations of what is so and what is not, conflicts with the fact that universities flourish or founder along with the rest of the social order and as an integral part of it.

We insist that universities have taken a primary role in the conduct of public policy, extending into the classroom, where coming generations are formed, the attitudes and ideals of the entire society. Universities are often seen as ancient foundations, begun in the centuries in which Western civilization reached maturity, formed in a single common model defined at the horizon of Western memory. But whether old buildings house new activities or quaint customs—odd garments on ceremonial occasions, from which deep voices emit stupefying platitudes—everywhere the old defines only form, the surface of things.

What really happens is otherwise. We interpret what happens in and to universities not by appeal to an abstract and age-old conception of an unchanging institution but by reference to practical matters of power and politics. For, in our view, on campus and off, in the marketplace and in the great bureaus of government alike, considerations of public policy—extending even to practical politics—imposed the national will and purpose upon the academy. We on the campus form an integral part of the country as a whole. When the nation knew its own mind, we knew how to nurture it. When the country lost its way, we found ourselves unable to recover it. What happens in the country takes place on the campus, and we who compose the campus form the reliable indicator of the country's health, its clarity of social purpose. And that is not for superficial political reasons, because public universities turn to state legislatures for support. It is for profound political reasons, because all universities, public and private, form an integral part and expression of the political order. So we take as our problem the task of correlating politics and academic culture, in this instance, the Cold War and the academy's golden age.

Whether funds come from private or public sources, donations of alumni or appropriations of legislative budget committees, foundations or federal funding agencies, scarce resources sustain enormous universities because people place their faith in the power of universities to carry out the national will. Indeed, universities have flourished, both in material and intellectual terms, only when they persuade society that they serve better than any competing institutions aiming at the allocation of those same scarce resources. And, as in the present age of uncertainty of will and unclarity of purpose, when universities fall on hard times, it is because ideas have failed, attitudes have atrophied, self-evident truths have fallen into desuetude, and, in all, the vision has failed. As we said before, money flows to vision: first comes the idea, then the means for the realization of the idea, and, in the end, people cannot be manipulated, but only compelled by the force of a moral vision of worthwhile enterprise, to support this vessel of vision.

That conception then accounts for the chapters of our story. For the campus formed a—perhaps *the*—principal battlefield of the Cold War. Winning that war required our side to marshall ideas to persuade, as much as weapons to compel. When war heats up, issues of purpose clarify themselves—us against them forms the most powerful ideology—and everybody joins the common cause. But in the twilight war fought in haze and fog, where vision blurs, and in a struggle that demands not so much overwhelming the other side with force so much as pursuasion of our side to stay the course, attitudes govern. Conceptions of good and evil dictate action, and clarity of purpose and a sturdy conscience form mighty armor.

The Cold War tested the will of our democracy against the steel of their autocracy, and, if the Communists gave up, as they did in 1989 and afterward, it was because our intelligent use of diverse kinds of force, economic and political as much as military, on our side was complemented by our power to learn from mistakes, theirs and ours; they knew only how to repeat ours and so they lost. The universities hardly served as ministries of propaganda, the places from which the political commissars of our armies would go forth. But they did respond through responsible scholarship to the country's call for science and technology, social science and wisdom, humanistic learning and insight. A nation engaged in a war like this one—in which only a few could imagine the details of victory or when the normal chaos of human affairs would return—looked to the academy for its particular gifts: criticism and objectivity, rigorous learning and unsparing self-criticism. Why come to the academy for more than applied science or the rules of psychological warfare? What brought the country to the campus for the particular specialities that the campus nurtured in its own terms: scholarship in research and teaching alike?

That is why it was no accident that the Cold War lasting from 1946 to 1991 between the United States and the Soviet Union overspread the American universities and defined their character. Here was a war of ideas, beginning with the scientists who created atomic weapons out of nuclear physics, then moving onward to the political scientists and historians who explored the parameters of violence and found a way to fight a war without blowing up the world. Even social scientists were called upon to find out how to form alliances despite differences in culture and social order, and to educate our representatives—both the official ones and the heroes of more discreet activities—in dealing with distant places, about which, until then, we Americans knew little and cared still less. The war was fought through science and learning, with imagination and intellect forming the counterpart to high explosives in hot wars. Universities then became the counterpart to that arsenal of democracy that American industry had made of itself, and Detroit's equivalent came into being in the think tanks and research centers, involving science and technology, social science, and the humanities as well, throughout the country.

Now, as a matter of fact, this country's newly empowered intellectuals—brilliant, thoughtful men (women came into play only toward the very end)—arose not so much out of the right as out of the center and the left. They recognized the character of the protracted struggle and, for the first quarter-century of the four decades' contest, dictated our part of its course. Succeeded by other men and women, who resolved matters brilliantly and with remarkable success, the policymakers of the late 1940s and 1950s turned to not only science and technology, but also philosophy and history, the study of religion and the social sciences, in their battle for the country's future in the world.

From the outset, George W. Kennan laid out the strategy of containment, which taught us how to keep the peace while making war, to the end, when Samuel Huntington interpreted the events of the 1980s and shone a light into the dim future. Throughout, the Cold War formed its battlefield in the context of values, attitudes, and ideals, on the one side, and in the contest of wit, imagination, and vivid intelligence, on the other. Our policy planners, making mistakes to be sure, kept their eye on the main chance; theirs merely repeated our mistakes. Our economists formulated a policy of disciplined prosperity and social harmony; theirs bankrupted their country and in the end lost the war. Our generals and admirals reinvented war, tactics and strategy alike, learning how to stand on high alert year after year, how to train armed forces for a large war that would not come, while fighting many small and medium wars that would break over us and test our will.

Nearly all the players in politics and public policy, economics and military life, and in the on-going cultural struggle over social policy, made their livings as intellectuals, book readers, and many were scholars, book writers. And they not only came from universities (only one principal player, Harry Truman, was not a college graduate) but also appealed to ideas, not solely to interests, in formulating public policy. (Truman, lacking formal education, was a voracious reader and a quick study, saving the country by decisions of a moral certainty that attested to profound reflection over a long time.) The Kennedy cabinet was made up in part of professors and deans; there was even a court historian on the scene in the person of Arthur M. Schlesinger, Jr. Presidents Johnson and Nixon followed suit. The interchange of professors and politicians—a Kissinger going from Harvard to the National Security Council, for instance—underscored the reality.

It was that this vast, enduring war, involving two generations of national life and demanding an ongoing investment of national treasure and will, in the end found its victors in the side best able to muster intellect and enlist the power not of formal propaganda but of important ideas. Science, not just technology; political theory, not just practical politics; public policy, not just disposition of this morning's crisis—these ways of imagining the world and sorting out its facts governed on our side, and in the end, those deeply academic vocations of mind, science, theory, and policy would sustain our struggle. Ours was a victory of imagination: the freedom to think the unthinkable. And, as everyone now recognizes, where imagination failed and sheer habit intervened, we on the campus made those decisions that cost us so heavily in national will and unity of purpose.

Politics—who may legitimately do what to whom, that is, the exercise of coercive power in realizing public policy—governs learning; universities form an instrument in achieving the national will; and the shape and goal of scholarship for professors and of education for students (and the two overlap for much of the way) find their definition in that same consensus that dictates public policy for all else. That is how, in a well-integrated democracy such as is ours, culture in the life of mind and intellect responds to the realities of power in the affairs of state. Proof and illustration for that simple—to us self-evident—proposition emerge when we look back at the years in which the Cold War began, along with my career, which commenced on the campus in 1950 and moves now into its fifth decade.

1

INTELLECTUAL ARMS FOR THE TWILIGHT STRUGGLE

In 1945, most of America's colleges and universities continued what went on in high schools: more of the same subjects, only at a more advanced level. In the next thirty years they so reworked their programs that moving from high school to college required a considerable intellectual retooling: not only learn more, but also learn in a different way, and not only take up new subjects, but also master new disciplines. By 1975 universities had redefined themselves and their purpose. No longer mere repositories of what humanity more or less knows, they had become bastions of criticism, sources of new ideas and fresh critical perspectives. The shift corresponded to the rising estimation of universities in the public mind. Once fortresses of privilege and emblems of wealth, with only the few able to contemplate study beyond secondary education, the academies opened their doors to a growing proportion of the population. In the decade before World War II, Jews were admitted one by one, and one was too many; blacks were rarely let in the door and, in many elite campuses, women as well. There was a near-exclusion of Catholics, who were stigmatized as people who believed everything the Pope told them to believe and therefore incapable of scholarship. After World War II, negative quotas had ended for Jews, blacks found a welcome, women came in numbers and even rose to faculty positions. Catholics, too, could aspire to careers in secular universities. Not only so, but everyone who could benefit from further study—and a great many who could not—would begin to treat tertiary education (beyond primary and secondary schooling) as an entitlement.

And, at that very same time, in those three decades, the country assigned to universities critical national tasks. These involved both education and research. Take research first: the Manhattan Project had left no doubt that science must serve in the country's defense and would find support in budgets for defense. But the political tasks, the cultural obligations, the economic competition—these too would require purposeful study of politics, culture, economics, and other disciplines of the social sciences and humanities. But now the academy confronted a hitherto-unimagined assignment in education as well. The revolution began when, in 1945, Congress contemplated compensating World War II veterans for their years of dangerous service to the country. So, the government offered returning veterans a college education—of all things. After prior national struggles, they had passed out money or land, but not education. Now, the GI Bill focused upon higher education (not exclusively to be sure). That remarkably high tribute—risk your life, go to college—found its match in the 1950s when the great philanthropic foundations—joined often by private giving, as well as by public funds from state legislatures and the Federal government—poured vast sums of money into higher education, scholarship and teaching alike. So at the very point at which, for one set of reasons, the country determined to educate at the tertiary level a large proportion of its young people, and the elite colleges and universities dismantled the barriers to excellence that had closed them off, the universities found themselves called upon for a second enormous undertaking as well: research and scholarship such as had characterized few universities and no colleges prior to World War II.

What was to change was the quality of higher education, not only the quantity. Entire fields of learning, in the social sciences as much as in the natural sciences, mathematics, and engineering, were redefined and renewed. Sociology and economics, statistics and political science, took their place alongside nuclear physics. What turned into a silly cliché—("the battle for men's minds")—contained a solemn recognition that the struggle played itself out in the realm of opinion and conviction. We had to make sense of other peoples' nonsense. The study of religion, formerly centered (where it flourished at all) on the truth or falsity of religious beliefs, on the one side, and the description by native believers of their personal beliefs, on the other, now began to ask the questions of social description and cultural analysis that now preoccupied the country. And the birth of the academic study of religion—religion, not religions, for analysis, not for mere description—stands for much else. Social sciences and humanities belonged on the front line, alongside engineering, mathematics, and the natural sciences of physics and chemistry and biology. It was an age of intellectual vitality such as the United States had scarcely known.

To set foot on a university campus in those days opened the way to paradise—at least, for an intellectual adolescent. I came on the scene a few years after the revolution had begun. In June, 1950, two great events took place—one for me, the other for everybody, including me—events that would define the next forty years in my life and in world history. First, I graduated from William Hall High School in West Hartford, Connecticut, and set my mind to the bright college years to come. I knew I was leaving West Hartford, suspecting never to return. And second, a few days later, the North Koreans invaded South Korea and turned the cold war hot. Other events—the guerrilla war in Greece and threat to Turkey, the subversion of Rumania and the take-over in Czechoslovakia, the conquest of the Baltic states, the conquest of Poland—all these happenings on the borders of the then-Soviet Union pointed precisely in the direction people feared: a new and final world cataclysm, a war fought with atomic weapons. We had learned the lessons of the 1930s, when Britain's anti-Semitic and incompetent establishment government fed country after country into the Nazi gorge, hoping to appease an insatiable appetite for world rule and ruin. We knew not to appease. For five years, from the end of World War II in 1945, we had done everything right, rebuilding Japan and Germany, punishing a handful of criminals and rehabilitating the rest, not assigning blame. We made none of the mistakes of Versailles and Weimar. But war had come anyhow.

Had World War III begun, we—my generation, which had followed the earlier war the way, these days teenagers follow rock stars—would have gone off to fight. For the American university, mobilized in the war just ended to do what it could, whether in science and technology or in education, nothing would have changed. The campus knew what protracted war meant. And everyone thought that Armageddon had come upon us. That is because, until then, no one had imagined the idea of a "cold war," at least, not a twilight-zone between war and peace such as the world would endure until 1989. True, the great statesmen of the age—Churchill, Truman, Marshall, De Gaulle—all had warned from 1946 onward that what followed victory resembled a truce, not true peace. In 1946 Churchill pointed to the Iron Curtain that had fallen across Europe.

But even with the Truman Doctrine and Marshall Plan, Communist subversion in Greece and takeovers in Hungary, Czechoslovakia, Poland, and the Baltic nations, cold war and no peace defied imagining. Few could conceive what was to come. Certainly, no one of my generation, too young for one war but ripe for the next, conceived a time of fighting but not total war, or peace that was no peace. It now turned out that World War III could be postponed, perhaps even avoided entirely, through the policy of containment and limited, local wars. Men would die, but the world would not come to an end. A different kind of struggle, one that few could imagine (although history could supply many parallels over time), had commenced, neither war nor peace, a struggle against mutual destruction but for a timely resolution. For a generation persuaded that nothing substituted for victory, the Cold War represented a difficult challenge: restraint and resolution at one and the same time.

I. THE COLD WAR AND THE ACADEMY

In June, 1950, we were to learn what the new kind of war entailed—and the American academy would never be the same. Walking by one academic office building after another on any American campus, an alert college president or provost or dean could imagine uses, in the national struggle, for nearly every subject. And the government would certainly provide the funds to support whatever that president could invent. Take area studies, for example—the joining of various social sciences in a task force to examine a given region of the world or a country, whether China, Poland, the Balkans, or the Near or Middle East. For the political consensus that somehow takes shape to guide America through history had come to precisely such a conception, of a time of neither war nor peace, an age of national service over a lifetime, a career in (for example) area studies, would yield rich results for the national interest. It would follow that area or regional studies would demand attention and support. Alongside area studies came comparative studies, where we would learn how to negotiate difference; interdisciplinary studies, where political science, anthropology, sociology, economics, and other disciplines would join together to deal with common problems; and other productive modes of academic interaction.

Everyone understood that the atomic bomb originated not in technology but in nuclear physics, as well as in physics in general, chemistry, and the other hard sciences, not to mention mathematics and (for ballistic missiles) astrophysics. Economics promised valuable lessons in the struggle: feed us, starve them, in the competition for scarce resources. Sociology, psychology, political science, demography, statistics—all had their contribution to make. When it came to the humanities, there were the languages of obscure parts of the world, not to mention the literatures of those languages and the cultures embodied in those literatures. So the National Defense Foreign Language Act financed study of everything but French or German or Spanish. World War II had left the lesson that language is power, Churchill having shaped the national will through well-crafted speeches, Roosevelt having done nearly as well, and (alas) Hitler having done best of all. So how could literature and English professors be left out of the legions of intellectual warriors? And since religion then as now defined the social order for many countries and life's purpose for much of humanity, the time had come to support the study of religion, for analytical purposes and not as a medium of indoctrination, within the curriculum. That was the point at which the academic study of religion in the United States came of age.

When the Korean War broke over us, ours was the first generation to learn the new rules of war for the academy. Stated briefly: the smart study, the rest fight. True, that decision expressed naked class interest and prejudice—the rich could afford to study, the poor would have to fight; whites would study, blacks would fight. The phrase "class warfare" took on new meaning. The new policy, without precedent in World War II, when everybody went sooner or later, also conformed to the requirements of the new kind of war. Academic deferments would allow young men to improve their knowledge and skills—and by the way would also make sure universities had the students they required to pay the tuition that supported the work of research that the country demanded. So on the campus it would be business as usual—but now, an unusual sort of business, as we shall see. For before World War II, research hardly defined the vocation of most American colleges, and even large universities placed only marginal value upon faculty research and publication. Everything would change.

For an uncertain few weeks, in that tense June of 1950, no one knew what change meant for those of us who headed toward a higher education. Then someone decided: we need highly educated young men[1] for the science, technology, and politics that would defend Western civilization in the coming struggle. So the male college students would enjoy an exemption from military service, only to join up mostly as officers later on (when, everybody hoped, the "police action" would have ended). The upshot was that while many of my high school classmates went off to die in war, like coming generations of college-bound students I was exempted

---

1. At that time women were not at risk, nor did anybody suppose they would serve in more than an auxiliary way. But, on the other hand, women also were not accorded their place in higher education, few emerging in graduate education in mathematics and the natural sciences and social sciences, not many more in the humanities.

and sent off to college. That decision underscored the critical role that the political consensus assigned to universities in the defense of the country and the Free World. We formed the intellectual armament, the fighting minds. Others would die; we would make sense of things.

An intelligent, if unjust, decision, but it was no accident. Wars last a long time, we now knew, and science and technology would ultimately decide the issue, as they had in the last two wars: Churchill's tanks, for instance, in World War I; radar and the atomic bomb, applied mathematics in code-breaking and submarine detection (to take a few instances among many) as well in World War II. For, people remembered the atomic triumph and knew that the geniuses must do their job, whether in radar, which had saved Britain in 1940, or in atomic science, or in any of the countless ways in which one country outwitted another. Further, everyone understood the power of great leadership, and men[2] with political insight and philosophical acumen, as much as those able to invent ultimate weapons, would make all the difference; the generals and admirals, the administrators of the economy and the government—these as much as atomic scientists would bring victory. A Churchill, a Marshall, an Eisenhower—they too would come from higher education.

Second, universities after World War II enjoyed a premier position among those who laid claim upon the scarce national resources; it was self-evident that for a strong, free society, education promised the surest way. The decision was natural. The country had decided, at the end of World War II, to arm for conflict by mass higher education of veterans of the conflict, if they wanted to go. Other benefits competed, but none really compared. The country determined to raise the educational level of the male population (few women were veterans), and that meant paying tuition, living costs, and other fees and expenses for everybody who qualified. More took advantage than Congress expected. But no one budged.

The face of the campus changed—probably forever. No one conceives a return to the gentle, exclusive age in which white Protestant males of old American or northwestern European family origin spent four years learning this and that before entering the family business or a guaranteed position. What changed—the nationalization of the academy, that is, the mobilization of institutional intellect in the service of public policy— changed irrevocably and, many then thought, also changed for good. The nation had reached a consensus, and the golden age of the campus dawned.

---

2. Once more, we note, women would not gain entry into politics for another two generations.

For aspiration, no limit; for money, none either. Whether it really was a golden age remains to be seen. The result is difficult to explain to young academicians today: in that era, whatever you could imagine doing, you could do. The perpetual negative of the contemporary campus—good idea, but no money—was unimaginable. For every good idea, and many bad ones, people found plenty of money. Ample funds to support graduate students, plenty of money for special projects of every kind—these to-day-unthinkable conditions prevailed. But money follows vision, and the conviction of the university as a place of authentic intellectual achieve-ment, true excellence of mind, and superiority of conscience and charac-ter—that utopian vision governed. Self-evidence protected the academy: when it came for support, people responded. And that was because the universities would form the arsenal of democracy, just as, in World War II, American industry had. What now was needed was the research, trans-lated into teaching, to make the country great and strong: atomic bombs of ideas which would win the Cold War. The Manhattan Project now rep-licated itself on the American campus.

But large-scale change takes place at a slow pace, and long before June, 1950, the universities had been changing. In fact, by the end of World War II, many of the trends that would shape higher education for the next two decades were already in place. Even before the influx of students taking advantage of the GI Bill and the infusion of cash from the federal government and private foundations, American universities had been marching away from the academic parochialism common before the Civil War. Yet such demographic and financial factors hastened the pro-cess, and to a degree, focused other trends.

II. BEFORE THE REFORM OF SECONDARY EDUCATION

What was it like to study in high schools that preserved the old ways, before the revolution in education that the Cold War would bring even to primary and secondary schools? When I went to high school, everything was cut-and-dried, obvious, and boring. I cannot remember intellectual challenges in any subject except for mathematics and any teacher truly imperious in her or his subject except for the great English teachers of the day. And, I had the impression, college would bring more of the same: do the assignment, get the A. I chose between a local college, Trinity, and Harvard, because I had never heard of anyplace else. What about Yale or Brown or Columbia or Chicago or Stanford? As a Connecticut boy, I knew only "Yankees" (descendants of the early settlers) went to Yale, and they were all anti-Semitic so I didn't want to go there. The only other college that I'd ever heard of which seemed a cut better than whatever we had in town was Harvard. Perhaps youngsters somewhere else, beyond West Hartford, knew as little about the world as I did, but it is hard to imagine. Besides, everybody said Harvard was better than the University of Connecticut, where my sister went, or Trinity, where my brother went. One student from our high school had gone to Harvard some two years earlier, which formed the basis of my comparison. Like politics, nearly all education in America was local. As usual, my perceptions placed me in the middle of the middle. I had never heard of Chicago or Johns Hopkins or Columbia or Cornell, all academically more ambitious places. The entire world of state universities existed on some distant planet.

Racism, beginning with the fully realized anti-Semitism of systematic mass murder, had gotten itself a bad name in World War II, and the then-accepted notion of exclusion from the world of intellect by reason of religious convictions or racial origins (including national origins outside of the select circle of northwestern European countries) now competed with a different concept altogether: that any qualified person could study and teach any subject anywhere. That notion took root first in mathematics (the first Jew on tenure at Dartmouth College was in mathematics, and he came when the college was a century and a half old) and in the hard sciences. Then the social sciences opened up with so many of the greatest minds coming over from Europe, where they had been victims of Nazism. And, finally, although much later, minorities started to teach English, history (including American history, although as late as 1960, the anti-Semite Carl Bridenbaugh lectured the American Historical Association about the dangers of foreigners in their midst) and classics. Except for a few small pockets of resistance, by the end of World War II, the idea of a free-thinking and meritocratic faculty had come to compete with, although hardly to supplant, all other visions of higher education.

To understand the revolution that was underway, we have to look back on the preceding century. For most of their history until the middle of our own century, colleges and universities simply added four years onto high school. The professors taught but did not evaluate their subject matter. The students learned but did not criticize what they were taught. Education equaled indoctrination, the acquisition of established facts, the mastery of unchanging paradigms. The prevailing policy stifled imagination, discouraged fresh inquiry, and effectively suppressed research, with all that that word represents in the realm of questioning established truths. Bright college years brought remarkably slight illumination.

American colleges, founded either by churches, ethnic groups, or state legislatures, had until the Civil War or even World War I, remained passive extensions of the pedantic notions of education characteristic of secondary schools, with the trappings of boarding school. State universities added an agricultural school. Dormitories provided a home away from home, and through deans and professors, colleges were surrogate parents, there to punish infractions of the rules, particularly the parietal rules. No one imagined high school teachers would pursue independent research, and of college teachers nothing more was expected.

What changed was not the university but the country that sustained the university. As America joined the larger world, so the university would overcome intellectual isolation. As American industry competed in world markets, so would professors take up the challenges of the marketplace of ideas. Free debate matched free trade, and prosperity—profits for industry, powerful propositions of great consequence for professors—would follow. National influence in intellectual matters then corresponded to national power in economic competition. So if the rise of faculty scholarship—and its symbolic link to invention and research—is linked to America's economic and diplomatic growth on the world stage between the Civil War and World War I, the connection is not coincidental. We shall see how the setting of national and global priorities routinely shaped the future of American colleges throughout the twentieth century.

III. The Advent of Scholarship on Campus

Before the Civil War, scholarship was not necessarily wedded to the university. Good work took place wherever it happened, and no one assumed—in Europe or, surely, in the United States—that the great work in science and the humanities would come from the campus. Quite to the contrary, many of the greatest ideas of the nineteenth century came from outsiders to the campus: a Viennese doctor, Sigmund Freud; a Swiss bureaucrat, Albert Einstein; and a German journalist, Karl Marx, exemplified all of those who made their livings somewhere off campus. Only a few of the great figures of learning can be identified with the life of learning and teaching that professors lead. But the idea of a casual scholar, a self-supporting autodidact devoted to a close and careful reading of data upon some revolutionary notion, was giving way to the ideal of an institution of scholarship, a legacy of nineteenth-century German universities.

The movement in the United States started at Johns Hopkins and Clark Universities. While Harvard remained a backward and dull bastion of ethnic and class interest (rich New England Yankees, but no New England Irish, Poles, Italians, French-Canadians, or Jews), and while Princeton embodied the values of the slave-holding South but not the Southern yeomen, the advent of research-oriented faculties at Johns Hopkins University in Baltimore and Clark University in Worcester, Massachusetts, in the late nineteenth century, enhanced the status of advanced scholarship at the college level. Where did research take root?

It was in what really mattered: the sciences of life and death. Medical research led the way onto the campus (just as, now, medical research is leading the way off the campus). Just as medical research spilled over into a reform of medical education, so, it would become clear, active scholarship in research would completely reshape conceptions of education. It would no longer suffice to tell people things that everybody knows: education would provoke a process of inquiry. The values of the researcher, the rationality, the questioning, the close examination of data, the testing of the known and the search into the unknown—these would give shape to a new theory of teaching, one renewing Socrates' notion that we learn through asking questions and answering them and criticizing the answers. The dramatic shift in research, as a matter of fact, involved the reform not of research but of the teaching in medical schools. In 1910, Abraham Flexner chaired a commission that found American medical schools no more than diploma mills, generating revenue for groups of doctors who barely had an interest in advancing the field. Flexner, who later made a mark guiding the work of the Carnegie Foundation, deplored the low standards of what was then regarded as medical education. The commission not only pushed higher standards, including a college degree, for all medical school applicants. It also supported the then-nascent movement toward medical research in teaching hospitals, which first took shape at Johns Hopkins Medical School in 1893.

The results of the Flexner report were twofold: It raised general standards in American medical education, particularly in student application prerequisites. It also placed scholarship above all other vocations as the most important distinction of a medical school. Medicine, once regarded as an ordinary profession suitable to scientific men who needed steady work, became a profession that, from 1910 on, was one of the most sought-after career paths in the nation. The excellence sought in medical scholarship then would in time be translated into a search for excellence in other fields, particularly those in the hard sciences, like mathematics, physics, biology, and engineering. Combined with an explosion in knowledge in the hard sciences, such fields foisted new standards upon universities.

Standards like merit, excellence, and initiative could not be earned solely because of elitist or traditional preeminence. Certain colleges—Yale and Harvard, for example—quickly joined the trend by launching professional and graduate schools; others, like Princeton, did not. We shall see how such decisions in the early part of the twentieth century had deep effects on the institutions.

Either way, the excellence sought by faculty spread over the classroom too; students could not remain immune to the fever of discovery. And for that reason, the basis of selecting a college shifted. For students, staying close to home or family loyalty to a particular institution had been the preeminent factor in college selection for decades. But such localism and provincialism gave way to excellence in academics. State universities still retained their coveted position, but among the Atlantic seaboard elite and growing middle class, it was not uncommon for the best and brightest to seek the very best, whether from near or far away. Because the exotic attracted, the familiar repelled, and this usually meant going out of state, to a private college. This perception, valid or not, remains true today, although more so for undergraduate education. At the graduate level, where admissions standards are significantly higher, state universities maintain a very high reputation. Graduate students go to the famous professors, who can lead them to the frontiers of learning and beyond, and whose repute will afterward also make finding a good job easy.

Church-related colleges, particularly Protestant ones, were learning that they could not accomplish their academic goals if they excluded non-believers; they needed some as students, and even a few as professors. So as the country became more diverse, church-related colleges began to reconsider criteria for appointment. But, while keeping themselves separate from the dogma of their founding churches or institutions proved central to their improvement, the idea of serving society—continuing the goal of serving the church—was not lost. The Protestant commitment to a worldly vocation would take a secular form. The college would now measure its success by its contribution to the social order.

In fact, because of a growing social acceptance of the purpose and meaning of higher education, many colleges—particularly state universities—devoted themselves more to particular goals. In research, this meant an expansion of scholarship in emerging or ignored areas. In teaching, this meant emphasizing relevant and practical matters over theoretical ones. In no sector of higher education was this experiment more prevalent than in women's colleges. Such institutions were wedded closely to a social agenda, making them not unlike their Protestant brothers a century before: weak to the whim of dogmatic vision. However, women's colleges were not engaged in mindless brainstorming. From them American higher education learned several values, and even as these were integrated into the mostly male private colleges and state universities by mid-century, the beginning of the Cold War found women's colleges still on the very edge of the new ideology of higher education. Only a few included important research in their academic programs, and only in a few subject areas.

But the face of the academy was changing, because minds had changed. What had formerly sufficed no longer was enough; indeed, in the great centers of serious learning, the genteel program of the nineteenth-century college or university (except for Clark and Hopkins) would no longer serve at all. But what then would serve? And, to begin with, where should discussion commence? Is the issue how to teach or what to teach? Predictably, at the core of this search for a new ideology would come a striking departure from past philosophical concern. The "how" would give way to the "what," just as in learning, the substance of education was taking over and surpassing the form, as new learning succeeded. During the first half of the century, most curricular debate focused on the way knowledge would be imparted. During the second half, many colleges, particularly women's colleges, debated the substance of that knowledge itself. It is not surprising that debate in the freshest terms would begin on the margins, at the women's colleges, not at those reserved for men. Freer and more able to contemplate the unthinkable, the women's college faculties asked the questions everyone else assumed were settled. With less at stake in the status quo, they went about reinventing the "what" of learning, particularly for the classroom. Everybody thought they knew what a college degree should represent; everyone would be proved wrong.

For example, the matter of giving preference to knowledge of contemporary significance, or relevance, resonated at colleges like Sarah Lawrence and Bennington. They surveyed their students, attempting to find out what knowledge and information each needed. They created curricula and areas of study that depended not on imparted curriculum from days gone by, but on the issues which many of their students would face upon graduation. Such a form of study, with its heavy emphasis on making all knowledge relevant, had its obvious pitfalls. Not unlike the controversy over the creation of "survey" or "core" courses in general liberal education, the student-directed curriculum was criticized. Some felt students would find the relevant studies of their college years mostly irrelevant five years later. Others said the generalized approach, later common in interdisciplinary studies, gave students the full expanse of knowledge without even a road map. Yet this was the point, as John S. Brubacher and Willis Rudy note: "Faculties like those of Bennington and Sarah Lawrence held the conviction that integration is something to be sought in the individual student, not in the curriculum."[3] The fact that these issues played themselves out strongly in women's colleges should not surprise. The same issues had been debated a generation earlier, with great emotion, at mostly male universities. Most colleges leaned towards a generalized approach, mostly in reaction to the growing specialization of knowledge. There was fear, compounded by the growth of knowledge, that the college experience would no longer include the moral and intellectual inculcation of society's future leaders.

IV. General Education for a Global Vision

During the 1930s, the University of Chicago, for example, set up a model not unlike a junior college, where the first two years of the undergraduate experience were devoted to rounding out a student's general education. The concept of a general education was emphasized at Columbia University during World War I, when some students there took a course called "War Issues," which approached common subjects from a historical, political, economic, and philosophical point of view. The apparent success of the course, combined with the fear over the splitting of the curriculum, gave way to Columbia's efforts to tie together learning into survey courses. Alexander Meiklejohn, first at Brown University and then at University of Wisconsin, attempted a similar approach at integrating disciplines in an approach to a single civilization, such as Greece, Rome, or the United States.

Meiklejohn's vision was to take a cue from events, and not from subject matter. Attempts at Columbia and Chicago followed the same logic; most efforts at general education yielded "core" requirements. Another lasting feature of the general education movement was the introductory course, taught by an esteemed professor in the field, preferably one who was still shaping it. The effect of looking at knowledge not simply as a collection of facts, but as a coagulation of ideas, was beginning to take shape.

After the war, however, general education remained hopelessly far from the mainstream, until Harvard University issued its Redbook, a commission report on "General education in a free society." That report, never adopted at

---

3. Brubacher and Rudy, p. 277.

Harvard, acknowledged the heavy impulse towards specialization, particularly in the natural sciences. But it found great promise for interdisciplinary and symbiotic work in the humanities and social sciences. For the first time, a prestigious university seriously considered previously marginal issues, such as the relationship between a student's education and his ability to coordinate it. Ironically, the general education movement—which was launched partly because so many faculty were becoming alarmed that their students had no grasp of the books and knowledge that shaped their own college educations—yielded a philosophy that emphasized theory over fact. Not to be displaced, however, were the core elements of such an education: Western civilization's great books. Some argued such books were the very essence of fact over theory. Others said they united knowledge, by forcing professors to find the philosophical girders of knowledge, something which had not been done since theology was ejected from the curriculum in most American colleges. Either way, some previously unheralded colleges, like St. John's College in Annapolis, Maryland, made their mark as a pure, liberal arts education institution revolving around these great ideas and books of human history.

Subsequent commissions and studies found American higher education greatly lacking in its support of the nation's "common culture." The Truman Commission on Higher Education, which in 1947 looked at a variety of issues within colleges, argued that universities ought to devote themselves to asserting American leadership in the world. It would be difficult to identify a more explicit statement of how universities were to enlist in the national struggle. Such internationalism aside, the Truman Commission said overspecialization had yielded little in the way of vision, educational or otherwise. At Massachusetts Institute of Technology, one of the nation's leading colleges in service to the nation's needs after the war, the faculty was pushed to accept such a mission, not by having top professors teach undergraduate survey courses, but by having such professors introduce high level research to still budding minds. The integration of research and introductory level work was at that point unique, but it proved a helpful model for other colleges and other subjects.

The strongest criticism of general education came from those who saw the results as diffuse: however, the biggest drawback was that few skilled professors could teach such survey and interdisciplinary courses. Demanding both in time and skill, such courses needed a seasoned professor who had reached the very top of his field. In certain circumstances, such professors were simply too rare to make the equation work. It became easier, therefore, for universities to embrace the general education ideal through introductory courses and loose-fitting credit requirements.

Still, the overwhelming growth of the economy after World War II, and its concurrent call for practical education, rendered the debates about generalized education moot. The lasting response to specialization, if there was one, was the growth of honors programs. Conceived in the early part of the century, such programs, which emphasized close faculty-student contact, won overwhelming approval of students. However, one wonders whether such approval was merely a reaction to the need for an even higher stamp of certification beyond the standard bachelor's degree.

V. THE PROFESSIONAL REVOLUTION AMONG THE PROFESSORS

What had occurred even before the outbreak of the Cold War to make universities less parochial and more geared towards excellence in scholarship? Certain subjects, particularly those hard sciences that had previously been categorized as "natural philosophy," had exploded with knowledge. Teaching as an exercise of repetition of long-learned facts had simply vanished as a useful skill, since knowledge was being created every day. Yet the changes in universities cannot be linked solely to what was happening in certain subject areas. The American economy, moving rapidly from agrarian to industrial to commercial foci, had created a new kind of student for the American university.

David Riesman and Christopher Jencks, in their sociological and historical study of American colleges, *The Academic Revolution,* noted that the liberal arts—hardly changed by an exponential growth in knowledge—grew in scholarly stature because many of the new college students taking liberal arts classes after World War I would not have attended college a generation earlier. Many of these students were readying themselves for a professional career, one marked by a meritocracy and expert knowledge. The GI Bill brought to a changing campus an entirely new kind of student—middle class, not just upper class; Catholic, not just Protestant; children of immigrant parents, not just children of longer-established migrants. And the campus presented a curriculum able to encompass the new classes of students, not class-indoctrination in the knowledge, possession of which would signify high class status (Latin, for example), but the education of citizens able to ask tough questions—and answer them.

That explains why, over time, American universities prepared themselves not only for explosive growth within the ranks of students, but in subject matter as well. By the end of World War I, American professional and graduate schools had begun to accept and seize the role of leader in various fields, including medicine, law, and engineering. As we noted earlier, prior to Abraham Flexner's scathing report on the country's medical education in 1910 to Congress, most medical schools were set up by groups of private doctors for profit. Of 155 schools, only 16 required two or more years of college of its applicants.The situation attracted the attention of Andrew Carnegie, who decided to wean schools off such habits by sheer force of his largesse. It worked. By 1928, after he set standards to go with his grants, the number of schools was reduced to eighty, principles of teaching had been established, and by 1945 American medical education had gone from one of the worst in the civilized world to the top. That American medical research would first meet, then define, international standards provided only an indicator of changes taking place elsewhere in the higher learning.

We realize, of course, that the political community, nearly all of it now college-educated, could not remain indifferent to the value to the country at large of the new intellectual resources of the campus. The growing influence of colleges in larger society was aided mostly by implications of scholarship in the effort to win World War II. At the urging of several advisers, President Franklin Roosevelt placed great faith and resources in university laboratories in developing technologies useful to the war effort. Chief among these, the Manhattan Project in the deserts of New Mexico engaged the nation's leaders with the promise of a column of insight independent of the nation's defense industries or agencies. Besides proving the value of independent scholarship, the effort to build the first atomic bomb garnered lasting loyalties, both from government leaders and the public in general.

The road carried traffic in both directions, to the campus from the community, from the community to the academy. The college thought of itself as isolated, often building walls about the campus to signify the protected preserve of serene intellect. Now the walls came down. "The ivory tower conception of the university has been largely displaced by a belief in the almost magical powers of the scholar-scientist," wrote Oliver C. Carmichael, the president of the Carnegie Foundation for the Advancement of Teaching in the 1953 *Current Issues in Higher Education*.[4] So while advanced scholarship had the effect of encouraging distance between scholars and the society they served, the opposite was true: the scholars proved their value in the most basic means possible. They helped win and end a world war. And, as we said earlier, they would win the Cold War, too.

---

4. Smith, ed., *1945–1970: Twenty-Five Years*, p. 39.

But the business of America is business. And if the political consensus settled on the campus as a national treasure, commerce and industry could not stay far behind. Indeed, if educated citizens were required to fight the Cold War, young people educated in the principles of management and equipped to make decisions in the face of the unknown would also have to come forth to manage the military industrial complex that had developed. And, given the country's unlimited faith in education and in the university as the center and source of education, we should not find surprising the formation of a new constituency for academic service.

In the business world, which a generation earlier had been run by entrepreneurs, seat-of-your-pants management no longer sufficed. A managerial revolution had created a market for professionals capable of managing and understanding the institutionalized growth common to American business and organizations between World War I and the Depression. In an earlier generation, future free-marketers sought college for connections and perhaps the erudition and honing it offered. But by the middle of the century, students needed an education—even a liberal arts education—focused on practical matters like business management and principles of understanding mass society. Moreover, American entrepreneurship, a fabled nursery for American businesses during the turn of the century, suffered a blow during the Depression, driving many bright prospects to seek "credentials and work for a big, safe organization [rather] than . . . gamble in the open market."[5] American universities were quick to realize this, offering a curriculum that bestowed such credentials. And if universities could bestow credentials in other fields, professional benchmarks from those fields could be applied equally to the universities themselves.

Professionalization of management found its match on campus in the professionalization of the professorate. New standards defined what excellence required, and rules would govern what in times past a college president's prejudice would dictate; promotion and preferment for instance. A half-century before, what counted as standards in American universities would hardly rate mention when the war ended. Professors had not been expected to publish, and tenure had come through longevity, the result of a popularity contest. Proof of changing conditions of employment on campus came in the form of two major trends by mid-century. Tenure would almost universally reward qualified professors, not merely out of good will, but because of accomplishment. In the end, professionalization came about because professors insisted on it. It was the faculties that

---

5. Jencks and Riesman, *The Academic Revolution*, p. 94.

demanded their administrations set out clear definitions of excellence. Once research began to be valued, it would quickly define the highest value; nothing could compete, because the commitment to research would redefine the traits of good teaching, too. Other forms of academic activity—service on committees, community service, for example—would receive little attention. When the old order changes, it leaves few monuments to itself. When the new order takes over, it takes no prisoners.

Such new standards—contributing to learning through publication, participating in national scholarship in your field—had the dual effect of protecting professors from being fired and forcing professors to meet minimum goals. Mr. Chipps would have to go—a lazy, time-waster, who taught what was, anyhow, no longer true; and Mark Hopkins could sit on his end of the log, until, without a student on the other end, he toppled over and drowned. The old ideal of surrogate fathers giving wise advice to fictive sons persisted in the formality of affirmation of "good teaching." But most knew good teaching only when they saw it, along with the art they liked but could not explain but that won their approval. Research was something else: palpable, measurable in circulation and influence and effect. You could read reviews, count the number of times reference was made to an article, determine the impact of a book. Collegial response replaced the vagary of student nostalgia in the long-term reputation of a university.

For state universities, which remained captive to the political whims of legislators, setting such standards, for both job protection and academic freedom, had an unusual effect. And it was a very positive one, securing for the future the primacy in the American research enterprise of state-supported education. Frederic Heimberger predicted in 1964 that state universities, because of their institutionalized protection for professors, would one day enjoy greater academic freedom than private ones. And while the coming debates over the relative merits of teaching and scholarship remained dormant, a pervasive feeling took hold that without tenure there is no scholarship. One wonders whether it has ever been defeated.

The result is ambiguous. On the one hand, the academicians got what they wanted: a critical position in the hierarchy of national priorities, broad appreciation for precisely the labor that they conducted, exact appreciation for what they produced. Until the end of the Cold War and the imposition of a social agenda in place of a national, political one, meritocracy governed, because results of an academic character concerning intellect and learning were what mattered. It would follow as self-evident that universities did what universities did and not something else. No one supposed universities could make up for the deficiencies of the social order.

No one even conceived that the academy was possessed of the appropriate resources to do so. But, on the other hand, while that concept of the academy would emerge only much later, the source for it derived from the notion, encouraged by universities themselves, of the academy as a place where the country brought its problems. Once universities critically addressed one set of national problems, people would naturally expect them to proceed to take up another. Even at the outset of the Cold War, that concept, vastly encouraged by universities themselves, would take root and lead in directions the research scholars could scarcely imagine.

But we have moved ahead of our story. Back in the late 1940s, meritocratic thinking changed American universities. If most universities were once governed by the principles of conformity and loyalty to the founding fathers of a college, with priority in admissions assigned to the children of alumni, by the end of World War II, professors pledged their loyalty to excellence above all. The war had exposed the potential. The expansion of funds for research was fueled largely by the war effort and its effect on the nation's understanding of the power of knowledge. But, as a matter of fact, the building blocks were in place even before then. Thorstein Veblen, the bohemian rogue scholar who demonized much of what he saw in several American colleges, died in 1929, just before the University of Chicago—where he had taught for several years—threw off the cloak of "shabby-genteel academics hired to provide a bit of polish." The college quickly began building a university based on the principles of organized and inventive scholarship. In the Cold War, the University of Chicago would achieve the well-earned reputation as the most authentically academic of all American universities, the one place where the pure ideals of learning governed. Preeminent in many fields, it would define for all of them the standard of excellence in dedication to scholarship and the labor of reasoned inquiry. In the season of riots in the late 1960s and early 1970s, Chicago's great president, Edward Levi, informed rioters that for disturbing the peace of the academy they could and would be thrown out. His was one of the few elite campuses that survived unimpaired and, indeed, intact. And among its greatest monuments, the University of Chicago Press defined the model of what a university press was meant to be.

Where government treads, private enterprise follows. Private foundations, which gained strength precisely at the time when America's colleges and universities were reaching this professionalized stage, hastened the process by setting standards tied to monetary grants. Here too, long before World War II, the academy could discern the coming age. Just as the Flexner Report, the work of private philanthropy, would reform medical education, so private philanthropy would point the way toward the reform of the academy in general. Andrew Carnegie, whose early notion of helping retired teachers avoid abject poverty was transformed into a sweeping vision of a private education foundation, tied his money to required standards unheard of before World War I, namely: admissions standards for undergraduates, anti-denominational hiring standards for professors, required endowments and matching funds, standard curriculum measurements, systematized finances, higher qualifications and salaries for professors, and encouraging research in unpopular areas, like the social sciences. Such standards were extended to black colleges as well.

Foundations supported and standardized the teaching of medicine, law, and social sciences. The Carnegie and Rockefeller foundations, in particular, created the huge sums of money needed for hard science research. The standards set before World War II were carried forward after the war, particularly in the social sciences, which were just emerging as a field. Later in that postwar period, even as federal government money flowed into certain areas of research, foundations were responsible for nearly a quarter of the budgets of American universities.

The Ford Foundation, founded in 1936, had not found its mission until immediately after the war, when it supported and supplanted many of the functions of the then-pervasive Carnegie Corporation and Carnegie Foundation. In particular, Ford allowed the nascent symbiosis of social and behavioral sciences to prosper. The concept of studying society using the tools of psychology was, at that time, virtually unheard of, and yet Ford supported institutional and individual programs in the area. In particular, Ford's dollars pushed economists to participate in urban studies; behavioral scientists to participate in anthropology, and ethnographers, etymologists, and personality psychologists to look at cultures and societies with a unified goal: to promote peace, education, democracy, and the economy. Where social science had previously existed, it was transformed by dollars from a fairly theoretical discipline to one that was answering questions asked by emerging areas, both at home and abroad.

VI. SCHOLARSHIP AND HIGHER EDUCATION: THE CURRICULUM CHANGES

It was one thing to impose high standards of research productivity, but quite another to educate people able to meet those standards. That meant, to begin with, enormous investment in graduate education, a vast increase in the number of people achieving the Ph.D., and a commensurate improvement in the standards of the degree. More people were needed—people of higher qualifications as well. It is quite natural, therefore, that the growing preeminence of scholarship during the postwar period was supported by a similar interest on the part of many colleges in graduate programs.

By 1950, there were five times as many graduate students as there had been in 1930. And during the 1950s, there were more doctorates awarded in America than there had been in all the previous decades combined. But most important, graduate school requirements and standards had reached a much higher point; in the nineteenth and early twentieth centuries, master's degrees had been awarded for longevity or as recognition for the equivalent of a fifth year of undergraduate work. Even in the 1920s, a Ph.D. was regarded as a "union card" to get a university teaching job and not much else. Within a generation, the requirement for an advanced degree was research, usually combined with some training in teaching.

While promoted as necessary to provide faculty to the burgeoning campuses of that period, the expansion of graduate programs was fueled by outside dollars—from the federal government, in particular, especially in the hard sciences. This, however, did not occur without considerable controversy on several campuses, even during the halcyon days following the war. Indeed, while the concerns were originally voiced in the interests of maintaining cohesion and financial balance between "practical" and "impractical" disciplines, the stridency of such opposition heightened when professors were asked about their political and national loyalties.

Such concerns aside, graduate programs reached their zenith not through the traditional schools of law, medicine and the arts. The professionalization of the American economy, with its concurrent need for standards and certifications, was serviced by American graduate programs. Schools of nursing, pharmacology, business, public administration, education, journalism, and agriculture, to name a few, transformed trades into professions, where advanced understanding of subjects mattered. And universities quickly learned that the best way to achieve national prominence was through graduate schools, not colleges.

Brandeis University, for example, was envisioned by inaugural president Abram Sachar as a model for general education. But Sachar also wanted a nationally recognized university—and found the going quite slow. He was forced to reconcile his original plans with the need to produce doctoral students under professors who were at the top of their fields. In the end Brandeis would find it impossible to compete with other Massachusetts powers, such as M.I.T. and Harvard. Distinguished neither in teaching nor in scholarship, it inherited the worst of both worlds. In the previous century, universities had sought to make their mark by aligning themselves with a specific religious philosophy, ethnic or racial group, geographic area, or simple exclusivity and social hierarchy. By the 1950s, there was only one way for a university to survive, let alone make its mark: scholarship. And scholarship required expensive laboratories, large libraries, and well-paid professors.

VII. A NEW BREED OF STUDENT

So much for who teaches what. We wonder, to whom was the new curriculum to be addressed? And this brings us back to the immediacy of the campus after World War II. By far, however, the largest external force on colleges immediately after World War II was the contingent of veterans. The fresh faces came in droves, attracted by the blank-check promise of a free college education. The effect of war veterans on college campuses is well-known. In 1945, when the country's population numbered almost 140 million, colleges and universities enrolled about 1.7 million students. The following academic year, there were 2.6 million students—a 35 per cent increase. The concurrent stress on universities to teach, house, and manage such an influx did not compare, however, to the attitudinal effect such students had on the campus.

These veterans, as noted by David Riesman, dispensed "quickly with the collegiate in the rush to make up for lost time."[6] They frequently sought to attain their degree in three years, rather than four. And by sheer numbers, they forced colleges to make better use of their resources, as in the development of year-round schooling. Having fought a war, these older students did not supplicate themselves to the traditions or juvenile perversities common to colleges before the war. Some had learned foreign languages, others history. They did not fear college, even though many would not have attended had the government not paid the bill. Perhaps because they were drawn from a relatively wide spectrum of American society, by sheer numbers they broke the control of the social and cultural elite, particularly at the nation's top private colleges. Coupled with the growing trend towards faculty professionalism and meritocracy, their presence helped create not only a larger university system, but also a brighter one.

The growing enrollment in colleges continued unabated even after the wave of war veterans passed. While the United States population crept forward at about 5 per cent a year, college enrollment doubled between

6. David Riesman, *On Higher Education*, p. 45.

1945 and 1960. Women, too, were entering college in greater numbers, and the institutions they were attending were just as ambitious as their male counterparts in pursuing talented scholars for faculty. Blacks, Jews, and Catholics all had developed interests in higher education before the war—although for different reasons. However, the war's lessons, brought home by having fought the Nazis in particular, eradicated any latent racism or bigotry against groups of traditionally unwelcomed applicants. Jews, in particular, had been thwarted between the two world wars. At colleges like Columbia, New York University, Harvard, Yale, and Rutgers, quotas effectively pushed Jews out of the elite colleges even after an earlier generation had proven their interest in attaining skills. But the quotas were relatively limited in scope—the private schools in the nation's Northeast used them, most others did not—and by the end of World War II, they had begun to fall away. Still, through the mid-1950s at Harvard and into the 1960s at Dartmouth, as if by magic, each freshman class comprised 10 percent Jews, and at Yale and Princeton, proportions were even lower, and the welcome accorded to these non-Christians even cooler.

Though many students were the first of their families to go to college, some were not. For even as many first-generation college students flooded the campus, the growth in enrollment was not exclusively rooted in lower to lower-middle economic groups. College had become a requisite for the upper-middle-class in particular, and if a high school senior's family included a college-educated parent, he was much more likely to see the need to carry on for another degree. A child of well-educated background had a 47 in 100 chance for entering college between 1915–25. Thirty years later, the same child had a 78 in 100 chance. Coming from an educated background also made a difference in completion. Having an educated father increased chances of completion by 50 percent. Indeed, while college was a first-time experience for many of the new breed, those coming from educated or well-off backgrounds were joining the college ranks in far greater numbers, too. The doubling of college attendance was not strictly limited to one ethnic, religious, or economic group. It was broad-based, and drawn from those most likely to perceive an education's benefits to receive its rewards.

The growing democratization of higher education did, however, run headlong into another trend. Many university leaders felt the elite universities should take advantage of rising enrollments not by expanding their campuses, but by making them more meritocratic. This, they argued, would improve not only their status, but their capabilities. And where, others argued, would the other students go? The answer, to the delight of those who favored expanding both the opportunities and lowering the costs of higher education, was public institutions. State universities had been launched on the basis of teaching agricultural and technical skills a century earlier. But by the decade immediately following World War II, they, too, shared many of the characteristics of private colleges. They adopted new subject matter, encouraged faculty to perform important research and generally sought the approbation common to the elite national universities. Moreover, the increased support and recognition accorded to universities in general was felt most in the state universities, where certain states created vast systems of interrelated campuses. California and New York emerged as leaders in supporting such growth, which was fueled largely by the populist dream of teaching the nation's returning veterans at cut rates. But while the state systems could easily fall back on the models and examples set by the private universities—or push them, as in the case of the Wisconsin and Minnesota, both leaders in curriculum reform—the impact of growth had even deeper impact on the nation's junior colleges, which had retained, to a large degree, the responsibilities of the old land grant institutions.

For junior colleges, the end of World War II promised two things: rising enrollment and a concurrent crisis over mission. Not unlike their four-year counterparts, the junior colleges faced external challenges which vexed the nature of the institutions. Where colleges were forced to adopt new standards to meet the needs of professional and graduate schools, junior colleges were forced to place themselves in contradistinction to colleges, which had "adopted," to a certain degree, the mantle of populism through the GI Bill. Junior colleges and their faculty were left to debate between educating for the benefit of transfer-track students, or instead, for those students geared for a two-year, terminal vocational degree. Not unlike four-year institutions, junior colleges were faced with the challenge between giving students a general understanding of information, or a more particular, practical education. These issues were borne out by the Truman Commission on Higher Education, the blue ribbon committee which, in 1947, laid out issues relevant to the then still-emerging junior college movement. Phrased in the optimism of the years immediately after the end of the war, the Truman Commission's findings linked higher education, and higher education for underrepresented groups in particular, to the long-range stability of the country. To gain the goal of allowing one-third of the nation's students to enter college-level programs, a goal self-imposed by the commission and reached by the middle of the 1960s, the commission placed great emphasis on combining technical training not only with general education, but with adult education as well. Towards that goal, the commission also suggested renaming the institutions "community colleges," both to emphasize this democratic ideal and to distinguish the fledgling institutions from four-year colleges.

To a certain degree, the tension between emphasizing the general instead of the technical was settled by the students themselves. Before World War II, most junior colleges were largely middle-class, and perceptions of the students held that they were below par. But following the war, these same colleges took in a more representative selection of the population, especially more students from blue-collar families. Subsequent studies, authors Steven Brint and Jerome Karabel say, show junior college students performing at the same level as their four-year college counterparts. Such students were increasingly interested in pursuing a four-year degree eventually, and not the two-year, terminal degree often supported by certain administrators and faculty.

Still, while students effectively put the issue to rest by choosing to pursue four-year degrees, support for community colleges continued from some unlikely quarters. Many of the nation's education leaders, apparently apprehensive about the limited economic opportunities available to many of the returning war veterans (and despite obvious evidence to the contrary), suggested that community colleges could exercise a winnowing effect on the incoming students. They offered a model where students would be routinely guided towards vocational and technical programs to keep them from developing undeserved hopes for success. James Bryant Conant, Harvard's president from 1933 to 1953, suggested in 1948 that universities ought to define their task only in terms of teaching the most promising, leaving the less promising students to community colleges. While apparently elitist, Conant's approach, similar to others reacting to a fear over the management of the nation's "human resources," anticipated an event which never came in the postwar boom years: a severe space crunch at the university level and an economic downturn driving down the demand for college-educated citizens.

Indeed, Conant's approach underscored a larger movement in American society, already discussed in this chapter: a movement away from higher education for the elite and a growing appreciation for the naturally gifted. Conant's preoccupation with filling university lecture halls with the most talented students available fed his interest, and others like him, to promote the cause of community colleges. The two-year institutions, starving for such ideological support, did not reject Conant. To the contrary, it took many more years before foundations and private money reached the same conclusions. But governments did take notice. In 1950, the state of New York launched its ambitious state university system largely on the foundations of seventeen community and technical colleges. As Brint and Karabel note, New York's entry into the expansion of community college market demonstrated that the community college, previously found mostly in Western states, was becoming a lasting institution. Only in states where universities feared community colleges' ability to woo students did the two-year schools not receive the state funding needed.

VIII. THE SECTARIAN AND PAROCHIAL INSTITUTIONS

American higher education presents a range of diversity unknown in most other countries: public and private; sectarian and nonsectarian; black, racially neutral, and all-white; segregated by sex and integrated; local, regional, national. But among the many types of colleges and universities that serve, three take pride of place: the Catholic, the black, and the women's colleges. And while critical to the education of enormous numbers of young people, all three types of colleges at the time of this chapter remained unchanged, indeed scarcely affected, by the revolution on campus brought by the requirements of a nation arming for the Cold War.

While Riesman and Jencks herald the period immediately following the end of the war as a period of growth and realization for universities, they point out that the revolutions in professionalism, particularity, and federal support lagged in institutions not prepared for such changes. For instance, black colleges remained hopelessly mired, compared to their white counterparts. Having fewer of the material advantages of white colleges—whether private or public—black colleges could not have aspired to reach the same level of faculty professionalism or research. However, notwithstanding relative poverty and discrimination in the parceling out of federal research money, black colleges reached the second half of the century behind because they depended on an antiquated model of higher education. As noted by Jencks and Riesman, black colleges remained a "caricature" of white colleges, with the attendant social forms: heavy influence of elitism, exemplified by fraternities and sororities, and petty dealings between faculty, administration, and students.

Not unlike most American colleges three decades before, black colleges focused on goals separate from the pursuit of knowledge. Because they held substantial influence over the black community, black colleges acted more as social stratifiers. Great care was taken toward the protection of student morals. Curriculum was outdated, based largely on high-school-level knowledge. And because black poverty was so rampant, and black opportunities within a mostly white economy limited, black colleges served the needs of the black, not the white, community. Black colleges trained professionals (i.e., doctors, ministers), but for the black community only. The focus on students being guided by the opportunity to use education to fill important positions within larger society did not exist to the same extent on these black campuses, as it did on white campuses of the same era. So the professionalization which affected national and state universities from the end of World War I did not have the same effect on black colleges. They remained, as Jencks and Riesman point out, several important steps apart.

Black colleges, because they were heavily dependent on the largesse of white benefactors, did make several important steps towards achieving the standards set by white colleges, a key component of their ability to join the academic revolution. But there was, to a certain degree, a need to satisfy the base interest of some kind of external force, usually identified as white society. "Instead of trying to promote a distinctive set of habits and values in their students, the Negro colleges became purveyors of super-American, ultra-bourgeois prejudices and aspirations. Far from fighting to preserve a separate subculture, as other ethnic colleges did, the Negro colleges were militantly opposed to almost everything that made Negroes different from whites, on the grounds that it was 'lower class.'"[7] This exaggerated ethos of black colleges was not necessarily shared by all blacks, and certainly not by all blacks two decades later. By the mid-1960s, black students in mostly white colleges not only rejected the political and economic values of their new institutions, but demanded a black sector within them. Before that time, most black students came from backgrounds where poverty was so pervasive that the concept of a college education simply did not register in importance; until blacks began to see the value of a college degree in terms of economic opportunity in the white world, black college students were not faced with the identity crisis which later evidenced itself in re-segregation.

While Riesman and Jencks identify black colleges as acting as a shadow to their white counterparts, the two authors also link the status of black colleges to Catholic colleges. Both shared an obvious demographic characteristic—their students self-segregated, or were segregated by external forces—and both kinds of colleges lacked the institutional tradition or inclination towards creating or supporting graduate programs. But both

---

7. Jencks and Riesman, pp. 424–25.

were posed, by the 1950s, with a problem. Both blacks and Catholics were being actively recruited to some of the nation's most prestigious universities, and while the groups maintained basic allegiances to certain institutions, it was hard to argue with the benefits of attending a national university, both because of opportunities and prestige.

That is one reason why, by the second half of the century, Catholic colleges could not afford to carry on the debates between parochial loyalty and scholarship. Even as such colleges reverberated with battles between Church dogma and potentially unsettling scholarship, Catholic colleges moved towards the mainstream And just as the Catholic institutions aimed at moving forward, they continued to benefit from a universal approach, preventing the splintering common in secular colleges among departments, faculties, and graduate programs. This unifying vision of education later provided Catholic colleges an immediate advantage over their secular counterparts in securing institutional purpose.

Still, as long as Catholic colleges lagged behind their secular counterparts in giving their faculty freedom to pursue their interests, latent distaste for "liberalistic academic freedoms" appeared to keep Catholic institutions solidly behind the times. In particular, Catholic colleges had not advanced on the issue of scholarship in social sciences and tenure in general. Most Catholic schools did not even aspire to the concept of a university; before 1945, Catholic University in Washington, D.C., was the only one in the United States. And even while Catholic colleges constituted a segregated sector of higher education, the schools remained aloof, not only from their secular counterparts, but from each other. Although they shared an association, the Catholic schools did not have the unifying element of an athletic league or an accrediting agency. As other institutions of higher education were moving quickly into an age of professorial independence, power in the Catholic colleges remained vested with the administration. This condition was certainly aided by an almost nonexistent tenure system: a 1942 study found that while 10 percent of non-Catholic institutions extended one-year professor contracts, 44 percent of Catholic colleges did. And while only 8 percent of non-Catholic institutions had no tenure, 65 percent of Catholic colleges had none.

Throughout the immediate decade following the end of World War II, Catholic colleges remained, intellectually speaking, "backwaters." This attitude was partly shaped by theology—Catholicism was not traditionally interested in a flexible attitude towards immutable or moral truths. But, as Charles Curran notes, the anti-intellectualism rampant in Catholic colleges was aided by the larger perception that declining standards of American morality were aided by most American colleges. That loosening morality, in this view, included the acceptance of communism or communist sentiments on secular campuses. In his 1949 address upon ascending to the presidency of Georgetown University, Father Hunter Guthrie explained the purpose of a Catholic university largely in terms of moral inculcation in an age of sin. As Curran summarized: "(He) paints a very negative picture of human beings at the midway point of the twentieth century."[8]

For the Catholic colleges, what Riesman and Jencks described as the Academic Revolution came, but not at the same pace as it did for secular institutions. The philosophical trend towards professionalism, especially among the professors, did not translate into a greater acceptance of tenure or of independent scholarship. Catholic colleges were not banned from benefiting from the GI Bill, but the heavy influence of the federal government did not alter the Catholics' chosen path. Changes were to come; just as the pace was set for the first half of the twentieth century by officialdom within the Church, so too, would the Church leadership help bring about the growth of scholarship in Catholic colleges. Changes in the occupational trends among Catholics required, to a certain degree, what decades of self-segregation could not: college administrators had to start offering first-rate professional and graduate training.

IX. TO BE YOUNG WAS VERY HEAVEN

To spend a lifetime on the American university campus—who would have dreamed, at the age of seventeen, that such a thing could happen to a Jewish boy from West Hartford? I was a typical suburban yokel, able to see horizons that stretched outward only to Bloomfield and Wethersfield and as far as my father's newspaper's printing plant in Southington. My father had founded and would publish until his death the *Connecticut Jewish Ledger*, the English-language general circulation newspaper then serving the Jewish communities of Connecticut and Western Massachusetts. In his office I learned how to work. Through junior high and high school I ran errands for the paper every afternoon after school, five days a week; we had *Hartford Times* stringers, by whom I was taught news writing, headline writing, news editing, layout, and make-up. By my junior year in high school I could do everything but sell advertising. I reviewed books from the age of thirteen, wrote editorials when our editor was away, and from the age of sixteen put out the paper when the news editor was on vacation. When I left West Hartford, I never wanted to walk into a

---

8. Curran, p. 33.

newspaper office again, and I never did. So the junior writer of this book took up a career in journalism—go figure!

What I didn't have is what I wanted. I had little formal education in Judaism: a smattering of the Hebrew alphabet, and nothing else I can remember. Yet from my twelfth birthday, I had always wanted to be a rabbi and never entertained any other ambition. I even bore the naive notion that what qualified one as a rabbi was learning, a conviction that, had I actually served in a pulpit of a synagogue, would have marked me as unsuited. Of my childhood, it suffices to cite two sentences I remember thinking time and again: (1) Let me do it by myself! (2) Let me take it apart and put it together to see how it works! These turn out, now, to form the keys to the lock of worthwhile knowledge.

Being born in that third generation beyond immigration of which Marcus Lee Hansen had said, "What the second generation tries to forget the third generation wants to remember," I had a keen interest in what made me different from my playmates, most of whom didn't go to Temple Beth Israel, the century-old West Hartford Reform synagogue. On my father's side my grandparents came to Beverly, Massachusetts, at the beginning of this century. On my mother's side, my great-grandmother came from Odessa to New York City; of the others I knew nothing. But my parents spoke only English, and my one living grandparent, my father's mother, did too, although she spoke to my father in Yiddish, which no one taught me.

My roots, such as they were, were sunk into the clay soil of the Connecticut River valley. Along with everyone else, young Jewish Americans were taught Connecticut history in the setting of Puritan Christianity, and drew pictures of Congregational Churches, celebrated our forefathers' Thanksgiving with the Indians, observed Christmas in school, recited the Lord's Prayer, and, in general, thought of ourselves as perfectly normal Americans, for everybody did these things. None of the Jewish students found this odd or off-putting. West Hartford for young Jews could have presented a malign face, had we looked at how things really were. I grew up before and during World War II, when America, inhospitable to many minorities and utterly indifferent to the presence of blacks, chose the Jews for special abuse: we had all the money, we were not bleeding in the war, and we had caused it all.

But to me, life seemed benign, anti-Semitism forming unnoticed background static, which I tuned out. I was pleased to be a Jew—but I wanted to be a Jew in the mainstream, not despite and not because of, being Jewish. If I would read everything, something Jewish meant the most. When my parents wanted to know what I wanted for my sixteenth birthday, it was Hebrew lessons (I'd never had any, in the Reform Temple in which I grew up). For the next two years memorizing grammatical paradigms kept my mind active. At that time, I found inspiring that statement of Moses in referring to the Torah or Teaching, "For that will be proof of your wisdom and discernment to other peoples, who on hearing of all these laws will say, 'Surely that great nation is a wise and discerning people'" (Deut. 4:6).

X. First Flower of Our Wilderness: Harvard Class of 1954

So from West Hartford I went off to Harvard. Now what was life like on campus in the years, 1945–57, when America turned to its colleges and universities to form a principal line of defense? It was paradise—an orchard of trees of knowledge, but without the snake (and, to be sure it was also Eden without God). When I found myself in such a world, I decided never to leave. From the day I set foot on Harvard Yard, in early September, 1950, until the end of the academic year, in May, 1951, I did not go back to West Hartford, in fear that, if I left, the place would disappear, like *Brigadoon*. And quickly too, but for my own reasons, I decided to stay for summer school and onward through to graduation, returning home only for ever-briefer spells. I went to summer school in 1951 and 1952 and graduated in 1953.

What I wanted for myself, from that September, 1950, onward, was to be what I wanted to be—a Jew and an American—and that meant, to make my life in the mainstream. A prior generation of Jewish intellectuals found an opening to American ex-Jews, changed their names, denied their origin, and gained professorships. None of them taught anything to do with Judaism and its sources, nor would they have wanted to. But since I had an intense intellectual interest in everything Jewish, I had the notion, then scarcely articulated, that I wanted to study Jewish things—but within the mainstream. I also was, and would remain, a religious person, who said prayers and kept commandments and valued and studied the Torah. I wanted all this, and I wanted it in the academy. And to me, then and now, the university's walls formed the broad and steady banks of that vast and flowing stream. I dreamed of bringing to the university that heritage of learning that Judaism had accumulated, not only learning another way of thinking but also teaching our lessons.

At Harvard I invented for myself a magical kingdom, the Disneyworld of an adolescent intellectual of that time. As to religion, with a friend I went to Friday evening services at a local Reform Temple and taught Sunday school. As to education, I took whatever I was supposed to take. And as to the social world of that day, I saw what I wanted to see, not what was there. In those days, gentiles rarely socialized with Jews; it would have been a gesture of enormous liberalism to invite a Jew into one's home. In the fall of 1950, I found everyone friendly, but no one, except other Jewish students, particularly interested in friendship. But, as in West Hartford, I also found most of the students not nearly so interested in their studies as I was. Still lacking all taste and judgment, I found everything exciting. Later in my freshman year, perceiving how things really were—dull and cold—I decided to finish up in three years and spend as much time in the reading room of Lamont Library as I could. That is where I passed my bright college years—never bored, but not part of the mainstream of college life.

For, as I perceived in due course, the Harvard class that entered in the fall of 1950 combined three separate student bodies: those who believed in learning, those who (rightly) valued the degree for what it could get them, and those for whom Harvard represented social prestige and family tradition, who (at best) would learn what had to be mastered to get the degree but wanted little of the learning. If I had to divide matters up in proportions, I would guess (and a review of the class reports over the past forty years confirm this impression) that well under a sixth really loved the learning. About two-thirds did the assignments because they wanted the degree so they could go to Harvard Law School or Medical School or get a good job in banking or insurance or whatever people did in those days. Somewhat more than a sixth came because their families qualified them to come. In my class—the class of 1954—John Updike and (the late) Christopher Lasch, who were roommates, stood for the authentically intellectual minority; David Pingree the still smaller group of those with scholarly commitment. For the innumerable future lawyers and judges, physicians and dentists—the smart and coldly ambitious—the list of distinguished careers in this and that would occupy many pages. Edward M. Kennedy and Sadri Khan, the son of the then Aga Khan and the uncle of the present one, constituted the socialites. Most of the people I met fit into the second group and struck me as not very interesting people. I doubt I knew the last-named group existed. I was a bottom feeder.

The loneliness of high school had ended. Plenty of others were smart and interested in learning. But I did not find all that many smart and engaged classmates. I had years of education to traverse, and beyond one stellar course early in my education there, Harvard was only marginally more interesting than Hall High School—although considerably more challenging. We were taught mainly by teaching assistants, who were graduate students employed to staff the classrooms. The great professors lectured to hundreds, but the actual work of teaching passed into the hands of young men only a few years older than ourselves and ill-equipped to offer more than a precis of what textbooks or professors had already told us. In due course I would repudiate the entire approach to teaching taken by lecturers, determining that there are better ways to impart information, but few worse ways to conduct education.

Only one course captured my memory and left not only a residue of learning but a sediment of enduring modes of thought. Thomas S. Kuhn's and Leonard Nash's course in the history of laboratory science changed my very notion of knowledge. They presented a general education course in the natural sciences aimed at teaching non-scientists what they should know about science. That course, the foundation of the 1962 book, *The Structure of Scientific Revolutions,* introduced me to the world in which facts bore no self-evident meanings, and truth required negotiation. It was a concept utterly beyond the capacity of a Jewish boy from West Hartford.

It was a course designed for the Cold War. Specifically, it began with a lecture on how, in time to come, we—some of us—would have to make decisions on the use of public funds for science, so we had best learn what scientific method actually accomplished and what it could not achieve. The premise, then, was that we future decision-makers in the national enterprise would have to know how scientists make decisions; the country needed us to know. How do scientists solve problems? It is not, we were told, by collecting information, but by forming a paradigm and testing it. That was an intoxicating vision for a teenager, for who thought in those terms? Who imagined such a world? Who could see knowledge as not a given but a gift? Who could view intellect as a medium for sorting out competing claims of plausible knowledge?

At Harvard, and I suspect, everywhere else, I hasten to add, not everyone conveyed such a vision either of what was at stake in learning or of what we do when we learn. Nash and Kuhn remain exceptional in my memory of teachers. That both men devoted themselves to the students also distinguished them at Harvard; most professors appeared aloof and indifferent. My honors' thesis advisor, a truly great scholar, routinely approved whatever I brought him—unread, I thought, and certainly without helpful comment. Acts of human kindness from Harvard professors of that era were seldom and probably unintentional. By contrast, Kuhn decades later claimed he could remember me standing by his lectern after class, vigorously arguing with him about the phlogiston theory or some other idea. That can only mark his own generosity of spirit, since I have no such memory.

In those days I did not even know that professors maintained office hours, at which times students were free to present themselves with questions or problems, and I am not certain that any of them did do so. I cannot recall a student's ever telling me that he had talked with a professor outside of class. I never walked into the office of any professor, excluding my freshman adviser and my senior honor's thesis director. In those days I did not conceive that I might ever join the ranks of those other-than-human immortals, those who declaimed from the unattainable heights of the lecture platform. Looking back, I realize, the Harvard professors of the day whose courses I took were intellectually rather ordinary men. The great professors were entertaining rather than rigorous. I cannot claim to have excelled at learning, only at getting A's. At that time, I did not know how I could define my own education or frame my own problems for solution, nor did I suppose that one could do so. So, it follows, I also did not imagine a life as a professor and writer of scholarly books.

My parting memory of Harvard was a broken leg. On April 11, 1953 I played catcher for the Harvard Phi Beta Kappa team (I was chosen in November, 1952, just into my third year) against the Yale counterpart. That is not a date easy to forget, along with the obligatory dates, my wedding anniversary and the birthdays of my wife and children. For a Yale ringer, who had gotten into Phi Beta Kappa at University of Kansas and actually knew how to play softball, slid into home plate. In my entire life I had never played in a game in which anybody slid into plate or even got dirty. I doubt I knew much more about the game than to try to hit the ball and, having struck out, not to throw the bat. In the field, I was put behind the plate, where I could do the least damage. So that day I was just standing there on the plate, watching the game, never imagining anything bad could or would happen. But something did. I suppose I should have learned, just knowing some facts can help a whole lot, like not blocking the plate with my leg.

XI. HENRY FELLOW AT OXFORD UNIVERSITY. ITALY, GERMANY, ISRAEL, ENGLAND

After three months in a cast and another three months on crutches, hobbling on a cane, I sailed on the *Queen Mary* for England. I have one odd memory of that trip. As I was getting my table assignment for meals, the purser asked whether I had any special dietary requirements. Instead of just saying no, I asked what he might mean. He said, "Well, for example, are you Jewish and do you want kosher food?" On the spur of the moment I said, "Yes, I am Jewish, so I guess I do." The answer was disingenuous; I just wanted to find out what would happen. For I knew little about my religion's dietary taboos. My mother claimed to keep a kosher home, but that meant she bought kosher meat. When she wanted to give me a great reward, she took me to G. Fox and Company in downtown Hartford for a bacon-lettuce-tomato sandwich and a strawberry milkshake. Those outside the faith will want to know that it would be difficult to violate more dietary rules in one fell swoop unless I ate such a meal on the Day of Atonement, when we Jews are supposed to fast, and at the same time had sexual relations with my sister while smoking a cigarette. (The possibilities of elaboration are endless. It suffices to say, many sins lurked between those pieces of bread).

So I found myself seated next to an American rabbinical student and his wife, one from the Jewish Theological Seminary of America, en route to the State of Israel for a year of study. The next morning, at breakfast, one day out of New York, he asked, "Do you want to study a *blatt gemara.*" I had no idea what he meant. He was asking me whether I wanted to study a page of the Talmud with him. I asked him what that was, and he explained. I had heard of such a book, the previous year having read A. Cohen's *Everyman's Talmud,* first published in 1931 and reprinted in the United States in 1949—a compilation of wise sayings on various subjects.[9] But I had never heard of anyone who actually studied the document, nor did I know why someone might want to. A gentle and patient soul—since dead—he did his best to explain what it was about.

My next stop was Oxford University, where I enjoyed a one-year fellowship that required that I not get a degree, not undertake formal studies, but rather read books, travel, talk to people, and, in general, learn and grow. I reckon I did. My fellowship awarded more money, if less prestige, than the Rhodes did. I had no idea what to expect to find in Oxford, which, I assumed, would excel in everything and show still greater brilliance than Harvard. What I found was a dull backwater. My teacher, in Jewish history, gave me an assignment. I did it and returned the next week. He had meant an assignment to last the entire eight-week semester. A dissertation I was supposed to do for him (it was on English Jews in the United

---

9. Just now I went full circle and wrote the new Preface of that title for Stocken Book's reissue—a touching moment for me.

States in the nineteenth century, hardly a demanding topic), I finished in a few weeks. I spent the rest of the year studying other things—Italian, the history of art and architecture, European history, this and that.

But Oxford presented surprises of another order altogether. To me, then as now, America represented humanity's best hope for decency and civilization. Not a perfect society to be sure, we aimed high and regretted when we missed. I had never known an American who hated America or did not express pride in being an American. But here for the first time I met people who genuinely despised my country and insisted we had started the Korean War. These were English students—Labor Party members, I learned—who attended Communist Youth Festivals in Eastern Europe and stood for a world-view different from any I had known. In response, I joined the one group of pro-American British students I could locate, which was the Blue Ribbon Society, the Conservative student group. I wrote articles for their magazine and filled a chair at meetings and understood nothing of British politics except who our friends were.

If unprepared in politics for this other world, in religion I was still less ready for what I found. For at Oxford I also met students who practiced Judaism in its classical mode ("Orthodox") but who also spoke good English (though with one or another of the strange accents of Britain) and had even read the same books I had read. In response, I began to reflect on the severe limitations of my earlier education. I attended their Sabbath meals from time to time and learned that a liturgy existed in Judaism that I had never heard. But for me Judaism at Oxford formed a hobby, among many. I gave just as much time to mundane things. I remember that when the D'Oyly Carte Company came to Oxford for more than a week, I spent the entire week attending the Gilbert and Sullivan operas they presented, night after night.

Nothing prepared me for the English climate, the shadows, the early darkness, the overcast days, the chill. New England gets colder but never so overcast or grim. And I had arrived toward the end of post-World-War II austerity, complete with meatless meals and ration cards for bananas and sugar. Matching the mood of the day, I encountered the gloom of a late-autumn season in Oxford and realized what I was missing: the sun. So I determined to go to the sun during the long (six-week) vacations between semesters. The choice then was Italy or Spain. Since in West Hartford I had grown up among Italian-Americans, whom I had liked, I decided I would take Italian lessons and visit Italy. To prepare, I also read all the art books on Renaissance art I could find, accounts of architecture, the cities and their history—whatever I stumbled across in the book stores.

I still did not know good from bad, I just absorbed it all. At this season of discovery in my life, Italy might as well have been invented just for me. Arriving first in Venice, walking into Saint Mark's Square, in December's mist and rain and gloom, I saw a scene I could not have imagined in England: a world of light and shadow, striving upward and inward, pigeons soaring over a nearly empty space. So, too, I found Florence, and the older parts of Rome. Italy from then on formed one boundary of my life. It explains why, not an artist, I married one and understood something of what her life comprised.

That dark autumn in Oxford, I made yet another discovery: the full meaning of what later came to be called "the Holocaust." This too came about by accident. In my first week in Oxford, I wandered into Blackwells, the remarkable bookstore. I noticed a mountain of books stacked up by the door, Gerald Reitlinger's *The Final Solution*. Since it had to do with the Jews, I bought it and went back to my room to read it. Reitlinger wrote the first comprehensive history, in the English language, of the massacre of the European Jews. In junior high school, in 1946 I remember reading in the Hartford Times extensive stories on the concentration camps, but these had made little impact. Europe was far away, of which I knew nothing, except that I was glad my great-grandparents on my mother's side and my grandparents on my father's side had left. If we had relatives in Europe, I never heard their names. If anyone of our family had died, no one I knew mourned. Surely my father's mother must have had family who perished, but she never spoke of them. So the mass murders formed part of the Jews' history, not my personal life. But in Reitlinger's book, sitting there in Oxford, I read accounts of what had actually happened. It was a horrifying, embittering and, as always when I read a book, a quite personal experience. For some weeks, I was not eager to engage in conversation with any gentile on any subject. How could people have done such things? What was this Christianity anyhow? And just who were these Germans?

And that is how a second boundary line was drawn in my life. For I was a Jew, and, now only eight years after the gas chambers had closed their doors one final time, I found myself drawn to see with my own eyes what manner of people, what kind of country, had done such things. So I went from Italy back to Oxford through Frankfurt, to see a German friend I had known at Harvard and to meet his family. The destruction of the European Jews formed a critical fact in my life from then onward, and I wanted to see the country that had done those things and to meet the people who had formed the population of that day. In its way, and in time, Germany offered its revelation too. What it taught was the facticity of Jew-hatred: bad public policy, but self-evident fact for more than one nation, more than one religion. I was to return many times over the coming decades.

The first visit showed me what to expect. At the Frankfurt railroad station, my friend's father asked me—in the point-blank way that Germans cultivate—"Herr Neusner, sind sie Katholisch oder Evangelisch"—"Mr. Neusner, are you Catholic or Protestant?" Sitting with me in the back seat, my friend, who of course knew I was Jewish, quietly answered my glance, indicating to me to chose only from one of the above, so I answered, "Etwas Evangelisch," by which I thought I was saying, "Well, some sort of Protestant." I reckoned that could include my Reform Judaism. Whatever the man heard, he was satisfied. For the next ten days I met the upper middle class of German society, lawyers and judges who had practiced and served in the Hitler period, a novelist who won a Hitler prize, manufacturers, senior staff at I. G. Farben—the lot. All of course had hidden Jews through the war, one per basement it would seem. Every one deplored Hitler's "excesses" against the Jews. All of course loathed Jews ("sie haben unseren Namen genommen," "they even took our names," Herr Rosenberg told me). They unanimously wanted to know why we (the United States) had not joined them in the war against Bolshevism, which we now were fighting in any event. Hitler was then all by himself, solely responsible. The rest was a bagatelle. It was not an easy time for me, but I learned what I had come to find out. Germans were no different from us. Anyone could have done what they did. The difference lay in anti-Semitism, which for them defined not an attitude but a philosophy of politics and culture. What I learned then was that that generation of Germans found it easy to forgive itself and tell the rest of the world to forget what had happened. The political regeneration of that nation would be long in coming to realization.

From Italy with love and Germany with horror, that summer, I came to what would mark a third life-boundary, the State of Israel, going with a British Jewish group on an eight-week tour. My father had helped to found the Connecticut Zionist Region; I was raised to take for granted that the Jews formed a people, one people, that they should found a state, and that Zionism was integral to our Americanism. I was fifteen years old when the State of Israel was created, and like everyone else at that time I saw it as the fulfillment of the Zionist dream, the happy ending to the awful story of European horror.

None of these self-evident convictions prepared me to encounter the normal everyday life of a real country and its sheer mundaneness. To me, being Jewish always made me special. There, I found, it was the one thing that made no one different from anybody else—an unimportant detail. I wondered how Israelis could ever be Jews. They certainly did not resemble any Jews I had ever known. That summer of 1954 I found still more puzzling the way the country presented itself to Jewish tourists who came to admire and then went home. Most of us thought of ourselves as citizens of the countries of our birth. Few of the British Jews with whom I traveled contemplated migration. For my European Jewish friends, to be sure, I represented an anomaly, because I did not see being Jewish and being American as contradictory, and they thought of themselves as not English at all. Still, not many regarded migration as an option to take seriously. The State of Israel for them did not present the final solution to their Jewish problem.

But the Israelis viewed us as potential immigrants and candidates for their military draft. Two typical encounters repeated themselves. The first was, "Have you come to settle?" The second involved how the country presented itself. One tour of battlefields in the recent War of Independence followed another, until we asked the tour directors whether there might be something worth knowing about what we were seeing besides where our guide, Yosi, was standing when an Arab Legion shell burst nearby. "Well yes," he said, "this happens to be the place where . . . ," and then a string of references to ancient Israel's history would follow. To our guides "Israel" stood only for "the State of Israel," and her history had commenced six years earlier. American Jews, the guides made clear, were destined for gas chambers too, all gentiles hated Jews, no gentile was to be trusted, and the State of Israel represented the sole place on the face of the earth where Jews could leave in peace. None in those days foresaw the forty years of nearly continuous war, sometimes cold, sometimes very hot indeed, that were to come.

Italy, Germany, Israel, Britain—these would from then on form part of my life—places I cared about deeply. More than that, foreign travel and study, learning foreign languages, pursuing curiosity about peoples overseas would define that life of learning I was to pursue. From Finland and Sweden to New Zealand and Australia, from Montreal and Toronto to São Paulo and Rio de Janeiro, from Swedish to Portuguese and Spanish— all of these places came to belong to me, and I to them, for shorter or longer periods. Going home was hard, like trying to leave Harvard in that freshman year. I prolonged matters as best I could.

En route home, loathe to leave England, I managed to find yet another student program, this time ten days in Stratford-on-Avon, seeing as many of Shakespeare's plays as possible and hearing lectures about them. When I arrived in New York City, to begin my studies at the Jewish Theological Seminary of America, where I was to remain from 1954 through 1960, I discovered not many thought it self-evident why I would go to Stratford to learn something about Shakespeare, rather than to a yeshiva to study Talmud. But just then, I didn't know more than that the Talmud existed.

XII. THE JEWISH THEOLOGICAL SEMINARY OF AMERICA, COLUMBIA UNIVERSITY

But I wanted to, and that explains my apostasy. All the prior years, from the age of twelve or thirteen, I had planned to go to Hebrew Union College, the Reform rabbinical school. Now, in Oxford, I decided to study at the Jewish Theological Seminary of America, the Conservative one. The reason was simple. I decided to study at what I conceived to be the more rigorous school, rather than at the one that people told me which offered a less suitable education. The decision involved educational, not religious considerations. As a Reform Jew, I would give everything its shot, but in the end decide on my own what I would practice and what I would neglect. But in fact it was a religious discipline that was demanded, and rightly so. Entering students had to sign a pledge to observe Judaism, with special emphasis on the Sabbath restrictions and the dietary taboos. The latter meant little to me. But at that time I smoked cigarettes, and I did not know whether I could give up smoking for one day a week. I tried, succeeded, and, the Monday following the first successful Sabbath, mailed off my application to JTSA. Why they admitted me I shall never know. I had no qualifications, in terms of educational preparation, for their normal course of study. And in my basic attitudes and values I never gave up the Reform Judaism I had made my own: the deeply autonomous and faithful Jew, who accepted the Torah as God's word—and then undertook to negotiate.

Mine was the first JTSA class comprised of more alumni of Harvard than of Yeshiva University, an Orthodox institution—three to two. Everyone knew something had changed. A few years earlier, a student lacking all preparation, as I did, would never have found a place at JTSA. But JTSA at that time had decided to admit students requiring remedial study in languages and texts, in an experiment aimed at broadening the kind of rabbis that the Seminary would offer Conservative synagogues. The administration recognized that the Orthodox could not forever supply their heretics to serve as Conservative rabbis but would in time retain their own progeny. So—people realized—Conservative Judaism had to find its own talent and inculcate in them the qualifications of learning and piety to serve in pulpits. Among those whom JTSA took in those years, none was less qualified for the school of that day than I. It was not only because of what I did not know—which was, in sum, everything anyone needed to know to do the work of the curriculum. It was also that I came with interests not broadly shared, with an education in history not widely appreciated, and with the fundamental conviction of Reform Judaism that being Jewish and practicing Judaism ought not bring about segregation, either of the Jews as a community or of individual Jews in their lives and careers. Still, I also did not know what I did not know. For, even though pleased with my prior Hebrew language study and proud of my encounter with the classical Judaism practiced at the Oxford University Jewish Society of that time, I found quite alien the authentic and natural life of Judaism I was to find at JTSA. And I soon would discover how much I had to learn.

A single story suffices. I arrived during the Intermediate Days of the Festival of Tabernacles, in early October, 1954, when, in synagogue worship, Psalms 113–118, called collectively, the Psalms of Praise or "Hallel," are sung. At the Seminary service, I lost my place and asked my neighbor where we were.

He: "Hallel."

I: "What's Hallel?"

To a practicing Jew, not knowing what Hallel is compares with not knowing how to throw a baseball. It was simply not possible that a student at the Jewish Theological Seminary of America could know so little about so much as I did. It would take me three years to master what most students knew upon entry. These were not easy years, but they also were not boring. By the end of three years, I had studied, in the original, all of the Mishnah, several entire tractates of the Talmud, and some Midrash-compilations as well. I would in time have no difficulty mastering the rest.

If that lay in the future, I did not have to wait long to find out what made it all worthwhile. Within days of my first year, I was to find my life's work: the Talmud. From the opening lines of the first chapter to which I was exposed, I found myself in a strange and wonderful world, a world of question and answer, thrust and parry, tradition and innovation, persistently fresh and original perspectives and modes of thought. I never doubted that I would struggle on that front until I could stand on my own. And there would be no other front, no other struggle. Nothing could afford so intense, so immediate a challenge of intellect and wit—but also of spirit. For at stake in the Talmud, I would find out, are the critical issues of shaping a just and holy social order. "Our sages of blessed memory" sorted out those issues and set forth the modes of intellect and inquiry, but also the disciplines of soul and conscience, that would teach holy Israel through eternity how to form a kingdom of priests and a holy people.

My Talmud teacher discovered that I would need a tutor to work line by line through the text we were to study, and, with my tutor, I found I had to memorize everything, since nothing otherwise made any sense. But as the text began to yield its meanings and exhibit its regularities and uniformities, even in the first weeks of study I found myself facing a subject of unending appeal, one that combined the two disciplines I had always appreciated: history, for its human appeal; mathematics, for its rigorous demands of clean logic. To understand the document demanded the capacity to reason and the ability to think historically and to use imagination in the reconstruction of the everyday of a piece of writing. Here, at last, I found the solution to that long-term problem of learning, where intrinsic interest met an unfailing challenge. It would never bore and never yield mere commonplaces and banalities. From late autumn, 1954, to this morning—any morning any reader opens these pages—no day has gone by that has not brought me its portion of the Rabbinic writing of late antiquity, those first six centuries of the Common Era (=A.D.) in which the canon of Judaism, of which the Talmud forms the pinnacle, came into being.

XIII. GRADUATE STUDIES

During the same six years, 1954–60, that marked my Rabbinical education, I spent a year at the Hebrew University and in a yeshiva in Jerusalem, Mir, mostly studying Talmud; in neither place was it so perspicaciously represented as it had been in those years at the Jewish Theological Seminary. During two years, 1958–60, I was in doctoral studies, receiving my rabbinical degree in June, and my Ph.D. in November 1960. The Hebrew University struck me as dull and intellectually moribund. The lectures recapitulated the reading, which is to say, the professors read their lectures out of their books. My initial impression of studying Judaism in Jerusalem left serious doubt that much would come of that particular center of learning. Time has confirmed that impression; the then-aging, great figures of the founding generation produced no successors. Servile students and dogmatic teachers, the Jerusalem school of Judaic studies, extending its hegemony over the other Israeli universities, would come to little. What Gibbon said of the Byzantine schools would apply: "Not a single composition of history, philosophy, or literature, has been saved from oblivion by the intrinsic beauties of style, or sentiment, or original fancy, or even of successful imitation."

But, representative of what was happening in American graduate education in those days, Columbia was something else. Themselves hardly scholars worthy of any ranking at all, the professors there assigned great books and helped us to understand them. Studying religion at Columbia marked the first time that I saw Judaism as not particular but exemplary, the Jews as not special but (merely) interesting. What made the difference was reading the works of the great theorists of religion, Max Weber and Emil Durkheim in the early part of our century, Mircea Eliade at that time. All wrote about religion in general and left me wondering how they had learned so much about Judaism in particular. One of the earliest readings in my first year of graduate studies was Eliade's *Cosmos and History: The Myth of the Eternal Return,* and as it happened, I read the book just before the New Year and Day of Atonement that fall in the autumn of the Judaic liturgical year. When, in the synagogue that year we said in prayer, "Today the world is born," I realized how Eliade had changed my grasp of things most dear and valued and Judaic. But how had he learned so much about Judaism? Then, reading Weber's principal works on religion—China, India, ancient Israel, for example—I entered into a world of analysis and informed speculation, the formation of hypotheses about the character of religion in general and the testing of those hypotheses against the data of particular religions. The texts that I had learned at JTSA took on an importance that transcended their own setting.

Here, I realized, was the path into the mainstream where I wanted to make my journey through life. Judaism could become a source of exemplary data for the testing of propositions of general intelligibility—a formulation I was later to learn from a friend of those times and afterward, Jonathan Z. Smith. And as much as I had found at JTSA, in the Talmud, the love of my intellectual life and the source of unending engagement, so I acquired in the study of religion at Columbia the context and purpose for my study of the Talmud. I wanted to serve as the medium for making public and accessible, important and illuminating, those most distinctive and particular documents of Judaism that defined the faith and dictated its character. These intellectual convictions dictated the career to which I would aspire, and I acted upon them, even though, as we shall see in chapter 2, at a considerable price. From that point I never taught under Jewish auspices or for a rabbinical school (except for brief periods as a visiting professor) and never earned my salary within the Jewish community and its sectarian institutions (with the same exception).

My university student years lasted from 1950 to when I completed my doctoral studies in 1960. So I prepared for my academic career in the very decade in which the country was reorganizing and reforming its entire system of higher education. And, as we shall see, that was the very moment at which the academic study of religion was finding a normal place within the organization of the curriculum.

Reading books was one thing. Going to class at Columbia and Union, another. About doctoral studies in those years at Columbia little need be said. We took courses, wrote exams, got degrees. I recall no distinguished teaching, apart from the wonderful books we read, no intellectual stimulation, no particular models of learning—nothing. The chairman of the doctoral dissertation committee, a historian of the Jews named Salo W. Baron, contributed nothing, being, himself, intellectually vacuous. He made his books by paraphrasing sources he never troubled to criticize and by paraphrasing the opinions of other scholars he never fully understood. The other members of the committee offered still less.

But one member of the committee, Morton Smith, had the reputation of offering stern criticism. So I brought him drafts of my chapters and got in return first-rate analytical criticism of both style and substance. I struggled for a while to find out the key to his criticism, which struck me as solid. I made little progress, having no model of what was good work. Finally, I took the train to Harvard and, in the Harvard archives, read his Th.D. dissertation, on *Palestinian Parties behind the Old Testament*.[10] A superbly argued and original book, it exhibited all the virtues of the American academy. Unfortunately, it also showcased the vices. For Smith's doctoral dissertation at the same time was tendentious, broadly idiosyncratic, and even uninformed. The work turned out ultimately to exercise remarkably slight influence in the study of ancient Israelite religion. But for me, then a young doctoral student, the vigorous and aggressive mode of argument and clear, forceful presentation dazzled, and from that work I learned what Smith expected—and rightly so.

The next chapters I brought to him showed what I had learned. He accepted them. The one memory I retain of graduate school comes from the day I came to get his criticism of the new work. Another person was in the room, and he did not acknowledge me but said to him; "This young

---

10. Stuck in what was then Palestine because of the outbreak of war and the closing of the Mediterranean, Smith had done his Ph.D. at the Hebrew University of Jerusalem. The degree was with a Classicist but pertained to Rabbinic literature, for Smith avoided meeting the standards of a given field by working with a

man has just written good chapters and is going to write a fine dissertation." I almost fainted. At any rate he went on to approve the dissertation, which won a prize. That recognition came to what is certainly the most conventional book I have ever written, one lacking all critical perspective.

The prize misled me for a decade. I would waste the next decade doing more work of an equally uncritical character, at the end reaching the conclusion that a century and a half of historical study had yielded nothing that could withstand the simplest questions of learning: How would you know if you were wrong? Why do you take at face value the allegations of your sources? I knew those questions from the New Testament and Old Testament scholars we had studied in graduate school. I remember, in particular, studying the writings of Martin Dibelius and Rudolph Bultmann on New Testament and wondering where I would find equivalent work on the Talmud and the counterpart documents of Judaism. My highest ambition was to write for the Talmud the equivalent to Bultmann's *History of the Synoptic Tradition*. But, in those days, I simply did the kind of historical work on Judaism, particularly on Talmudic times, that people then thought worth doing—and did it as well as anyone else. My work could have been done in 1200 or in 1900, but it should not have been done in 1960. The world had learned lessons in criticism that had yet to reach my field.

XIV. THE KENT FELLOWS OF THE NATIONAL COUNCIL ON RELIGION IN HIGHER EDUCATION

My graduate years found their real purpose and defining context elsewhere than at the Jewish Theological Seminary or Columbia University. My definition of the ideal professor took shape in an extracurricular enterprise that made all the difference thanks to a fellowship-granting agency that gave not only money but education and purpose. From 1957 through 1960 (and for several years afterward) I was also a Kent Fellow of the National Council on Religion in Higher Education, a Protestant group founded by a professor at Yale University that nurtured young graduate

---

scholar of genuine achievement in a subject said scholar in fact did not know at all. European academicians lend themselves to that dubious enterprise. The result is not a good one in the case of Smith's dissertation. In my *Are There Really Tannaitic Parallels to the Gospels? A Refutation of Morton Smith* (Atlanta, 1993: Scholars Press for South Florida Studies in the History of Judaism), I have shown that that work bears profound flaws of method and argument and shades over into obfuscation.

students and professors, aiming at raising a generation of college teachers devoted to teaching, on the one side, and to a positive view of religion on the campus, on the other. The council made a place for diversity of interest, commitment, viewpoint, religious conviction, and personality. The Kent Fellows, young and old, turned out to define the field of the study of religion for the next generation, and for me, the meetings kept the promises I had heard the academy make. We met every summer for an intense week of study, called "the week of work," and those weeks completed my education for what would become my career.

I learned three things from them: first, that the study of Judaism belonged in the mainstream, not in a ghetto, and was wanted elsewhere; second, that gentiles included Christians, whom I now learned to admire and respect and with whom I found myself quite at home (as I never had in West Hartford, Harvard, Oxford, or, all the more so, New York City); and, third, that what was of greatest worth on campus was the work of education, both in the classroom and everywhere else. For education was meant to change people, their intellect as well as their character—a profoundly Protestant concept of reform, which matched the Judaic conviction that Torah-learning affected character and conscience. The lessons of the Kent Fellows' meetings defined my ideals. The group would last as we knew it only a few years; in the unrest of the mid-sixties, it was taken over by people who lacked the intense scholarly commitments that the organization honored in my time. At that time, the group I had attended every year from 1957 through 1963, which had been devoted to biblical literature and the history of religion, was disbanded by the new managers because it was "too scholarly." Or, so they told us in so many words. Arguments made no difference; we could not meet again. I never returned. But I had already encountered a harbinger of what was to come upon the academy: denial of the freedom to excel. Our group evidently had made other groups in the same program feel bad about themselves. We could do nothing about that, so we had to disband.

XV. ACADEMIC SNOBBERY

The good lessons from the Kent Fellows competed with another that I'd learned while I was in New York City, at JTSA and Columbia. It was a bad one that took me decades to unlearn: namely, that, in higher education, value depended upon location. Achievement, reasoned argument, wit, and imagination—these gifts of intellect and spirit registered only when the right people—meaning, people from the right places—exhibited them.

What I learned at Harvard, Oxford, Jerusalem, JTSA, and Columbia was snobbery.

Like Americans in general in the 1960s, I thought that the best and the brightest should rule, and where a person came from indicated who was best and brightest. A labor saving device, academic hierarchism made it unnecessary to listen to what someone said. If the person came from the right place, what he said was so; and if not, one did not have to pay attention at all. So, in my time, we knew at Harvard that we were the best, and so too at Oxford, we lucky few knew we were the best. So too at the Jewish Theological Seminary, we knew we were in our field by far the best; and of course, everyone in the Hebrew University knew that Jerusalem was the center of the world; and no one at Columbia doubted where true scholarship took place. Of those delusions, the closest to truth was that at Columbia, where, in the late 1940s and 1950s, the social sciences—whether economics or sociology—were redefined by the seminal minds of a generation. But the study of religion excelled elsewhere, although in graduate school, I did not know that fact.

But for me, the conviction registered that if a person taught at Harvard or Columbia, that person's opinions carried greater weight than those of someone at an inferior place (for the stupidity of the day, the names "Yale" and "Podunk" served equally well). I would spend most of my career near, or in, Ivy League universities and their counterparts. It took thirty years to learn the truth that good people are where they are, good work comes from the accident of intelligence locating itself for odd and unpredictable reasons. Königsburg mattered because Kant walked its streets—and ceased to matter when he stopped walking. I did not have the maturity to recognize what mattered is what one accomplishes. For too long I thought it important to teach in the Ivy League, even if only at the bottom register. In chapter 4 I shall tell the story of how I determined to leave Brown and go to the University of South Florida—which only commenced its existence in the year in which I got my Ph.D. The lessons of my education took years to unlearn—three decades in fact.

I remember that in the early 1970s, when I had reached the conclusion that the university that then employed me, Brown, having fallen into the hands of mediocre people, was beginning to decline in its standards of excellence, I talked with other universities hardly so high in the academic hierarchy. These included Sir George Williams University in Montreal, York University in Toronto, and some American state universities. My doctoral teacher at Columbia, Morton Smith, a product of Harvard and Jerusalem, warned me off: "Don't go to the academic slums, you'll never get listened to." As it was to happen, Smith remained at Columbia where he was heard and, as a result, ended up an academic pariah. People heard when he announced his "discovery" of a fragment (the original of which he showed no one) that "proved" Jesus was "really" a homosexual magician, and therefore Smith marked himself as a charlatan and a fraud, and his discovery a hoax.

Now, looking back, I wonder how to explain how universities yielded a pecking order meticulously determined day by day by appeal to minute changes in indicators of status. I am inclined to invoke the Cold War and its impact upon the campus. Why so? The reason is that, in former times, only a few universities aspired to a more than local status, and most found satisfaction in educating a town's or state's future citizens. Some few universities claimed national standing, but that was solely by reason of the excellence of the facilities for research that they sustained. Why the broad indifference to the pecking order? In those simpler times, little was at stake in a college's comparative standing in competition with that of others. Now, billions of dollars, both public and private, would flow into the universities, and some would grow rich while others fell by the way. So the natural snobbery of upper-class colleges and universities—those serving American families of ancient lineage, such as Harvard and Yale—gained reinforcement in the need to establish self-evident precedence.

If funding agencies could be persuaded that Harvard was best because it was the best, then decisions in the competition for funds would readily resolve themselves: favor Harvard over "Podunk." And then assume that whoever teaches at Harvard has survived a process of selection that assures that the most intelligent people will serve at the "best" universities, the next most at the next best, and on downward to the dreaded Podunk. Among public universities, a comparable competition would range a state system's "main" campus (Berkeley and UCLA were chosen originally for political reasons to serve the northern and southern constituencies of the imperial state) against its subordinated and satellite ones, which were blamed for spreading resources too thin. By the 1980s it would become clear that in one field after another, no correlation existed between the high standing in the hierarchy of universities and the excellence—the substantive impact upon learning—of specific departments and fields. But for a long time the campus valued the sizzle over the steak, and some gave ourselves indigestion for that stupid reason.

XVI. THE COLD WAR AND ME

So—to return to my own story—I wanted to stay not only in the academy, but in a very special and peculiar corner of the academy. And that shows in a small way how private and personal interests intersect with the vast public issues addressed by a nation engaged in a protracted, dangerous, twilight war. In that detail, a huge inflow of money created a competition that in former times scarcely existed. But equally at every other important turning, I now realize, I found my place only among the possibilities defined by public policy.

First, because money was flowing onto the campus, fellowship support proved ample. For ten years I pursued full-time study, without support from my family, rarely gainfully employed for more than a few hours a week, and yet emerging with three degrees and no debt whatsoever.

Second, the expansion of the curriculum encompassed even the study of religion, which invented the category "religion"—not just various religions—and determined to define itself. The campus opened its doors to new subjects, and, among them, the study of religion enjoyed broad recognition, being centered on values but not sectarian, interested in the condition of humanity but not theological.

But the third determination of public policy would make the greatest difference to the character of the campus, and, along the way, to me. Our country, forced to face outward, now had made its commitment to world leadership. Taking on the responsibilities that brought us into dialogue with cultures vastly different from our own, the nation turned to the universities for guidance on the exotic and the bizarre. Fields of learning capable of undertaking comparison and contrast—political science, sociology, anthropology, for example—found overseas those new intellectual challenges to broaden the scope of learning.

The humanities curriculum, which formerly bore the burden of the nation's intimate culture—the values-defining subjects of literature, history, philosophy, religion, all within the framework of the Anglo-American heritage (in sixth grade we studied British history, but never Latin American history, for instance)—now assumed new tasks. The new humanities would admit the study of India and China, Russia and Poland, Japan and Indonesia, old countries formerly ignored, new nations formerly unimagined. For the nation at the head of a diverse coalition of nations had to know its allies. On the campus that required not only area studies of formerly neglected parts of the globe, but a determination to find a place for difference of other kinds altogether.

In that context of a broadening scope of interest and widening range of sympathy, the campus was ready to pay attention also to the study of Judaism. But the academy at that time placed its highest priority upon academic disciplines, defining learning by distinguishing one approach to knowledge from another. That meant that one practiced sociology upon a particular social order, anthropology upon a specific culture, political science within a defined realm of political power and activity. The specialist in Italy then would emerge from political science to study Italian politics; such a person never imagined that all things Italian would come under examination, but from no particular perspective whatsoever.

The disciplinary approach to learning then required the academic study of religion to define itself: what is it, about religion in general, that you investigate when you examine your data, the particular religions of specialization? Formerly, the study of religion required a rabbi to teach Judaism, a priest to teach Catholicism, a minister to teach Protestantism, and a former missionary to teach Buddhism or Hinduism or other constructs fabricated by the West. Now that kind of department found itself labeled a zoo, where each species was placed on exhibit in its own cage, but where zoology was not practiced. We needed to find a better way. The academy knew that way; it was our task to explore it. "University" meant a place where the whole universe came under critical examination by everyone endowed with wit and reason. Room for everyone, but the same rule of intellect for all—these defined the terms of admission to the campus.

So, too, the hour was ripe for a person who specialized in the study of Judaism within the discipline of religion, particularly a Jewish boy from West Hartford, via Harvard and Oxford and the Jewish Theological Seminary, the Hebrew University and Columbia University, who aspired—the natural aspiration of a third- or fourth-generation American—to be a Jew in the mainstream of American life. An America open to the world and now curious about itself defined its universities in such a way that tensions between the particular and the general, the private and the public, the special and the ordinary, would prove stimulating and productive, but never come to resolution.

The campus defined itself, within the humanities and the social sciences, as that place in which, in intellectual terms, people would seek to understand both the world and our own country, sorting out difference in the determination of the nation's—and the world's—destiny. Of one thing I think all of us were certain: the academy would form the center and would draw all that seemed peripheral into its core. Reason, rationality, civil discourse, respect for difference in a quest for reconciliation and renewal—these formed the mission of the university. No wonder those of us who loved learning and drew vitality from a natural curiosity would never leave. It was paradise and worth any price.

The opportunity presented itself at the very moment at which I happened along. The twenty-five years from 1945 to 1970 mark the moment at which the nation called its elite to the campus. I wanted to be one of those called and chosen. It was not because nothing was too good for colleges and universities—I never knew of any other times—but because, for those of us alive then, nothing was impossible. And everything we did was worthwhile.

The upshot would be that I would spend my life bringing into the mainstream of academic life and culture that most obscure and sectarian and special piece of writing, the Babylonian Talmud. I would aim at making that document not only accessible, but important and interesting as a source of examples relevant to the general inquiry of intellect and education—something people would take for granted they would like to know, or at least, know about. Therein lay the challenge of my career: to make intelligible and consequential to everyone something which had always been treated by its creators as special and, moreover, something which made me distinctive, too.

But—to move along with our story—for entry into the academy and for the academy's entry into politics, there was a price to be paid, though not just yet. True, the re-invention of the academy, between the end of World War II and the crisis represented by Sputnik in 1957—the opening of the doors to new populations, of the classroom to new subjects, of the faculty to kinds of persons formerly excluded—matched the new circumstance in which the country found itself. Now public interest intervened in settling those questions that the academy had formerly decided for itself: who teaches what to whom. And, for its part, the academy undertook to engage itself with that broad range of public policy and public service that would in time persuade students and professors alike to enter politics not as citizens but as something else: privileged teachers of the public interest, guardians of the common good.

An agreement had been reached, inchoate and unarticulated but all the more powerful and pervasive because of its self-evidence: universities would become agencies of public policy. In exchange the national consensus would accord to universities a critical position in the determination of public policy. Along would come the resources required to maintain that position, resources in dimensions of which the academy formerly could scarcely dream. When, alas, the unthinkable was thought, the dream turned to nightmare. But the glorious decade of the 1960s was to intervene, when the terms of the agreement on self-evident requirements of public policy for higher education were meticulously observed. For the campus it came down to this: you give us the money, and we will give you the truth. And for a while that exchange would prevail; it was an innocent moment, I suppose, when the political establishment believed government works, and the academic consensus trusted its own judgment.

We who identified ourselves with Harvard and Oxford and the Jewish Theological Seminary and the Hebrew University and Columbia—or a similar combination—of course knew who was the best and the brightest. And when our counterparts in government pronounced public policy, we of course knew they had to be right. After all, many of them had been professors—economists or sociologists or political scientists or historians—all of them were college-educated, and, whether they were a Kennedy of Harvard or a Johnson of Southwest Texas Teachers College in San Marcos, everybody knew what really mattered. And that was the smarts—which we, above all, possessed.

In the golden age of the academy, we turned out not so bright as we supposed. And, as we now know, the best and the brightest led the country to disaster. But a mark of our stupidity would persist: we did not know we were, or could be, stupid. And, for my part, I would nearly destroy my career before it began because I, too, did not know what I did not know, which was a subset of stupidity: how not to say precisely what I was thinking at any given minute.

2

SPUTNIK!

I. THE GOLDEN DECADE

Higher education followed the trajectory of Sputnik, the first manmade earth satellite, launched on October 4, 1957. Facing the challenge of Soviet technology, the country, alarmed, determined to provide the universities with whatever they needed to meet the challenge. For the next decade or so, the two words the campus never heard were: "No money." Massive rivers of money flowed onto the campus, as to other hubs of the knowledge industry. If research corporations, defense industries, and other centers of study shared the wealth, universities above all—growing in size as they took a still more important place in the country's imagination—profited.

We Americans were no longer Number One. But the threat affected not only our national self-esteem but also national security. For the Soviets had intercontinental ballistic missiles, and dramatically showing off their throw-weight, they called into question our confidence. When, three years later, John F. Kennedy ran for president on a platform of improving national security, many accepted his claim (since shown spurious) that we stood naked before our enemies. In the span of time from Sputnik to Parrot's Beak—that is, from 1957 to 1970, when the United States invaded Cambodia—the country turned to the campus to meet the crisis.

II. THE INTELLECTUAL EXPANSION. AREA STUDIES

Sputnik stands for a much more profound revolution on campus. The campus at this moment also opened its doors to formerly ignored or excluded groups and subjects. For me, as I shall explain explain, the single most dramatic development of the 1960s proved to be the opening of the study of religion to encompass traditions and religious communities beyond Christianity: first and foremost, Judaism. So not only science and engineering and the social sciences expanded, so also too did the humanities. If we ask ourselves why, at just that time, university humanists discovered an importance in subjects formerly not recognized at all, we may point to three factors.

First, in the 1950s, America had assumed a preeminent position in world affairs, with the result that Americans began to take an interest in parts of the world formerly beyond the horizon. Accordingly, Russian studies were born, and concurrently the conception of area studies took shape. An area or region such as the Soviet Union, or the Near and Middle East, or North Africa, might provide the focus for diverse disciplines and their practitioners: historians, literary specialists, not to mention anthropologists, geographers, sociologists, political scientists, and scholars of religions. After the iron grip of the established areas and regions—Western Europe first, America second—was loosened, area studies would encompass the whole of human civilization The first important break with convention lay in the establishment of American studies as a recognized field not only in literature and history but in everything else: including social history, the economy, folklore and folk life, archaeology, anthropology, the Afro-American experience, American Indian studies. All of them constituted facts about a single area, a given region. Once the field of American studies was established, the principle of area studies was acknowledged, and a wide range of area studies programs could follow. Moreover, once universities made a place for regional studies, it would be difficult to include one region while excluding another.

The second reason for the new inclusiveness is that groups whose opinions were formerly submerged or ignored now began to appear in college classes. Whether constituted as a group by race, ethnic origin, religion, or sex, these groups wished to make their presence felt in higher education. Most could not state exactly what that could mean. But they knew they did not wish any longer to be ignored, treated as though they were invisible. Who were they? Jews, no longer restricted in numbers, and Catholics, no longer subjected to unconcealed bigotry against their religion; then blacks, Puerto Ricans and other Hispanics, Asian-Americans, American Indians, Scandinavians, Italians, and Poles; and women—the list is long and varied, depending on the region of the country and its ethnic and racial composition. The members of the list shared the aspiration to enter the academic curriculum. But with the enormous diversification of the constituency of universities—with Jews no longer carefully counted one by one and made to feel they did not count at all, with blacks no longer completely isolated, with other groups no longer forgotten, with women no longer merely tolerated so long as they acted as men wanted them to—universities clearly had to change. They had to accept fundamental changes already taking place in the character of American society and culture, and they did. The curriculum of a university serves as an enormously effective statement on what matters and what does not matter in America. These two factors—a change in the nation's politics and a shift in the nation's list of recognized groups—joined with yet a third to give birth to the new humanities.

That third factor affected the universities alone. It consisted of the effects of the tidal wave of growth that followed the arrival of the baby boom generation on campus. Not only was the generation coming of age in the 1960s much larger than any before it, but a higher proportion of young people chose to go on to college. The size of this college generation imposed an enormous burden by forcing old universities to expand and by leading other educators to found new universities, colleges, and community colleges. What followed in the age of unprecedented expansion should have surprised no one. New teachers had to be hired. These teachers could no longer be drawn only from protected castes—the "Anglo-Saxons" and those who acted like them. The old Americans could no longer supply the necessary numbers of professors. As women demanded recognition in the curriculum, so some women found a place in faculties. Jews, including those who did not apostatize or repudiate their origins, joined in numbers unthinkable a generation earlier. When I came along, I presented myself as a Jewish specialist in Judaism—a person of a formerly tolerated class, a subject scarcely welcome in the established academy at all. And, at just this time, I found a place for both myself and my subject.

The day Sputnik was launched in 1957, I was a rabbinical student, just heading into doctoral studies in religion at Columbia's joint program with Union Theological Seminary. I did not foresee the impact of Sputnik on my own career; I scarcely dreamed of having an academic career at all. A senior official of my seminary saw how crestfallen I was that day and knew what was wrong. He was planning to migrate to Jerusalem and had cut his emotional ties to this country. I had no such plans and could not imagine doing what he was going to do. He said to me; "I know why you're so upset today. It's your American patriotism, isn't it?" I admitted that Sputnik injured my pride in the country that led the world in science and learning—but expressed fears for the strategic balance that kept the peace too. Still, I think Sputnik did more injury to our national pride than it did to our military prowess.

But the effect of Sputnik was to make the late 1950s and early 1960s precisely the right time to start an academic career, even in a subject not yet broadly accepted in the academy—religion—and worse yet, in a subfield of that subject that scarcely existed at all. Today, that generation which came on the scene in an age of expansion leaves in a time of despair. For, when the tide comes in, all the boats in the harbor rise, and Sputnik marked the academy's high tide. In response to the Soviets' technological triumph, people drew incommensurate conclusions. It seemed the skies were falling— on us. So, in near panic, the country determined that its future would be defined by learning—science and technology—and more to the point, people also took for granted that the universities were where learning takes place.

III. A METEORIC CAREER

The expansion of the universities' budgets, with emphasis upon research scholarship, persuaded deans, provosts, and presidents to invest in any subject likely to produce solid, published results. Left with discretion over their budgets, moreover, the administrations tried to keep some balance among the components of the curriculum, strengthening the humanities along with the more favored social sciences and the most favored natural sciences, mathematics, and engineering.

To show the impact upon the careers of the starting generation of that age, let me set out the dates of my progress from an instructorship to a full professorship. The path took eight years, but I walked it only for four, 1964–68 (later on in this chapter, I will account for the other four, 1960–64). First came the lean years:

1960–61: instructor in religion at Columbia University, completed the Ph.D.
1961–62: assistant professor of Hebrew, University of Wisconsin–Milwaukee
1962–64: research associate in the Lown Institute at Brandeis University
Then came the fat years:
1964–66: assistant professor of religion, Dartmouth College
1966–68: associate professor of religion, Dartmouth College
1968: appointed professor of religious studies, Brown University

The difficult years came about on my own account; the good years represented what was happening in general. So let me talk about the representative, good times first. Since, in the academy, we work on a long lead time, I spell out what these dates mean. In March, 1964, my life began afresh when I got married, and then, in autumn, 1964, I set my foot on the academic ladder with the appointment to Dartmouth College. A year or so later, late in the autumn of 1965, my chairman, Fred Berthold, called me in to tell me that the college was promoting me to a tenured associate professorship. Scarcely two years after that, in February, 1967, I received an offer of a full professorship at Brown University, to begin a year and a half later, an offer that Dartmouth matched. So in not much more than three years I moved from bottom to top. Such career leaps these days—when younger people laboriously climb career-steps by the stairs, one by one—can scarcely be believed, but, at that time, people zoomed to the top by elevator.

But that tells only part of the story of a charmed career during those remarkable years. During that same span of time, I received five offers of tenured associate or full professorship. None of these offers derived from endowment, for, at that time, Jewish donors had not discovered the idea of endowing chairs in "Jewish studies" (whatever that might mean) or paying universities to teach what they wished (largely: "Jewish history" and Holocaust studies). In addition to Dartmouth's and Brown's, others came from Duke and Columbia and Stanford. When dealing with Brown's offer, in February, 1967, I declined to visit Princeton to discuss a possible appointment, and other universities were in touch in various ways as well. The reason was that I did not think I could raise observant and faithful Jewish children in Hanover, New Hampshire, and I saw Princeton as not much more promising. At that time, too, the Religious Studies Department at Brown competed on nearly even terms with that of Princeton's in scholarly commitment and promise. All the choices lay in my hands. I could go anywhere and do anything I wanted to. When I tell beginning assistant professors about such times, they find it difficult to even imagine them. And, it goes without saying, my career proved representative, if not average. Many moved ahead easily, and few had reason to give up or lose heart. On the campus, all things were possible, and great things, entirely probable.

From a first-term assistant professorship to tenure in a year and some months, from a tenured associate professorship to full professorship in another year and some more months—these indicators of expansion found their match in provision for research. The university not only grew in size but moved ahead in intellectual ambition. Money to pay for learning, free time, systematic study and self-improvement—those funds flowed easily. True, the academy would turn out to pay a price for those years of abundance. For an attitude took shape at that time that today provokes needless conflict. It was the conception that teaching and scholarship formed distinct vocations. That is, publishing scholars do not teach much or very well; teaching scholars are not expected to publish at all.

In those days people supposed that scholars required "free time" for research, and the freedom was from teaching. Consequently, ample funds devoted to research removed the "burden" of teaching—I don't think it is a burden at all, but an absolute requirement of worthwhile scholarship and publication—from professors able to show they could make good use of research opportunities. As we shall see, that concept—that teaching is a burden, that research and teaching form contradictory demands, and that research not only takes precedence but finds teaching an obstacle—formed the nucleus of the crisis the academy now faces.

Without teaching, as much as without publishing, scholarship proves academic in the awful sense of the word: desiccated, formal, and divorced from reality. More of that later on. Here it suffices to say very simply that within the calendar of teaching—two or three courses in a given semester, six to nine class hours a week—if they want to, people can find ample time for students and scholarship. People now realize that professors who do not publish cannot claim for that reason to be superior teachers, and people who do publish bring to the classroom riches of intellect and commitment inaccessible to the sterile majority of professors. But in those days, with plenty of money, the fabricated tension between research and teaching would be invented and supported.

Dartmouth wanted superb teaching by productive scholars. So at that time, did Brown. And both schools, like most, also maintained high and rigorous standards of education: honors programs and theses, examinations that required knowledge, not just opinion, and serious attention to grading students. Beginning professors today find such an age beyond all imagining. When I came to Brown, I found many publishing scholars who also took pride in first-class teaching. Dartmouth's administration in particular spent money on training the professors to make us better scholars, and therefore better teachers.

What in concrete terms could we do that young scholars cannot do today? A single example serves to capture the flavor of paradise. In the early 1960s Dartmouth College got a sizable grant from the Ford Foundation for a comparative studies center. The directors of the center came to me with the following proposal: If you organize a seminar for professors, bringing to the campus the greatest scholars in the field, we shall compensate you with ample time off. Neither you nor the other participants will have to teach at all for two quarters, and you'll only have to teach one course for the third; and the seminar will stretch over the years 1965–66. Budget for visiting seminar professors? Whatever you need. We also will provide secretarial assistance, to record the seminars, which you then will publish.[1]

---

1. This assignment yielded the *Report of the 1965–1966 Seminar on Religions in Antiquity.* Hanover, N.H.: Dartmouth College Comparative Studies Center., 1966. Reprinted, 1984.

I agreed, on the natural condition that qualified undergraduates might attend, which they did. Dartmouth took education more seriously than most elite colleges and universities in those days, and that proviso pleased my colleagues. The seminar—the comparative study of religions in antiquity—paid its participants to study with great scholars. I brought to the campus the giants of the day—Gershom Scholem, Richard N. Frye, Erwin R. Goodenough, Hans Jonas, Thorkild Jakobsen, A. Leo Oppenheimer—and we faithfully read their books and listened to them as they set forth their modes of thought and argument and laid out their principal results. For nearly two years the seminar members as well as undergraduates worked their way through the classic scholarship of the early and mid-twentieth century in the intertwined fields of antiquity. The great scholars raised our sights, showing us possibilities of learning that few of us on our own could have imagined. That was what money bought. As if that were insufficient, the American Philosophical Society and the American Council of Learned Societies gave me grants for my work as well.

And I stand for a great many others for whom research funds flowed abundantly. For, if the period immediately following the war was marked by an unencumbered devotion to scholarship and research, the trend reached its apex within the following decade. The money which encouraged excellence through scientific method, through advanced work in the humanities, and independent thinking was not available immediately after the war. Even as federal programs like the GI Bill changed the face of the academy, federal dollars remained an afterthought, or at least a subject of hot debate, in the nation's leading universities. The Massachusetts Institute of Technology took federal money; Harvard did not. That sedulous purity came to an end in 1957, when even Harvard turned pro.

IV. MOVE OVER, DEANS, PROVOSTS, PRESIDENTS— WE'RE FROM THE GOVERNMENT, AND WE'RE HERE TO SOLVE YOUR PROBLEMS

For prior to that year, the challenge had been to lead, to use America's intellectual talents to understand a changed and changing world. Educational policy remained the province of the educators, the support of which remained the worry of educators, for whom the benefits accrued largely to educators. But guiding the world's leading nation soon became a much less abstract notion, and educators no longer would retain sole control over the enterprise. America's universities were not simply asked to lead, they were asked to catch up.

As we said, the Soviet launch of Sputnik I in 1957 signaled a new competition with the globe's other superpower. If knowledge had been a tool in the leadership of the world, the Soviet's preliminary mastery of satellite and outer space technology proved knowledge a tool in control of the world. Science, which had led universities into the world of advanced scholarship and its uses, was to lead it through another challenge.

Federal interest in science soared after Sputnik, even if the Soviet satellite represented a relatively minor scientific achievement. Indeed, it was not so much the science which frightened the nation into pouring money into scientific endeavor; it was the fact that American capabilities were in question. By 1959, government support had more than doubled to $356 million from the $169 million given in 1955. Such funds flowed directly to certain researchers and projects, allowing them to bypass local administration and creating pockets of specialized fields that few administrators could understand.

At certain universities, projects associated with federal research took shape. The University of California administered the Los Alamos Scientific Laboratory; Johns Hopkins University sponsored the Applied Physics Laboratory; California Institute of Technology ran the Jet Propulsion Laboratory. The federal government's involvement with such projects cannot be ignored. At those and other schools, the government created matching grants for construction of facilities, paid full construction costs, made lease arrangements, and so on. The fact that such institutional arrangements took the place of a federal, cabinet-level, science department should not surprise. The federal government employed a strategy of allowing universities to act as administrators of federal research grants. The arrangement proved to be a fruitful one. Where the government viewed science as a way to measure up to the Soviet threat, it did not meddle in the creative enterprise of scientists, which had already enjoyed several decades of relative freedom.

The government's largesse produced not only advanced scholarship funding, but also directed the nation's leading scientists to overhaul the science curricula for high schools. Subsequent federal funding aimed directly at helping promising students financially. By 1968, student aid programs were roughly equivalent in size to research sponsorships.

And not only in science: in the following decade, even without a coherent national policy on higher education, the federal government bankrolled the advanced study of foreign languages and cultures, national endowments for the arts and humanities, low-income students' tuitions, programs in medical science, and so on. Institutions like the National

Institutes of Health and the National Science Foundation, which directed university and institutional research, took a major role in guiding the nation's scientific community. The concept of government involvement in higher education was welcome at first, although it earned a certain amount of enmity in later years. But after the Sputnik scare, American universities embraced the opportunity to take emerging institutions and make them great.

V. THE CHALLENGE OF MASS EDUCATION: TEACHING AND RESEARCH PART COMPANY

Other Western countries, concerned with egalitarianism, refused to allow some of their universities to prevail over others in funding and mission. In the United States, however, state legislatures quickly crowned certain universities with heavy research functions while leaving other colleges to serve less-prestigious purposes. In California, for example, the state's Master Plan, drawn up in 1960, dictated a multitiered system of colleges and universities, with student opportunity strictly regulated according to class rank and grade point average. The idea, according to its authors, was to increase availability to the throngs of students coming up through the state's school systems in the late 1950s and early 1960s, but without sacrificing the quality of the state's main university campuses.

The result was, as in New York, a state covered with campuses, mostly community colleges, with virtually no geographic area ignored. Filling the myriad campuses with students was no problem, either. From 1958 to 1970, community college enrollment went from 386,000 to 1,630,000. The California Master Plan became the model for other systems, including the states where population growth has continued unabated since the 1950s: Florida, Texas, and Arizona. This age, when state legislatures assumed greater interest and responsibility for higher education, created what Clark Kerr, the president of University of California at Berkeley between 1958 and 1967, described as the multiversity, an institution of such complexity that its unifying force was its nameplate. Location of campus, research focus and other factors paled in comparison.

At the core of the state systems just being developed at the time was the research university, with a concentrated level of excellence in the faculty and graduate studies and the state's finest undergraduates. There might, in certain cases, be two or three of such campuses in a single state; usually there was just one. Below that tier was the four-year college, primarily a teaching institution, which functioned as a second-string school with occasional excellence in certain fields, like the geographically dependent sciences of oceanography, or particular forms of study, like drama. And then, at the lowest tier, was the community college. As in the California system, community colleges were open to anyone with a high school diploma, and they retained a vocational purpose.

The impact of the political separation of education from research would make its mark for decades to come. Universities that took shape at just this time appointed faculties who were supposed to excel at teaching, but that excellence was signified by disinterest in research. Consequently, entire faculties of nonpublishers entrenched themselves at the second or third rank state campuses, with the long-term consequence that mediocrity—at both teaching and research—found a home. To take one case among many, the University of South Florida, founded in the same year as the University of California at San Diego, would form a battleground for some decades between the few who wanted mass education to excel, and the many who were well-served by low standards, beginning with the faculty. Legislatures supposed that research cost too much to spread around, but no one then calculated the costs of institutionalizing a public policy of removing research from some universities and concentrating it in others.

For the community colleges, the lowest status did not translate into meager financial support. In fact, the community colleges benefited most from this system, which emphasized open admissions and the widening of access to state-sponsored education. Once the orphan child, the community college became a central cog of the state systems, and careful attention was paid by legislatures to spread the wealth. In 1968, in Florida, California, Texas, and Arizona, the country's fastest growing states in the last twenty-five years, community college enrollment was well over one third of total college enrollment. In California, 61 percent of students in higher education were filling community college classrooms in 1968.

But as enrollments at these open institutions went up, some critics argued that instead of widening access to higher education, the two-year schools were merely siphoning away promising minds from the four-year universities. And as middle-class students saw universities as an essential step to entering the professions of their parents, an inevitable clash occurred. Studies showing how students from low socioeconomic groups—particularly blacks and Hispanics—appeared to be choosing two-year schools instead of the four-year colleges upset educators immensely. While broadening the total base of students, the systems had in fact created a sharper division between rich and poor, white and black, urban and rural, than had existed before. Even at Harvard University, where pre-World War II enrollment was drawn heavily from the Boston area, some felt that growing meritocracy in admissions created a more homogeneous student body than before: white, suburban, and middle-class.

And so, just as Kerr described the multiversity, the university was not insulated from the world around it. No longer a jumping-off point for the rich and famous, universities became meritocracies. But those meritocracies were based on conditions the universities could not control, namely the unequal opportunities available to white and black, North and South, urban and rural, rich and poor.

But concerns over this dichotomy were still on the horizon; higher education, as an industry, grew unabated. Federal tax policy, which encouraged more corporate support of the nonprofit universities, jump-started institutional giving. From 1950 until 1970, voluntary giving increased by 675 percent; state allocations to state universities grew during the same period by over 1,000 percent. And even with a greater emphasis on attracting talented students, regardless of their financial needs, tuition proceeds grew by over 1,000 percent.

VI. PROFESSORIAL GOVERNANCE

All this new money presented an opportunity for universities. As author Richard Freeland points out, "funding could be found for almost any worthwhile educational proposal."[2] Such a situation made decisions easy, for without a scarcity of money, salaries could go up, standards could go up, production could go up, and opportunities for students could go up. But there were challenges, for without a set of clear goals, universities could easily waste the money. The federal initiative to improve the nation's scientific acumen, performance, and literacy shaped the sciences; in other areas, unless guided clearly by donors like foundations or governments, programs could flounder. The answer to the challenge, framed not at the time but obvious only in retrospect, was to allow the universities to be guided by their professors.

Authors Christopher Jencks and David Riesman identified this trend in 1968, arguing that institutional control rested with the professorate. Professors created powerful webs of associations, extended their learning well beyond the knowledge of their supervisors, and consolidated their control over the definition of tenure and academic freedom. Federal money channelled directly to certain projects and professors made this possible, but so did an apparently false assumption, made just at the time of Sputnik, that America was entering a professor shortage. Such a fear was created largely by the bubble of student growth moving through the country's educational systems. Predictions of a "tidal wave" of students were

---

2. Richard Freeland, *Academia's Golden Age*, p. 93.

grounded in reality. During the 1960s, total college enrollments went from 3.6 million to 7.9 million. The growth most directly affected public campuses. In 1950, about one of every two college students had attended a private institutions; in 1970, three out of every four attended a public school. The baby boom generation had been identified as a challenge to the academy as early as 1955, when a Ford Foundation-sponsored study said universities would, by 1970, train only one out of three new Ph.D.'s they would actually need to teach. "To expect that by 1970, the proportion of college teachers holding the Ph.D. degree will have declined from the present 40 percent to 20 percent is not statistical hysteria but grassroots arithmetic," the foundation wrote.[3]

The assumption of an impending professor shortage pushed universities to pay their professors more, lower teaching loads, improve standards of living and benefits, and abandon the idea that the professor should remain beholden to administrators for ideological support. With universities seeking out a consistent stream of talent, administrators were forced to support the goals of professors: stronger tenure, stronger ties to disciplinary associations, and greater reliance on those associations for certification and standardization of accepted research. These pluses for professors gave way, however, to deep weaknesses. As Kerr identified in 1964, the shortage of professors was driven by demographics. And if universities could be yanked to and fro by the need for professors to feed a demographic surge, this would—and did—expose a major weakness within the institution. That is, a demographic-driven university would find itself overextended following a drop in the birthrate. Universities, all at once and frequently without any clear notion, expanded their student base, their faculty, and their commitments. But did they articulate for anyone what they were trying to do?

Kerr, who led the Carnegie Council on Policy Studies in Higher Education, found universities lacking in this regard and foretold disaster. Competition had increased not only between universities, but between universities, industry, and government. While professors benefited, universities suddenly created an uneven system of governance. Some fields, mainly the hard sciences, led all others in prestige and rewards. Others, like the humanities, were at the bottom. This inequality appeared to be a hallmark of the age. Indeed, the concept of balance had left universities. One generation earlier, debates swirled about the strengths and emphasis between a practical and general education, research and teaching, limited access and universal access. By the mid 1960s, those debates were settled.

---

3. Ibid., p. 93.

The ideal university attracted federal grants, allowed faculty to specialize and insulate themselves from the generalized concerns of undergraduate education. The undergraduate body itself was drawn not only from the smartest, but from a growing middle-class society that saw higher education as a crucial step to a prestigious career.

The problem with this, Kerr and others have argued, is that universities became ill-prepared to wield their power. As universities became essential institutions, both to the national defense and the national economy, the rules that governed on the campus appeared as frayed wires—exposed, dangerous, and difficult to predict. How, for example, would the campus reconcile its influence over the middle class with the lack of opportunity afforded minority groups? And slowly, even the academic world was beginning to realize this danger.

Even by the end of the 1960s, academic commissions proved a harsh judge of graduate programs in particular, finding fault with a system that remained very much the province of professors. Graduate education, which some felt promoted pedantry and narrowness over service to society or undergraduates, came under particularly harsh attack. The Assembly on University Goals and Governance, which convened in 1968 and found fault with the professorial bent toward publishing at the expense of all else, nevertheless said the most stimulating teaching came from individuals engaged in "significant scholarly research."

A series of commissions, financed in the late 1960s by private foundations, professional organizations, and the federal government, took universities to task on a variety of other issues. To some, criticism of universities at the peak of their financial and political success seemed incongruent. In retrospect, however, much of the criticism was well-founded. Kerr, for example, chaired a Carnegie Foundation commission on the economic condition of colleges; there he reiterated his concern that universities were dependent on bodies filling classrooms, not on excellence or compelling vision. Other reports, like the one written by a federal commission chaired by Stanford president Frank Newman, said universities, despite their increasingly open enrollments, were more stratified economically and racially than they had been in the past. Newman's report also seized on one of the prevailing conclusions for the decade's volatility: students appeared unconvinced that universities had anything to offer them. Voluntary drop-out rates were much too high, Newman's report argued, indicating either a failure by the university to explain a mission, to be more than a status symbol, or, as Freeland has guessed, a by-product of males entering college to avoid the draft.

The fact that some of the nation's worst student unrest occurred at the finest universities, public or private, seemed to exacerbate the concern of higher education's leaders. Why, if one generation earlier universities had been regarded as opportunities for growth, did the current generation find it a mere forum for discontent and angst? Some observers, like Newman's commission, argued that students did not have the choices they once had. Virtually every institution, particularly every public university, transformed itself into a research-oriented, liberal arts school where solving basic problems took preeminence over applied work. With professional programs subsequently ignored or disbanded, students had only one kind of university experience to choose from; and that, Newman's commission argued, may not have been the one best suited to their skills or needs.

But the system—created by federal funding, student growth, and the university administrators themselves—rendered such conclusions mere intellectual exercises. For all their concerns about framing a vision for public or private universities, most administrators relied on the method that had worked for two decades: they persisted in their belief that programs pioneered at prestigious national universities, at the expense of any other kind of programs, were the surest means to excellence. The fact that university leaders said one thing—namely, to appeal to all students and create a multiversity—and did another has surprised historians who have studied that period. Freeland, in particular, argues that despite the battles for change, the war had been won for staying the course. General education, service to society, development of young undergraduate minds—all these things were hardly mentioned in criticisms of the American university in the late 1960s, a mere two decades after several commissions voiced them. Instead, universities, conscious of the flow of federal dollars to a select group, aimed for prestige above all else. We have already noted the example of Brandeis University, which abandoned its earlier hope to become a haven for general education in a quest for prestige. Freeland, noting this trend, and Riesman and Jencks, who identified it first, said such ambivalence about anything other than research could be linked directly to an "institutional ambition expressed in an ongoing competition for resources and prestige."[4]

This was, in short, the peak period for the professorate, because no other group within the university maintained either the authority or the power held by faculty. The students, who had by 1964 begun to chafe at the restraints of the nation's institutions, and the administration, which

4. Freeland, *Academia's Golden Age*, p.117.

had lost any semblance of control over an individual university's purpose, would each have their day yet. But until 1968, no one could challenge the faculty.

This presented both opportunities for success and failure. Using such
financial and political power, professors could shape the universities to
their needs. Academic departments, an important sub-group since the early
part of the century, began to oversee crucial decisions, like tenure and
curriculum. Such self-rule allowed professors to intensify further the specialization of their fields. This came, some felt, at the expense of teaching
and synthesis of subject matter. In particular, the power wielded by professors created a cycle of prestige-seeking. With only a handful of large,
private schools and some public universities garnering a large amount of
the federal dollars, and with these same institutions attracting the best talent, newer, smaller and less acclaimed universities felt compelled to imi-
tate, and not differ from, their bigger brothers.

VII. THE CATHOLIC, BLACK, AND WOMEN'S COLLEGES

For the chronically depressed Catholic and black colleges, the imitation
became unavoidable. Both aspired to swim in the mainstream. The external pressure to allow faculty to serve goals other than the institution's
parochial purposes became inexorable: professors with strong credentials
would simply walk away from institutions which did not permit them sway
in all issues academic. Internal factors, too, played an important role. In
Catholic colleges, the decade after the Second Vatican Council in 1962–65
was marked by an increasingly nonsectarian view toward knowledge-seek-
ing and academic freedom. When twenty-six leaders of Catholic schools
met in Wisconsin in 1967, their assertion that Catholic universities must
be universities in the "full modern sense of the word," they meant giving
their faculty greater freedoms to do things other colleges had been doing
for decades. For example, Thomas Aquinas' astronomical and scientific
findings would not remain unchallenged in science classes. But would, as
many argued was the case in 1968, Catholic colleges seek to maintain the
Church's teachings in purely classical terms, integrating new knowledge
solely for the sake of making sense of it in terms of faith? The answer to
that question was found partly by chance, partly by internal dynamics, and
mostly by external force.

Aside from the growing trends within higher education toward professionalism and scholarship, the Catholic colleges grew to accept a new
reality: American Catholics had become a part of the American middle

class, and their choices in higher education would reflect that. Their increasing secularization potentially widened the gulf between the traditions and norms of most Catholic schools and the habits and upbringing of most of their students. This gulf was further reflected in the faculties, where senior professors aspired toward providing moral guidance to students; younger faculty, trained in non-Catholic colleges, aspired to teach and participate in the full life of research and scholarship. To attract both the students (who were keenly aware of the prestige bestowed by the liberalized, private and non-Catholic universities) and talented faculty (who knew they were wanted elsewhere), Catholic colleges did away with many of their distinguishing attributes. Hence, what once were the hallmarks of Catholic colleges—obligatory Mass, Catholic-themed classes in economics, biology, and history—quickly disappeared from campuses striving to attract the very best students. Issues of quality aside, Catholic schools benefited from the growing use of college as a stepping-stone to middle-class society. From 1960 to 1969, enrollment more than doubled, going from 180,000 to 400,000.

During this period, Catholic colleges and universities—in particular, Boston College, Loyola of Chicago, and Saint Louis, Notre Dame and Fordham Universities—spent their energies reconciling their main purpose: to become great schools while remaining Catholic institutions. There was wide consensus among the leaders of this movement that the combination was not impossible, and what's more, would offer a fresh perspective in American higher education. Many of the faculty hired by Catholic colleges away from public schools remarked that they enjoyed greater freedoms in their new atmosphere. Such remarks prompted sociologist Andrew Greeley to remark: "Catholic colleges have no monopoly on paternalism."[5] Yet the effort to lure better faculty remained elusive. During the 1940s and 1950s, most Catholic colleges hired faculty, both clergy and lay, who had not attained a doctorate degree. They did not participate in the professional associations which marked that period's growth of faculty dominance. They carried a heavy teaching load, and spent a great deal of time on extracurricular activities with students. Even theology, which remained a required course for most Catholic students, was one of the most poorly taught on the campus, with faculty trained almost exclusively by ordination and not by doctoral standards.

By 1968, a much different picture had emerged. Sociologist Andrew Greeley's expansive studies on Catholic education understate many of the crucial trends. The pressure to conform to national, nonsectarian standards

---

5. Andrew Greeley, *From Backwater to Mainstream*, p.117.

yielded vast improvements at the larger, Catholic colleges. At schools with 5,000 or more students, 39 percent had doctorates; at schools with an enrollment of 1,000 or less, only 26 percent did, Greeley notes. In a trend not limited to Catholic colleges, the bigger the school, the more likely it was to adapt the qualities of the nation's elite universities. Not surprisingly, considering both the federal research money and prestige that went with such size and quality, smaller schools literally dropped off the map. In 1969, 68 percent of the Catholic colleges founded before 1956 ceased to exist.

And yet, while the vast number of Catholic colleges envisioned an end to clergy as faculty, most had not adopted some of the most contemporary aspects of a university. Namely, tuition and fees remained a crucial source of income (nearly half the budget, as opposed to non-Catholic schools, where tuition constituted only a third of the budget). Federal research money, which constituted about 25 percent of the budgets of American universities, represented 6 percent of Catholic college budgets. That is partially why Greeley and Riesman and Jencks, among others, foresaw a mixed future for Catholic colleges. The Catholic colleges remained very much behind their nonsectarian peers. They were held at the mercy of factors which had very little to do with learning, for their students and faculty were largely drawn from a changing ethnographic group. They had not settled the internal issues relating to their sectarian purposes. And, as Greeley illustrates routinely in his studies, Catholic colleges were still unlikely to come under the control of the determined, professional attitude which took hold of many American schools, both public and private. They harbored many of the separatist fears that had created the schools in the first place. But in a changing America, the use of higher education as a means to ethnic identity proved not only flawed, but dangerous.

For historically black colleges, the connection between national priorities, group identity, and higher education shook the roots of their ranks between 1957 and 1968. For that was a period when America, taking a look at its black citizens (most often because blacks demanded the attention with successful legal challenges to racism), found its education system the very symbol of its treatment of blacks. From that perspective, and from the set of goals issued by courts and federal authorities, came a series of events that black colleges could not have anticipated and barely survived.

The slow desegregation of white colleges, which began in 1946 in Texas with the introduction of all-black Texas Southern, later Texas El Paso, and which reached its peak with the 1964 Civil Rights Act, took away the most prominent reason for black colleges to exist at all. That, combined with a massive migration of Southern blacks to Northern states, pushed black colleges to accept a far different sense of priorities. For one, whereas black colleges previously saw themselves as serving Southern black society with vocational training and teacher-preparation, they now saw that black institutions were looked at with disdain in an age of integration.

While such an age demanded that black colleges ready students to move into white society, most were ill-prepared to do so. Very few offered more than undergraduate degrees, and one—Howard University—did most of the graduate training. Of eighty-eight historically black colleges, both public and private, only thirty provided any graduate schooling at all. Most of that training was for teachers, who took classes on a part-time basis. Like Catholic colleges, black colleges were below par compared to the elite national universities. But compared to white colleges of their size and in their region—mostly the South—black colleges ranked favorably. The number of doctorates on their faculties, the number of volumes in their libraries, the size of their endowments, and the number of doctorates granted—in all these categories, black colleges, particularly public colleges, were nearly even with their white counterparts. Whether such comparisons mitigate the obvious lack of quality in most of those institutions, white or black, is debatable. Colleges in the South remained, as a whole, far from the mainstream of growth and excellence common to large public and private schools.

Among black colleges, as among Catholic colleges, those with the largest faculties and enrollments tended to view the future in terms much different from those of their original mission. Namely, the larger ones sought to emulate the large, national universities. And as national universities and national markets opened up for blacks, the smaller colleges could not compete. The natural advantage they held before civil rights legislation—serving a single community under rules and expectations set by that community—was wiped away. In 1953, fourteen black public schools had six hundred students or less; in 1967, only two did. Not surprisingly, during this period, black colleges were not only the beneficiaries of more state assistance (through court-ordered settlements of the "separate but equal" lawsuits in the mid 1950s), but of greater oversight. Whereas in the 1940s, black schools were not accredited, in 1957, they were finally invited to join the Southern Association of Colleges and Schools.

But just as the standards set by American higher education were finally reaching black schools, the elite national universities began to seek black students for their campuses. Such a search—far different from the search for black athletes decades earlier—was accompanied by provisions for such students, many of whom had not attended high caliber high schools, as their college peers had. At this time, black enrollment in Northern colleges more than doubled, from 45,000 in 1954 to 95,000 in 1968. While civil rights legislation had forced open the doors of white colleges in the South, no legislation was needed in the North.

The hallmark of history for black colleges—and their fate, it seems—is to be intertwined with the issue of race, racial policy, and justice in America. To have their fate tied to such issues, during the time of desegregation, meant a widening of opportunities. But increasingly, as Frank Bowles and Frank DeCosta discussed in their 1971 study of black colleges, *Between Two Worlds*, that close relationship with contemporary political and racial issues forced black colleges and black students to face challenges uncommon to the American ethnic experience in higher education. The rapid availability of education to blacks during this period was not combined with a rapid development of skills to enjoy the benefits of such an education, as was the case for women, Jews, Catholics, and other minority groups. Blacks did not have a professional middle class of any note, their colleges did not train professors or professionals (other than teachers), and the white colleges which welcomed black students rarely took into account the preparation needed for such students. Added to this mix, and largely because of rampant poverty and poor schools in black America, there were simply not enough black college students.

So for black colleges, which once enjoyed a monopoly on the students, faculty, and professional standards of black America, this was not an easy period. Some realized the challenges ahead and oriented their training to new fields. At Morehouse College and Fisk University, for example, vocational training gave way to preprofessional fields and subject matter. This followed a pattern common to mostly white and small liberal arts colleges, like Swarthmore and Williams, where most undergraduates proceeded on a track toward graduate school. In an absence of another vision, every college seeking to survive did what the leaders did. They added professional training, mitigated the influence of traditions and sectarianism, and sought out a niche with which to attract students and faculty.

As Bowles and DeCosta describe, the choices forced upon black colleges during this period were precipitated by the choices provided black students. "The question of the capabilities of the historically Negro colleges . . . has now been accomplished, not by study and analysis . . . but by the decisions of high school students."[6] That the fate of black colleges lay in the hands of their clientele—an advantage during segregation and in 1968 a challenge—would remain a truism throughout the rest of the century.

If black colleges reacted largely to the needs of clientele, the picture during this period was much different at women's colleges. Most—especially the prestigious Seven Sister schools concentrated in the Northeast—recognized

---

6. Frank Bowles and Frank DeCosta, *Between Two Worlds*, p. 218.

in the trend toward liberalization of faculty and students a dramatic challenge. Not unlike the black colleges that found their best professors and students seeking the prestige of the nationally known private and state universities, the women's colleges had to look deeply at the meaning of their existence. In her comprehensive history of the Seven Sisters, *I'm Radcliffe! Fly Me!*, Liva Baker explains that the history of the women's liberation movement, mixed together with a certain amount of alumnae starchiness, provoked a serious question for the future of these colleges during the 1960s. As soon as men's colleges, particularly those of the most prestigious ilk, accepted female students, the financial, academic, and institutional futures of female colleges plummeted. Virtually every school considered going coeducational or creating alliances with nearby men's colleges. Vassar toyed with the idea of moving entirely to New Haven to melt into Yale University's vast structure. Eventually, in 1967, it decided against the offer, but announced it would welcome male student applicants.

Baker's analysis of the coeducational trend bears repetition. Where women's colleges enjoyed relative geographic closeness with each other or with men's colleges, a relationship of shared resources and faculty produced a happy medium. The coordination found in central Massachusetts between five colleges and universities exemplified this arrangement. But for colleges too far removed from such opportunities, the choice was simple: either stay all-female or accept male students. In 1972, a survey revealed that of the nearly three hundred women's colleges that existed at the beginning of the 1960s, barely one-half remained so. Forty percent were coeducational or had merged with a male institution; another 11 percent didn't exist. Baker found, too, that student quality had dropped. Where many students of top caliber once looked only to the Seven Sisters, such students had started applying to the formerly all-male bastions of Yale and Princeton.

The crucial issues for women's colleges, not unlike those for black colleges, were not framed in terms of the academic revolution which had overrun virtually every university in the country. These issues focused on a political and social goal of female excellence, but in what? For an earlier generation, the prestigious women's colleges produced, in Baker's estimation, high-pedigree wives for social climbers and aristocrats, or community activists and teachers. Academic excellence appeared not to be a goal, and as such, it wasn't. When the female liberation movement moved forward in earnest, and when spokesmen were drawn from the nation to make the case for equal rights, women's colleges provided precious few leaders. Baker's frustration with the condition of feminism at the

Seven Sisters proved illustrative. She pointed out that in Mount Holyoke's 1974–75 bulletin, the college boasted equally of the career of Ella Grasso, the first female governor ever, and the marriage of an alumna to Henry Kissinger.

The crisis of competition with the men's colleges rendered such attitudes passé; Baker argues some women's colleges ignored that until it was too late. Indeed, when the future of a special interest university appeared in doubt, as it did during this period among women's colleges, those that succeeded were not the ones who wavered. The larger issues, however, of educating young women and producing female faculty remained hardly addressed. Women's colleges were still not the place for graduate work for a talented mind. Even when women took classes with men, professors found them passive and mysteriously incapable of expressing either intelligence or dullness. Baker attributes this passivity, both on the part of the students and the colleges themselves, to a long-standing inability to take greater control of the feminist agenda. This may be so. However, when that agenda did find its way into women's colleges and those coeducational institutions where women found acceptance and power, the results were not what Baker envisioned.

Ultimately, in an age when two dozen American universities propelled themselves above all others by near monopolization of federal research money, when such institutions sought new forms of power and prestige, the sectarian institutions of the blacks, the women and the Catholics found themselves flat-footed. But each did react. They had to do so. Part of the reason for the growth of the national, professional university was in greater accessibility, not just for rich and poor, but for male and female and for black and white as well. And for the traditional minorities of higher education, such accessibility extended options never known before. How could the institutions which catered to their special needs and interests appeal to them, compared to the clearly superior national universities?

We know the answer. These schools found no satisfaction in remaining sectarian, and neither did their natural clientele. Women's colleges sought men. Catholic colleges sought lay faculty. Vocational black schools sought professional programs and better-trained faculty. But the trend toward imitation and coagulation was not for the sectarian institutions alone. The same transitions were found among mostly white male colleges. The small liberal arts schools were adding graduate and preprofessional programs. Why was this happening? Why, indeed, except to become the one thing that mattered at that time: a full-service university with a powerhouse faculty?

The lure of prestige exerted powerful control over all institutions, except, perhaps, those American colleges that by design never aimed at attracting a research faculty. In California, for instance, a system of nineteen state colleges was suddenly declared a university system, even though only two campuses—UCLA and Berkeley—granted doctoral degrees. This, author Martin Trow notes, had the effect of a self-fulfilling prophecy: calling an institution a university would make it so. Why was this happening? Again, as Sputnik drove the federal government into a full-court press to regain the nation's technological prominence, it sought out excellence, which invariably existed in the nation's largest and most prestigious universities. In 1968, federal support for higher education had jumped to $2 billion, far outpacing inflation and gross national product. Most of that support went to a select group of institutions—about 30 percent of the federal money went to ten universities during the 1960s.

Why certain institutions benefited where others did not in some cases depends on circumstances too specific to be addressed here. In other cases, however, the simple reason why ten universities could woo federal research money with ease was their pre-Sputnik facilities, prestige, and faculty. And the effects of the money are well known. For instance, research dollars could easily pay for the construction of new facilities, particularly libraries and laboratories, which proved a magnet for top scholars. Prestige flowed from such minds, and as Trow concludes, the cycle drove up student enrollment and selectivity, foundation and endowment funding, visiting professorships and international connections—and, without fail, more federal dollars. Again, considering the preeminence faculty held, and their ability to circumvent administrator supervision, it is not hard to see why the list of preeminent institutions in 1950 remained unchanged in 1970. Talent gravitated toward the most free and advantageous situations. That is why, when universities in the Southwest—like Texas, Rice, and Houston—wanted to launch themselves into the nation's top echelons, they did it with cash. They hired away professors—sometimes entire departments—from other top-rank schools. The lesson was clear: excellence not only could be imagined in concrete terms, it also could be bought.

VIII. VISION PROBLEMS AND THE NEW SPECTACLES

As Jacques Barzun noted in his 1968 study of the American university, "Barely twenty years ago the working of a large university ... could be sketched in a few strokes."[7] Barzun bemoaned the loss of cohesive curriculum and the growing derogation of skilled teaching. His complaints notwithstanding, the general focus of higher education had changed rapidly toward specialization, and away from the casually educated erudite professors. Gone were the rituals of classical education: Latin, Greek, and natural philosophy. In its place grew courses in foreign languages, hard sciences, and social sciences. And at colleges which once evoked the ethos of a particular institution—the Jesuit's Georgetown University, for example—fields of knowledge unrelated to the college's original purpose, like foreign diplomacy, were developed to meet the demand in the public sector. And Georgetown exemplifies what was happening everywhere.

This trend toward specialization and professional education frustrated those who still supported general education requirements for undergraduates. Earlier in the century, University of Chicago and Columbia University both created "core" curriculums and required their students to master a block of knowledge. Then, immediately after the war, there was a sense that the nation needed leaders with a "common cultural heritage toward a common citizenship," as the 1947 report of the President Truman's Commission on Higher Education put it. This commission's view toward opening up colleges to more people was just one goal. The commission also linked national goals to the agendas of the nation's colleges, and to a certain extent, provided the impetus needed for such social-oriented subjects in the social sciences and humanities, thus allowing students to participate in policy rather than to simply study the nation's ills. To a degree, such an effort dovetailed with the nation's general sentiment to an agenda shared by institutions, disparate ethnic groups, and individuals.

The war had ebbed, but patriotism did not necessarily give way to isolationism, intellectual or otherwise. Many in higher education, especially George Zook, the New Deal Democrat and University of Akron president who chaired the Truman commission, favored pushing universities toward complete public service, especially toward solving problems. However, the issue was largely settled toward the side of specialization. General education, while a goal for most, depended largely on the structure of a curriculum: were students required to take a certain course, or were they asked to take a course from an approved group of selections? Ideological visions aside, the issue was settled for the benefit of the specialists, who appeared to have the support of both students, who favored choices, and foundations, who tended to support certain scholarly projects. This, as

7. Barzun, *The American University*, p. 4.

Riesman and Jencks point out, contributed to the growing shift in power toward faculty scholars, who were not captive to the efforts of administration to gel disparate subject matter.

Freeland bemoans this trend, not because of the freedom it afforded, but because it destroyed any impulse toward creating a shared vision for higher education. "In the early postwar years, educators had not worried about the capacity of their institutions to formulate policies and act in an orderly way; debate was about the actions they should take. By 1970, this was no longer true."[8] The flow of federal dollars had pushed universities to copy one another, to seek sameness. The leadership role once seized by American educators in applied fields was left behind; building a prestigious university meant having a strong arts and sciences faculty and not necessarily a good business school. Most American colleges were abandoning any principles which once had separated them, but at what cost? Some have argued, as we have already noted, that the greatest casualty of this period was the relationship between professors and their students. Author John Coyne reflects in his Berkeley memoir that his professors not only would give the same lectures, but would tell the same jokes, make the same gestures, and pause at the exact same moments, as they had in lectures several semesters before. What's worse, perhaps, is that the students knew. They sold copies of the notes to each other so that they didn't have to attend classes.

What resulted from the loosening bonds between faculty and their students can be measured in many ways: the deception of faculty that research constituted a professor's purpose in life, the deception of parents that the very best minds at the expensive private schools were teaching their children, and the deception of the students themselves, who imagined universities to serve a purpose to society and community. When student revolts began on college campuses in 1964, professors and administrators found themselves lacking an explanation for the chafing that had caused the rebellion. George Kennan, in a 1967 speech at Swarthmore College, said the Student Left had reached conclusions without considering facts, other opinions, or even the art of debate. Kennan's summary of the Student Left, and subsequent research into the area, both demonizes and mythologizes a series of protests led by rebels who may have had very little interest in setting any goals for universities or their own educations.

Columbia's students put on the country's first great spectacle. The statement by students at Columbia University—who had seized a series of

---

8. Freeland, *Academia's Golden Age*, p.116.

campus buildings in 1968, including the president's office (they smoked his cigars!)—serves a useful purpose for analysis of this question. The revolt at Columbia focused on mostly institutional, as opposed to academic, concerns. Students took to task university researchers doing work for national defense, the university's expansion into nearby Morningside Heights and Harlem neighborhoods, and the university's embrace of capitalism. What, among those concerns, was focused on academic issues? Other histories of the period offer precious little proof that the student rebellions of the 1960s focused on anything to do with improving the quality of education.

Let us not allow the mythologies and pedagogies to sway our story. Were the concerns academic, in the sense that they were focused on what had happened to the promise of their education? The evidence is hardly conclusive. On the one hand, students involved in the revolt closed campuses with strikes, burned professors' files, destroyed campus libraries and facilities, and accosted other students who did not succumb to their threats. At Columbia, one student, who had fought to keep the university open, wrote to administrators that his four years and $8,000 had been wasted. "I have witnessed the destruction of a once honorable institution. I have seen a once great university become a third-rate political tool for a mob of Vietcong flag waving animals. . . ."[9] John Coyne's *The Kumquat Statement*, a narrative on the Berkeley rebellions and riots, described a campus torn not by academic debates, but by simple anarchy. Some of those rebellions—the Peoples Park riot in particular—had nothing to do with the intellectual enterprise of the university.

And yet, the students' concerns were not entirely tangential to the task of the university. At several campuses, students argued against accepting research money, especially for defense-related work, from the federal government. Some argued that the university's natural meritocracy destroyed the collectivist, socialist ideal of the New Left's ideal classroom. And professors, hardly innocent in their sympathy for the student's antiwar stance, actively encouraged the rebellion. One Berkeley professor, Coyne reported, read a congratulatory telegram from Hanoi at a student rally. At Berkeley, a drama department class awarded credit to students who performed in a pornographic play involving simulated sexual acts, including some with faculty actors!

At some campuses, black students held that black studies departments—without supervision or even the standards of the rest of the university—should be established. "Expertise is simply the mental form of

9. John Coyne, *The Kumquat Statement*, p. 204.

'keeping people in their place'," students wrote in their Columbia protest statement. Kerr's earlier analysis of the university—and even Barzun's 1968 observations—seemed to be reflected in such complaints. Undergraduates felt that universities did not serve them. They described universities as "knowledge factories" which are incapable of synthesizing the skills of the specialist with the mission to explain. Michael Rossman, a leader of the Berkeley disturbances in 1964, mimicked the typical college classroom, where students appealed not to learning, but to psychological petting of the professor. His essay, "The Totalitarian Classroom—A Learning Game," which was published in 1969, provides a clear view that the student unrest of the late 1960s had an intellectual and academic dimension. So, given the possibilities, the student rebellions were not linked solely to political concerns.

However, the student demands and protests of the period do not always share this vision or this concern. In fact, what distinguishes student rebellion is not the concerns voiced—which ranged widely and had few common strains—but demography. Serious debate about the consequences of accepting federal funds occurred within the ranks of faculty long before such issues concerned college students. A menu of student concerns during the period reads like an outline for ideological disunity: the draft, race, Vietnam, socialism, corporate recruiting, sexual liberation, cultural and chemical experimentation, divestment, student facilities, ethnic studies, due process for students, faculty hiring and minority representation. When academic issues were addressed, they were addressed within the realm of these other issues. They were not the wellspring of these other issues and, as far as historical proof is concerned, barely play a role in the larger student uprising.

And yet the administrators acquiesced—and acquiesced, and acquiesced. No demand went beyond the limits of credibility, and every nonnegotiable point students put forth was conceded, without negotiation. At the elite schools in particular, the administrations sought peace at the price of surrender. The rest of the country looked on amazed and drew its own conclusions. Only a few state universities capitulated, but the California and Wisconsin cases stood for them all. Except at a handful of schools like University of Chicago, student rebellion set the agenda for academic and intellectual policy. Student strikes shut down classes and entire colleges. Army officer training programs were kicked off the prestigious campuses. College presidents who thought of themselves as sympathetic to student demands found themselves the declared enemies of such students. "Each chancellor found himself holding a middle ground between the demands of small but ingeniously provocative groups of demonstrators, and angry phone calls from Sacramento threatening intervention if campus peace were not restored immediately," wrote William McGill, the chancellor of University of California's San Diego campus in his memoir, *The Year of the Monkey*.[10] McGill, like many of his colleagues, was utterly mystified by the tactics of the New Left, and could not deal with their provocative actions. His campus remained wracked by disruptions throughout his reign, much to the consternation of Governor Ronald Reagan, who built a solid political following by taking an unyielding stand against student protests. Reelected, he went on to the presidency, buoyed by the national revulsion at the destruction of higher learning by the Left.

At San Francisco State, by comparison a smaller and less prestigious school than UCSD, a semanticist named Sam Hayakawa presided over one of the few examples of a college wresting control away from anarchists. Hayakawa became president in 1968, succeeding two presidents who had allowed the following to occur: the routine shut-down of the college by radicals, the beating of the student's newspaper staff, disruption of the inauguration of one president, the use of college funds by the Black Student Union to buy guns, and so on. Hayakawa's technique for subduing such activity was simple. He ordered the college to remain open and brought in police to restore order. He denied paychecks to striking faculty, allowed the police to make mass arrests and to set high bail for the arrested, and negotiated with some student groups while ignoring anarchists and militants.

Coyne's analysis of Hayakawa's actions shows a considerable bias toward early intervention. But such intervention may prove correct. For when Berkeley administrators attempted to wrest control of a plot of land from a united band of civic do-gooders, militant anarchists, street people, and others, they found that they had allowed disrespect of university authority to become not just aberrant behavior, but a persistent condition. Their failure to set standards for university authority throughout the decade made it difficult, if not impossible, to quell a public park disturbance in 1969, Coyne argues. Indeed, by allowing the university to become a staging ground for the New Left, Coyne said administrators set their own fate into motion. The university was no longer an institution to itself, with its own successes and headaches. It had, whether in the cities of New York and Oakland or the countrysides of Iowa, become enmeshed into the societies around it, not as a symbol of the nation's effort to wage an international battle against Communists, but as a symbol of Communist sympathies and rogue revolutionaries. The simple failure to instill control and order over

---

10. William McGill, *The Year of the Monkey*, pp. 82–83.

a campus not only meant the temporary loss of use of a library or an office; it demonstrated a fundamental loss of control over the public's confidence. And despite the examples of Hayakawa and others, campuses by the 1960s were no longer benignly disrupted. They were disruptive. And that disruption, whether through student riots that destroyed Berkeley's Telegraph Street or the counterreaction by National Guardsmen at Kent State, was to haunt the nation's universities for decades to come.

IX. GETTING FIRED (1)

Public affairs and private life do not match. The tough times for me came at the beginning of the decade, at the zenith of the golden age, and the good times came at the end, when the then elite universities were beginning to disintegrate. But I made my own problems, because I thought the campus required plain truth, and, worse, I believed in the promise of the university and aspired to make my career there and only there. It was an aspiration natural to the golden age, although that same judgment endangered my career before it got underway. And at the end of the decade, as the campus began to disintegrate, that same vision blinded me to what was happening. I could not conceive that paradise could change, nor could I foresee that universities would abandon their calling to excellence. So I chose a school with a shallow and recent tradition of scholarship, which was to pander in its own strange way to precisely those disruptive impulses destroying elite universities throughout the country. But in saying so, I have gotten well ahead of my story.

Let me start back with the beginnings, 1960–64, probably the best years the American academy has ever known, but the most difficult in my career. I got my chance at the mainstream, but was nearly drowned, pulled down by hands reaching out from the nearby backwater. For in those times I learned that that academy to which I aspired comprised quite ordinary people, of whom I was one. It was not composed of the giants of intellect and imagination, conscience and wit, whom I had created out of my quite ordinary teachers and then took for models for myself. When I went to Dartmouth and took my first steps on the academic ladder, I knew that while that ladder led upward, its top touched no heaven, just another mundane, unredeemed spot on earth. The cordiality and collegiality of Dartmouth surprised me, and I never took for granted the human excellence of colleagues and administration of that period. In making my commitment to the academy, in those four years, I learned to keep my eyes wide open and to know precisely where I headed, and with whom. For experience taught me—too soon, I reckon—that even in those, the best of times, the academy was driven not only by rationality and love of inquiry and governed by people engaged in intellectual problem solving, but also by deeply human traits of character as well. I entertained few illusions; none would have survived, for I found the same jealousies, the same sense of grievance and entitlement, that sometimes embitter the world beyond the campus. But these realities struck early on, so no illusions clouded my vision. Nothing disappointed me in the many difficult years that were to come, because my expectations of the academy to begin with took shape in adversity, much of it caused by my own blunt, New England speech.

The direct, plain speech of the New Englander—that was the one lasting lesson that West Hartford's mostly-Yankee (and sometimes overtly anti-Semitic) teachers taught us: say what you think, simply and directly. As New England's poet Robert Frost showed, beneath the surface of simple words lurk dark and complex thoughts. But for us the power of words corresponded to direct, simple, and uncompromising clarity. Say what you mean, mean what you say—my English teacher in eighth and ninth grades, a downeaster from Maine, never ceased to tell me. And she also is the one who, seeing students publicly ridicule good work in class (it was a ninth grade class report, which I read aloud, comparing the Russian and English literary characters of Boris Goudonov and Macbeth, complete with records of the corresponding operas), whispered in my ear, *Illegitimae non carborundum* ("don't let the bastards wear you down"). That was a lesson she knew from her own observation that I would need to master, and a lesson that I did master. Years later I would take as my motto, *Since you can't join 'em, beat 'em.* To that I added, *or at least, beat 'em up.*

Plain language in the academy brought great rewards—after all, you're reading this book!—but it also cost much. In book writing for decades I was to reap the reward for the fact that no one ever missed the point of what I wanted to get across—at least not through my failure to say bluntly whatever was on my mind. But alas, I paid the price upfront. For my first job was very nearly my last, and however abundant the resources on campus, four years of struggle had to pass before I was to gain benefit from the expansion. But when I did, it was for the right reason. It was because people in the academy wanted me for what I knew and could do, when people in the world of Jewish learning did not. In retrospect, I realize, the fault was mine. I made enemies I did not have to make—not then. I told them what I thought; I needn't have. It would have come out through the work I would do, which would call into question the foundations of their scholarship in the history and religion of Judaism.

My teachers at the Jewish Theological Seminary of America, sorely provoked by me, had from the first tried to get rid of me.[11] That they tried in 1960 proves that at that time they thought they could control the field. But even then, the academy had opened its doors sufficiently wide for me to squeeze in. Clearly, a realm of learning beyond the control of the parochial institutions, whether Jerusalem's or New York's or Cincinnati's, was taking shape and would make space for me. Ten years earlier, before Sputnik and the vast expansion that came afterward, the parochial schools, with their control of how and by whom and for what purpose Judaism was to be studied, would have had no difficulty in destroying my career. Now it proved impossible. Control of learning on Judaism had passed from their hands, and I was the first to benefit from that fact.

Precisely what they—the professors of JTSA or Hebrew Union College or the Hebrew University or the various Hebrew colleges—wanted to control is hardly clear, even in retrospect. I cannot point to any intellectual issues. At that point my scholarly work was imitative and derivative, no threat to theirs. Into the earliest 1970s I had never criticized anybody, but only had taken the results I could use and had gone my own way, doing what at that time I thought worthwhile. At stake were matters that on the surface were not intellectual, but were, instead political and personal— I insulted JTSA—so the story is a simple one. It begins with the—to me— amazing day on which I got an offer to teach in a university, and, of all universities, Columbia, where I was then completing my doctoral dissertation, having taken the required courses and passed the various general examinations in a year, 1958–59.

In 1959–60, during my final year at JTSA and Columbia, the then chairman of the Department of Religion at Columbia, John A. Hutchison, whom I had known through the Kent Fellows and who had recruited me to the Columbia–Union Ph.D. program (and who first told me that there was an academic field known as religion), asked me to teach at Columbia. He said, "Next year you will be an instructor, but as soon as you complete your doctoral degree—I assume early in the coming year—we will promote you to an assistant professorship. Columbia appoints only on an annual basis, but you will be appointed year by year, until you come up for tenure. I promise." I did not know that he would leave within months, and that there would arise a Pharaoh who knew not Joseph. So I accepted in

---

11. This was not the first such effort. At the end of my first year there, the faculty entertained a motion to throw me out; Abraham Heschel objected and stopped it from happening.

the same minute, and of course, a few minutes later, everyone I knew also knew. As it turns out, that appointment lasted for a week, although it wound down for an academic year. I was fired before I began to teach.

The reason why begins a week after the Columbia offer, when, having heard about my appointment, the then dean of the Teachers Institute of the Jewish Theological Seminary of America, Seymour Fox (who went on to a powerhouse career at the Hebrew University of Jerusalem and in public education in the State of Israel—another career in the mainstream) approached me. Fox was one of the few figures at JTSA I respected; a remarkably effective administrator, in aura he reminded me of Brodrick Crawford in *All the King's Men*. But he was honest and forthright and a genuinely effective personality. He was known as an empire builder, and I thought the empire he wanted to build was entirely worth constructing. So he asked me to teach part-time at JTSA while teaching at Columbia, a fairly standard arrangement in those days. Would that I had said, "It's a wonderful invitation, let me give it thought," or perhaps, "Can we discuss it once I've started work there and know what is expected of me?" Any of a dozen courteous refusals would have sufficed—except to me.

Now, to understand the arrogance and rudeness of my answer, you have to know that I was simply a yokel with strong opinions and no tact. I did not admire JTSA. Despite the extraordinary subject that we studied—the classical writings of Judaism—I found the classes boring, adversarial, and punitive, the professors full of contempt for the students. The professors, with a few exceptions, were haughty, remote, and inaccessible, creating an environment rancid in jealousies and intrigues. In other words, JTSA was a quite ordinary and standard academic setting, no different from what I would find later on at Brown University. But, with little tolerance for the human condition, I took everything personally. I did not understand the unredemption of humanity, nor could I grasp that erudition in no way guaranteed the presence of character and conscience.

As it happened, Rabbi Fox and I were passing through the lunch line together—not a place for the serious discussion of weighty affairs, one would suppose—when he made what he (correctly) thought was a standard, cordial proposal.

"Jack, would you like to teach for us next year?"

We had not progressed from the soup to the tuna fish before I replied, "Seymour, I would never teach at the seminary under the present administration."

Silence.

The conversation faded. He could think of nothing more to say. And I did not have to say anything further. For I knew exactly what I was saying and I meant it: I think this is a dreadful place, and while thankful for what I learned here, I'll be glad to get out.

I now realize that such sentiments could resonate for more than a few impatient seniors in colleges and universities everywhere, those who have had enough formal education and are ready for the next stage in life. In my years in graduate education, I came to expect rudeness and insolence from students completing their doctorates—those who worked out, at my expense, their resentment at having, in their mature years, to take criticism of their work, however valid and well-meant it was. Through sullen discourtesy they said: Enough! However, I could not bestow the doctorate they wanted without the education they despised. But formal education from age five to age twenty-eight does exact its costs, and more than a few of my doctoral students may have exacted from me, in turn, the vengeance that JTSA unleashed on me for my own rudeness and insolence in that earlier incident.

But the provocation was there at the seminary. JTSA had special problems. It was a very small school, and as a seminary, it created psychological strains as the professors conveyed to the students the tensions of a tiny community and sought friends and allies among them. At JTSA, as in other small academic communities, students not only found themselves privy to the local gossip but imputed to the community struggles for pre-eminence. They traded the gossip and the opinions of one about the other, importance out of all proportion to what was at stake, which was, in intellectual terms, nothing. In my years at JTSA, I was much taken by the great theologian, Abraham J. Heschel, and I knew in detail how he had been and was abused by his colleagues, none of them his intellectual equal in either scholarship or theological depth—or in humanity. When he had published what he thought his greatest work, on the theologies of revelation in Judaism, the regnant politician of the faculty, Saul Lieberman, had told him it was "Purim-Torah," meaning a travesty, fit for the Jewish Mardi Gras, not scholarship at all. With such a mean, second-rate tyrant in charge, it was no wonder the prevailing atmosphere had left me, among others, eager to leave. All this I conveyed in that one, unspeakably arrogant and intolerant sentence, which echoes in my ears even now.

Don't misunderstand. I do not regret the decision, which rested on the integrity of my commitment to a life of academic teaching in the mainstream. I did not want to teach at a Jewish seminary, and I also did not want to spend more time teaching, just to make money, when I should be investing my time into advancing my education (learning new languages and texts, as I'll explain) and also working on my next book, whatever it would be. For life to me would find its definition in what, at a given moment, I was doing. The decision affirmed everything I believed. But, if I could, I would turn time backward and convey my decision in a more ordinary, mannerly way.

Still, I think the outcome would have been no different if I had. For it would have exceeded all reasonable expectation to hope that the JTSA administration and faculty would permit such testimony that teaching somewhere—anywhere—else compared with teaching at JTSA. Not only so, but that any JTSA alumnus would reject the stupefying honor of teaching at JTSA lay beyond all imagining.

JTSA professors of that date took for granted they were superior to us students. First, they were born in Europe (most of them) and we were mere Americans. All knew Yiddish and German—the languages of Jewishness and scholarship, respectively. Most had studied in the ancient *yeshivot* of Europe, the only places, in their view, where one studied the Talmud. Perhaps they resented us for our unaccented American, or for our youth, or, in the case of some of us, for our capacity at learning. I cannot speculate on the foundations of other peoples' attitudes and emotions. But none of us ever thought we had to apologize for having been born in the United States. Nor did I concede that there was only one way to know anything, or only a single, unique question to answer through knowledge. But I do know as fact that, in that place, at that time, people were expected to aspire to that unattainable height of teaching at JTSA. So rejecting the invitation, discourteously or courteously, stood for rejecting the self-image of the place as the very center, on earth, of the study of God's word in Heaven.

Indeed, in more secular terms, I remember an incident some years later, when I had just been appointed to the Brown faculty, which at that time was considered an accolade in the academy because of the presence at Brown then of several truly great scholars. When I reported the good news to a JTSA administrator, Vice-Chancellor Bernard Mandelbaum, he said to me: "It is good for you to teach in the bush leagues for a while; later on we'll bring you back here to the major league." But even as a student I had concluded that the published scholarship JTSA produced was sparse and dull, mere collections and arrangements of information, not daring solutions of long-standing problems. Only one scholar mattered there, and it was Heschel. He wrote books anyone might want to read. He alone, unlike his colleagues, then aspired through his books to change his readers and repair the world. Most of the others were at best erudites, but at worst, *idiots-savants*. Only in so small and parochial a subject as the study of Judaism could the empty illusion find credibility that not publishing marked authentic learning, and publishing collections of footnotes in the form of a commentary to an uninterpreted, unintroduced text (such as Lieberman, the eminence of the place from the early 1950s to the late 1980s produced) indicated great scholarship (or scholarship at all).

By 1960, I could articulate my conviction that the study of Judaism will thrive only in the mainstream of academic life and could not go forward in the mental ghetto that thought to monopolize the subject. Like the other centers of scholarship on Judaism—the Hebrew University and Hebrew Union College–Jewish Institute of Religion—JTSA had persuaded itself that within its walls labored all, or nearly all, of the authentic scholars in the study of the Torah. They believed nothing of value took place anywhere else; if a book was not published by one of its senior professors, it was not worth reading and did not have to be read. And, as I said, since few of its professors ever published (Heschel was the only genuinely creative scholar of the lot), writing books by definition blighted one's reputation. An occasional article, in an obscure and unread journal, in Hebrew, sufficed.

Nothing would ever change for me. I had ruined things, and I would never be forgiven. More than a decade after getting fired, when I had reached the senior rank at Brown, on May 15, 1973, I came for the first time to lecture at JTSA. I had been invited by some students, through the intervention of a dean, Neil Gillman, an old friend from my student days. With two exceptions, the entire faculty boycotted the lecture; lest I miss the point, Gillman told me, "The reason the faculty did not come to your lectures is that no one here thinks you have anything worthwhile to say."

"Then why did you invite me?"

Silence.

X. Publishing Too Much

When I was a rabbinical student, I published regularly in all manner of magazines and newspapers. From Oxford I had sent an article based on my thesis to *Commentary*. An assistant editor at that time and friend from then on, Nathan Glazer, wrote back, "We can't use this, but we'd like you to write for us." When I came to JTSA, I called on him and met the then editor, Elliot Cohen, a Southern Jew who loved Judaism and wanted *Commentary* to serve as a medium for the renewal of Jewish culture. For the next six years, from 1954 to 1960, I wrote for the magazine quite regularly, and not there alone. I printed a weekly column in my father's newspaper, did a monthly column of Jewish classics translated into English for the *Jewish Digest*, and sent off articles to most of the Jewish magazines of the day;

in general, I made myself a player in Jewish public affairs. By the end of the decade, I would be publishing in the scholarly journals in the field of religion as well.

From the start, other students objected. The senior class banquet at the Jewish Theological Seminary in June, 1955, included a will, and when it came to me, the clause read as follows: "To Jack Neusner we leave a text for his commentary." The message was, you may be writing in *Commentary*, but you don't know any texts; you are an *am haaretz*, that is, an ignoramus. In that setting, the meaning was, you have no right to publish. It was a cruel, public insult, received with great laughter and applause. It was not the first, or by any means the last. I had had the instinct—I could not claim it was mere wisdom—not to attend the closing banquet, but the news reached me in a minute or so.

The students did not stand alone—not by any means. By the end of my first year, as I said, that fact led the faculty at JTSA to debate throwing me out of the school. No one accused me of not working or not learning, or inadequacy to the task. The charge was that I published—not too much, but at all. The opposition of Heschel saved my place there. But to correct the "problem," Louis Finkelstein, then chancellor, called me to his office and in a not very cordial way objected to my publishing articles and book reviews in *Commentary, The Reconstructionist*, and all the other Jewish journals and newspapers of the day. "This is unseemly. You don't know enough, you should spend your time studying Torah." He did not mean to censor me, he said. But, in his exact words: "If you have anything worthwhile to say, you should print it in the *Harvard Theological Review*." I took him seriously and called his bluff. Not long afterward I did publish an article in the *Harvard Theological Review* and proudly brought him an offprint. It was an article that would have its afterlife. He glanced at it, reading perhaps a paragraph. His only comment was, "Well, you certainly do write very nicely, don't you?" I knew precisely what he was saying—and so did he.

Let me digress and tell the rest of the tale. Scarcely a decade later, in 1973, in my *Rabbinic Traditions about the Pharisees before 70*, for good and substantial reasons, citing chapter and verse, among other prior work on the Pharisees—all of it in fact—I dismissed as simply not historical Finkelstein's own study *The Pharisees: The Sociological Background of their Faith*[12] I called it merely a partisan-political document of the New Deal. In that work, long a party-document of JTSA, he had described the Pharisees as New Deal reformers, plebeian intellectuals struggling against the patrician Sadducees. He even explained arcane legal decisions on cultic purity by appeal to class status and class interest. And in the 1930s, when the work had been published, nobody laughed! In my *Pharisees* it sufficed to dismiss his account

---

12. Reprint (Philadelphia: The Jewish Publication Society of America, 1946).

of the matter by pointing out that (1) not a shred of evidence sustained his view; (2) his implausible and obviously anachronistic reading of matters was read into the data, not derived from them (who in first century Jerusalem had heard of Franklin D. Roosevelt—or Karl Marx, for that matter?); and (3) every line of the work moreover represented a quite gullible paraphrase of whatever the sources alleged as fact, lacking all critical perspective and demonstrating mere fundamentalism. Today Finkelstein's historical work finds its place on the shelves of curiosities of discredited scholarship, to which we send students only to entertain them on a slow afternoon. No one dreams of finding the historical Pharisees there.

But Finkelstein embodied the atmosphere and attitude of the then prevailing approach to the study of Judaism, its arid academicism, its narrow-minded philological positivism ("If you know what the word means, you know what the man said, and you can determine what really happened that day"), and, above all, its imperial sterility: don't publish until you're dead—or we'll kill your career. Used to the rules of the ghetto, with its total control of learning, Finkelstein responded in his way—and not only to me, but to everyone with whom he disagreed. And so did anyone else in command at that time of institutions of learning in the Judaic sciences. But Finkelstein was to serve his reputation poorly by failing to cope with change. His final scholarly statement brought him only ridicule, and before he died he stopped playing a role in Judaic learning.

Let me explain. Along with many others, Finkelstein took the path—well trodden in a field controlled by a few monopolists—of silence, for which the German academy provides its own word, *Todschweigen*, killing by ignoring. *Todschweigen* means people are not to cite or discuss that of which they do not approve or with which they disagree. And, if they practice *Todschweigen* properly, they will control the flow of learning. Whereas in Jerusalem the professors practice thought-control over intellectual life, protected by distance and even by a language barrier (the students do not read foreign languages), *Todschweigen* works. But the foci of public activity in the Judaic humanities now prove so diverse, the centers of power (such as it is) so numerous, that *Todschweigen* no longer works. In despair, the Judaica scholars of Jerusalem spent years pointing out how they would not cite my work deemed beneath contempt—so people went looking to see what Jerusalem would not cite. In the Hebrew University Library, for decades my books were kept under lock and key (along with the pornography). Then students picked the lock and read the forbidden books (or perhaps it was to stare at the forbidden pictures).

Finkelstein naturally would respond to my 1973 comments on his work in the only way he knew how. He assumed himself in control of learning.

He would ignore, and at the same time murder with his silence. But, alas for him, this exercise would play itself out long after he himself survived as scarcely a curiosity from a strange and bewildering past. Specifically, ten years later, in the second volume of the *Cambridge History of Judaism*, which he edited with W. D. Davies, a New Testament scholar, he printed a chapter on the Pharisees that simply ignored everything written on the subject after his book had appeared a half-century earlier. Finkelstein's chapter elicited comment in all the reviews, which unanimously expressed surprise at the man's unscholarly treatment of his subject. The chapter discredited the volume, and the dreadful reviews severely embarrassed the publisher, Cambridge University Press. That press simply waited out the scandal of the second volume, postponing the publication of the third volume of the same series for a decade—and simply cancelled the planned fourth volume altogether.

But in the ghetto, *Todschweigen* worked. No book of mine would ever be reviewed in the scholarly journals of the State of Israel—not one out of 550. Now back to our story of the nearly fatal day on which I told JTSA I did not want to teach there.

XI. Getting Fired (2)

That was the setting in which I had had the temerity to decline a position, however humble, at JTSA. And my reason was simple: Columbia was paying me what I needed to support myself, and I wanted to spend the rest of my time on learning. I was a true believer in the promise of the academy. I wanted to be a historian, working on the Jews' history, with attention also to their religion; only later would the field of the study of religion define my work. I went to Heschel and to Salo Baron, professor of Jewish history at Columbia University and chairman of my dissertation committee, to ask their advice on what to do next, my dissertation nearing completion. Heschel advised me to study Yiddish and work on the history of the Jews in Eastern Europe, explaining that, at that time, the scholarly literature on the history of that thousand-year-old and massive heartland of Jewry, now wiped out, scarcely matched the importance of the subject. Baron advised me to study the Jews in Babyhonia and therefore to take up the language, Pahlavi, the Middle Iranian dialect that was used for the written sources of the Iranian rulers of Babylonia in Talmudic times.

I wonder whether anyone has faced just this choice before; setting Yiddish side by side with Pahlavi surely contains its own incongruities. I chose Pahlavi and planned to study with Ilya Gershevitch, a teacher at

Cambridge University, in the year that he taught at Columbia, as I did, which was 1961–62. (I went on for two more years, 1962–64, with Richard N. Frye, the great Harvard Iranist, learning what I really had wanted to know, studying with another exemplary citizen of the academy) So I had made my choice: live on what seemed like a princely salary ($5500 for 1960–61, but my apartment rent on West 113th Street was exactly $100 a month), teach my courses, study Pahlavi, and start my next major work, which would be a history of the Jews in Babylonia in Parthian and Sasanian times—what was also called "the Talmudic period."

So much for what I was thinking in turning down the JTSA offer. What they were thinking we may readily imagine. Indeed, we need not imagine at all. For when I started teaching in September, I found out. Specifically, at the end of the first week of classes, rather awed and frightened by the experience of talking so much and actually being listened to, I called on the then acting chairman of the department, John Krumm, who was also chaplain of the university. It was on one of the intermediate days of the Festival of Tabernacles (Sukkot). My former teacher and then colleague, Jakob Taubes, had admonished me not to take off any Jewish holidays, on grounds that Columbia does not recognize private vacations. I replied that none of these was private; I did not invent the calendar of Judaism or its holy days; I would make up the time (which I did). I planned to explain to the acting chairman when I would make up those classes. Before I could bring up the subject, he said; "I'm glad you came by today, since I have news for you."

I: "What is that?"

He: "We have decided to terminate your employment at the end of the present academic year. Get another job."

I: "Why?"

He: "We do not require your services, we will use the position in some other way." He offered no other explanation, and I left, the holiday—and much else—ruined.

The "other way" quickly clarified itself. It was the same way, but with another person in the job. JTSA got what it wanted. Contrary to what Krumm said, Judaism would continue within the curriculum, but through part-time instruction, by the JTSA Talmud teacher, David Weiss Halivni. He would do what I had declined to do. Halivni would teach at Columbia part-time and at JTSA full-time. But it was not a stable arrangement; many decades later, he took a professorship at Columbia and left JTSA altogether.

Readers need not be detained by reports on how the decision devastated me. My father was to die two months later. In the aftermath of my being fired, Columbia University Press, which had orally accepted my dissertation for publication, rejected the book. The editor did not even give a reason. He did not think he had to. So it was not an easy time. Of the response of others little need be said. It suffices to say that when I reported the decision to Hutchison, then at Claremont, he replied with sympathy for me and outrage at his former colleagues, but, after all, he had left. Morton Smith expressed sympathy but did nothing and offered no suggestions.

Baron indicated that he had known about it in advance and voiced neither surprise nor opposition. He said he would recommend me for some other positions, which he did, at Texas and at Wisconsin in Milwaukee. In that interview, I pointed out to him that the promises made to me at the time of the appointment meant nothing. I cited to him the verse in Jeremiah referring to the Jerusalem authorities as "a den of thugs," and told him Jeremiah could as well have spoken of Columbia University. He said, "Bite your tongue." How valuable his recommendations were is difficult to say; I was not Milwaukee's first choice, and I had the impression that I was Texas's only plausible applicant. For some years afterward Baron wrote recommendations for me for competitive fellowships, none of which I got. When I ceased to request his recommendations, I succeeded in every competition. From his example of academic ethics I learned, if you cannot say something good in a recommendation, don't say anything at all.

But if in citing Jeremiah on the priesthood of Jerusalem I was right about the Department of Religion and those in charge of Jewish studies at Columbia, I was wrong about Columbia. The academy in those days treated its own word with honor. The university not only tried to make amends but twice, and in the next few years, offered me positions. When the news that I had been fired broke, I turned to Peter Gay, then in Columbia's history department, who brought the story to the dean of Columbia College, Peter Palfrey. The dean intervened and instructed the department to renew my appointment in its original terms. Horace Friess, who had taught me in his graduate seminar, called me in (Krumm the hatchet man made himself scarce from that point on) and announced: "The dean has forced us to renew your appointment for a second year, which we will do; but I assure you we will get rid of you then, or as soon as we can, no matter what. You will never get tenure here. And if possible, we won't keep you after next year. You are a worthless person." Friess was active in the Ethical Culture Society, so I did not doubt his word.

Why all this? I did not have to wait long for an explanation. Jakob Taubes, with whom I had studied at Columbia, some years later told me in so many words what I had long found reason to suspect: "The JTSA people said you are worthless and don't know anything. That is why we got rid of you." That message had come to me from JTSA for many years, and I found no reason to doubt Taubes's explanation. Since that same JTSA had the prior year awarded my Columbia doctoral dissertation their Abraham Berliner Prize in Jewish History, the sum of $1,000 (an astronomical sum to someone making $5500 a year), I found the charge of total incompetence difficult to take to heart. But, in context, no explanation was needed. I represented what JTSA (and other centers of study of Judaism) found difficult to contend with: someone who carried the subject into the mainstream of public academic life. Their nightmare came true; by the late 1980s, JTSA found itself unable to make appointments to its professorial openings, its first, second, even third choices turning down the offers in favor of university positions. Most of its faculty would come from its own alumni, particularly those without the choice of a university professorship. And in the competition with universities for the best students, the seminary struggled with equally disappointing results.

Did I really pose such a threat to the parochial scholars and their institutions? I should not have thought so. But they certainly did, then and for all time thereafter. My plan was to open the sources to all comers, lay out what they said, spell out what I thought, present my results as an exercise in public argument—the advocacy of reasoned positions through full exposure of evidence and argument. That was not the style of the scholars of Judaism. They confused their opinions with facts, cultivated obscurity, and practiced obfuscation. They did not spell out sources and explain why they thought the sources supplied facts; they just footnoted them as facts. They did not translate and explain the sources. They did not undertake large-scale presentations on major problems. And they did not nurture public debate.

For my part, then as throughout, I did not just allude to sources, I translated them, shared them with readers, and specified how I understood them. The sectarians, whether in the rabbinical seminaries or in the Israeli universities, addressed a tiny, homebound audience of specialists, dealing with problems of no broad intellectual relevance or even interest. I tried to formulate large questions and to answer them in ways others could examine and test. Most scholars in the area in which I worked (things were different in other areas in the study of Judaism) produced little, and what they wrote bore slight consequence. I produced a lot, and I aimed at making a difference.

Above all, the senior scholars, parochialists to a man, wanted to be consulted and to censor, to pass their opinions, and to dictate who would live and who would die. But I did not ask people in advance what they thought of my ideas. I published what I thought right and responsible, and let others criticize in print—no harm done. But public debate was precisely what the sectarians did not want—for the same reason that made them sectarian. They wanted to control, not argue; manipulate, not engage in reasoned discourse. In the 1970s a gentle, brilliant rabbi, Max Arzt, a vice chancellor at JTSA who embodied the finest ethics of the Judaism taught there, gently asked me, "Why don't you visit Lieberman once in a while?" He explained that things would go better if I occasionally called on Lieberman—the JTSA icon of the day and Heschel's tormentor, as I mentioned earlier—and asked him his opinion about something or other. I explained that I had written to Lieberman and asked him a question about a word, and he had not replied; and, further, Lieberman knew nothing about the problems on which I was working and was neither a historian nor a historian of religion. Whatever he had to say he had published, and I had extensively used his edition and commentary of an important text. But I could not think of any reason to cultivate the man by pretending to find interesting what was, in fact, a dull and ordinary mind. So I said, "No, Rabbi Arzt, much as I respect your advice, it is not good advice for a scholar to take, only for a politician. And I'm not running for anything— or from anything, either."

Not checking up front for permission to speak before I printed an idea represented my breaking ranks. I thereby violated the monopoly that had controlled the subject and had excluded competition: other ideas, other viewpoints, besides those of "our crowd." So whom they could not control, the principal voices would destroy. Whom they could not destroy, they would at the very least discredit. Would that at stake were issues of learning or intellect! But all that motivated anyone was politics. At that, the naysayers excelled, and—not surprisingly—I did not. But there was a more fundamental problem that I embodied. Mine was, in fact, one of the first entirely normal academic careers in that field. Independent to a fault, I also stood alone. That is to say, I was then nearly quite by myself in insisting that I would be paid only by the academy and would work only in the academy. My career represented a change in the conditions of the academy, and even a more irenic personality would have faced enormous obstacles in doing what I did.

Until then scholars of Judaism found university employment on a part-time basis while serving synagogue congregations, later on moving into full-time professorships (as in the instance of my contemporary, Joseph Yerushalmi, who left a pulpit to assume a professorship at Columbia), or served both synagogues and professorships (as in the case of Isadore Twersky, who for his entire career would work both as professor at Harvard and as rabbi of a Hasidic synagogue in Brookline), or worked in Hillel Foundations and then transferred to the faculty (as in the case of Judah Goldin who went from Hillel to JTSA to Yale and then to University of Pennsylvania). It was rare for someone to earn a secular Ph.D. and immediately enter into secular employment in a mainstream university. But the way was open, and I picked up the pieces of my shattered career and moved on to Milwaukee. I would soldier on. By that point in life, I saw no choice and aspired to none.

XII. NOT DEFROCKED BUT UNSUITED

I cannot imagine a young scholar less qualified for the work at hand than I was when I reached Milwaukee—less qualified in temperament, and less prepared in experience of what was a very new and inexperienced university. I understood nothing about that situation and, moreover, came to town nursing a considerable disappointment of my own. But I determined to make a go of the appointment. It took just two months before I realized I was unsuited to the requirements of that position. At that time, University of Wisconsin–Milwaukee was scarcely two years old. It was fabricated through the union of the University of Wisconsin extension, the old Milwaukee Normal School (which over the decades acquired successively more elegant titles, until at the end it was Wisconsin State College at Milwaukee), and various odds and ends of the Wisconsin system located in the city. All were joined together and the conglomerate was renamed UW–M— to be made famous through Fonz of *Happy Days*.

Now, in that early time, not much else changed besides the name. UW–M kept the old Normal School professors and deans. Appointments at impressive salaries were advertised in Wisconsin state teachers' colleges publications, but not in the national professional society media. Consequently the faculty was recruited from the ranks of people tenured for accomplishments of an-other-than-academic character (whatever they might have been). Supposing Milwaukee anomalous, I thought tenure in the system generally was rewarded for longevity, sloth, intellectual sterility, and academic passivity. I would learn that I was right—but not only about Milwaukee. But there, as in many of the newly anointed state university campuses of that time, publishing scholars were few and ostracized. Nullities ruled. The chancellor of that day defied even the lowest standards of public prose left behind by the Eisenhower administration as he pronounced barely literate banalities in the name of the new campus. Within days of my arrival I realized that I had made a mistake. It was when I brought the dean's secretary my requisitions for a dozen bookcases for my scholarly library, which I had shipped from New York City.

She: "That's a lot of bookcases. What do you need all those books for? Are all these books for instructional purposes?"

I: "None is. Anyhow, how would I know the difference between a book for an 'instructional purpose' and one not for such a purpose? And what might that difference be?"

Clearly, she knew and I did not know. I got half the bookcases, and the other half of the books stayed in boxes. It was just as well.

Then again, the UW–M library ran a weekly truck to the Madison campus, bringing back books from the main library for our use. Working on my history of the Jews in Babylonia, I wanted to survey the journals in ancient Near Eastern studies, to find out what had been done on Parthian and Sasanian Iran. Madison had a superb collection of journals in all the scholarly languages. I requested twenty-five to fifty volumes a week, since I could review the contents and copy the articles I required. The head of the service flatly refused to bring me what I requested.

"You can't possibly read that many books in a week."

"But I need to consult the journals and find out what is in them, then copy the articles I will use in the course of research."

"So what's the difference between a journal and a book? You can't read that many books in a week."

The local synagogue, which had a first-rate scholarly library on ancient Judaism collected by a former rabbi, had promised to contribute the entire academic part of its collection to the university when I arrived. No one else uses it anyhow, the rabbi told me, and we want the university to have it. This included rare and valuable monographs and complete runs of old journals. Alas, somehow the rabbi found a reason not to follow up, but I would be permitted to borrow one book a week, for a week.

I would soldier on. But my education reached the climactic lesson a month into the year, when I undertook to organize a lecture series on Jewish studies in the university. I had in mind to introduce the new department and its field to colleagues in various disciplines, inviting a philosopher, literary critic, historian, and political scientist to talk about Jewish studies within their disciplines. Since I took for granted that colleagues and students would want to know how the new subject fit into the various disciplines, I turned to leading figures to place our subject on display in accord with its various fields. I turned to the leading lights of the day (and long afterward), including Arthur A. Cohen in philosophy of Judaism, Arnold J. Band in Hebrew literature, and Ben Halpern in political science, and Morton Smith in history. Their lectures accomplished my goals and ended up in print in the journal, *Judaism*.

But when I was organizing the series, I met trouble I had never anticipated. To understand it, you have to know that my position was financed by the local Jewish community. It was through an organization called the Wisconsin Society for Jewish Learning, a group set up by a local Reform rabbi to sponsor Jewish learning at the University of Wisconsin in Madison. Now UW–M would get money, too, and that was the basis of my position. But one problem quickly presented itself. The society thought that I was its employee and was supposed to do what it wanted me to do, and, more to the point, not to do or say what it did not want me to do or say. I had no such understanding. I had never heard of a lay group supporting a professor and censoring him. And I regarded teaching about Judaism on the campus as an academic activity, with no connection to the special pleading or particular interests of the Jewish organizations that, collectively, think of themselves as "the Jewish community." It never entered my mind that local Jewish lay leaders would have to sign off on what we did on campus.

When I set up the series, I asked the society for a small grant to supplement the university's budget for the project. The president of the society—some sort of physician, I recall—called me on the phone to discuss the matter. His message was simple; cancel the lectures. I remember that the call came toward the later part of a Friday afternoon, and I was boiling eggs for supper. (Before I was married, I lived on yoghurt, cold cereal, and, for an ambitious meal, a boiled egg and crackers and cheese, never learning how to cook or wanting to learn) When the phone rang, I supposed it would take a few minutes. I left the eggs to boil.

The president of the society explained that the society did not plan to make the grant I had requested (it was $200, which even in those days was not a huge sum) because the society did not approve of the lecture series. I explained that the purpose of the series was to contribute to the intellectual program of the university a clear understanding of what we do in Jewish studies and how we in that subject relate to the disciplinary structure of the university in the selected fields (all of which had expressed an interest in the project) of history, philosophy, literature, and political science.

Yes, the society president said, "But I am telling you that we don't want it. So drop it, cancel it. First, you didn't ask our permission. Second, we don't think the lecture topics are interesting. Third, we never heard of the people. Fourth and most important is"—and this was why he called, and these words ring in my ears even today—"We really don't want the Department of Hebrew Studies to be that prominent and public. The *goyim* will get jealous." I heard his voice, in impeccable American, an educated man in the middle of a perfectly normal professional career, calling me back to the ghetto.

The president of the society supposed he was talking to an employee. I was some sort of local talent, comparable to a program assistant in the local Jewish Community Center, or, perhaps, an assistant rabbi in a synagogue. The society, in other words, had thought it was hiring a junior culture officer to "represent" it on campus and give a few courses, a kind of glorified Sunday school teacher, but with a fancy title. It did not have in mind the introduction of the subject, the Jews, their history, language, culture, and religion, into the center of university life. The society surely did not think that Jews should be so visible as, in the nature of things, my work was making them. So came the startling statement: "We don't want this lecture series. We won't pay for it, and we want you to cancel it."

I: "I simply don't understand."

He: "It's too much, it's too public, we don't want it. We just want you to give some classes in Hebrew and maybe a little history. You're doing too much."

To make his points, the president talked at me for nearly an hour; it was growing dark, and the Sabbath was coming. I told him, "Thanks for your call and advice, Now I will tell you my decision. My decision is to go forward with the series, and I hope you come. I'll have no trouble to get the money somewhere else," which was true. In the University of Wisconsin of that day, it posed no problem; the Madison campus was in the hands of first-rate academic leaders. They knew UW–M would require reform. So I simply explained the problem to the dean in Madison, who immediately authorized the required funds and wrote a strong letter of encouragement. The University of Wisconsin at Madison enjoyed remarkable leadership, and my impression was that the Wisconsin legislature also understood the rules for maintaining a great and free university.

The conversation with the society president had dragged on long enough for the water to boil away, the eggs to explode, and the pot to turn red hot. Cleaning up the mess, I reached the decision to leave Milwaukee at the end of that academic year—come what may. Fortunately, in those times of prosperity, I had the opportunity. During my job hunt the preceding year, I had been offered a two-year post doctoral research appointment by the Lown Institute for Advanced Jewish Studies at Brandeis University.

I wrote to the head, Professor Alexander Altmann, asking whether the position might be offered again. He replied immediately and re-offered it, and I accepted the position that same day.

The offer in hand, I went to inform the dean. Would that young professors today could have so good a morning with so obnoxious a dean as I did that day. As deans will, he took over control of the conversation, assuming I had no business and he had the only business.

He: "You know, I've been meaning to talk with you. You do too much."

"Too much?"

"You publish too much, you work too hard, you ask too much of the students, and you just go and spoil things here. Why last Sunday I drove by the building"—UW–M occupied what looked like an old high school building, and my office was in front on the ground floor and was visible from North Downer Avenue—"and saw the light on in your office in the late afternoon. What were you doing on a late Sunday afternoon at the office?"

"I was working on my new book."

"That's what I mean—it's too much. Why don't you take Sundays off?"

"Well, what difference does that make to you."

"Well, you just do too much."

"So you have no complaints with my teaching?"

"No. The students like you."

"With my record of publication?"

"No. It's just too much."

"With my organization and management of the Department of Hebrew Studies?"

"No, the papers come in when required."

"So you have no legitimate complaint and no reason to say what you said?"

"Well, you do too much."

"Well, I guess I should give you this."

I handed him my letter of resignation on the spot, got up and left without another word. I did not look back.

I finished out the year and no one bothered me again. The lecture series attracted excellent crowds. In these days, when Jewish audiences will come to lectures only if the subject is the Holocaust or the State of Israel, it is nice to think back to a time when I could fill a hall for a lecture by Arthur A. Cohen on Jewish philosophy and theology. The lectures themselves accomplished their purpose. I recall, in particular, how Arnold Band explained the relevance of the study of Hebrew literature in the university to the broader interest of

American culture by drawing within itself the various literatures and cultures of the world at large. It was from that lecture that I learned to think in such terms, although many years would pass before I could formulate matters so well as he did.

True, I did get an anonymous letter from a local Jew (I knew the writer was Jewish because he said so). He responded to a letter that I had written to all the members of the local Zionist organization, and especially to the Labor Zionists, the party that Ben Halpern supported, telling them about Halpern's coming lecture and urging them to attend. The writer took offense at my letter, asking by what right I had (1) the temerity to set up Jewish lectures in that community, (2) why had I not gotten permission from the rabbis, and (3) anyhow who was I to call upon the local Jews to come to the university to hear (the case in point) Ben Halpern?

"The Jewish community objects to this program of yours, and you had no business running it and using our name."

The unsigned letter made a point I should not have had to learn on my own, which was: never take the affairs of the Jewish community to heart but focus solely on the intellectual disciplines of learning in the academy. The writer was right to say, you are on the campus and have no place among "us." And he made it clear: "We don't want you, trust you, value what you know or what you do, or want to hear what you have to say." When I decided to try to make a career in the mainstream, my decision bore implications I had not perceived. The decision was right not only for the right reasons, but for the wrong ones.

For decades afterward, I had a nightmare that I was back in Milwaukee and would wake up upset, calmed only by the knowledge that I was somewhere else. When, nearly thirty years later, I was reaching the decision to leave Brown University, that nightmare recurred time and again. When I reached the University of South Florida in Tampa, the nightmare never came back. But from then on, I expected absolutely nothing from the "organized Jewish community"—the bunch of lay *schnorrers* and *berokhah*-brokers, the fund raisers and bestowers of rabbinical blessings, empty-heads one and all—and I was never to be either surprised or disappointed.

XIII. PARADISE

Brandeis meant living in Cambridge, just a short walk from Harvard Yard, studying Pahlavi and Iranian history with Richard N. Frye, haunting the bowels of Widener Library—the paradise of the subhead—and spending all my time for two years on research. Next to the Cambridge University Library in England, Widener is the best-managed and best-stocked research library in the English-speaking world, and therefore, in the entire world. I spent work time at home, reading and writing, and the rest of my time simply walking up and down the shelves of Widener, examining all the books I could find on whatever subject I was pursuing at that moment. For two summers and two academic years, 1962–63 and 1963–64, I wandered in those stacks and happened upon the accumulated knowledge of one topic after another.

Another chapter of this paradise was learning new languages—a different path into the unknown. For me in those two years it was to be more Pahlavi, Farsi, and Armenian (by accident, I really wanted to know something of Armenian history). In the first summer, 1962, I took Farsi (modern Persian) as background for Pahlavi; in the fall, another semester of Farsi; in the spring and summer of 1963, Armenian history and Classical Armenian (to write a little article, "The Jews in Pagan Armenia," forgetting the little Armenian I knew within a few months but retaining a lifelong interest in all things Armenian), and, throughout, weekly sessions with Frye.

In his mastery of everything Iranian, Frye showed me what a scholar of greatness could accomplish. I doted on the rich learning of his books as they appeared, the fresh viewpoint and the willingness to take risks. But it was in his breadth and generosity of spirit that he drew me into my work and offered a model of how the scholarly life may form a worthwhile human being. Lacking in pretense, vigorous in his devotion to his ideas, trusting his instincts and cultivating his powers of wit and imagination, Frye defined the ideal postdoctoral guide: always there when I wanted him, never there when I didn't.

I had plenty of time to study with Frye and pursue my reading in Widener and my work on my *History*. All the Lown Fellowship required in exchange for $5,000 annually was that I have tea with Professor Altmann once a year and attend occasional lectures under the institute's sponsorship. Altmann himself took no interest at all in my research. When I brought him my dissertation, which was published in the early months of my stay at the institute, he did not open it. In the first year I completed my *History of the Jews in Babylonia,* Vol. I: *The Parthian Period,* and started Vol. II: *Early Sasanian Times.* Altmann did not ask what was in the books. The Brandeis postdoctorate is acknowledged in the prefaces. For his part Altmann never acknowledged receiving the books that I wrote under his sponsorship and mailed to him upon publication. I never understood why he had appointed me, but it hardly mattered so I never cared to ask. Teutonic, distant, cold, disdainful, supercilious, uninteresting and uninterested, he never got in the way. And he saved my career at a disastrous hour, never asking me why I worked so hard (which I never thought I did). In context, his not caring was much to be desired over the UW–M dean's caring.

In those days, great scholars moved to Cambridge upon retirement, to gain access to the Harvard library. So I had the good fortune to meet yet another truly authentic scholar—a learning intellectual—and to gain entirely fresh perspective on my own area of interest, which was Judaism in late antiquity. He was Erwin R. Goodenough, the historian of religion, who, like me, worked on Judaism (among a wide range of other subjects that he mastered). After a miserable career at Yale, where he was highly productive as a scholar and therefore marginalized and isolated, Goodenough shook the dust of New Haven off his feet and moved to Cambridge and carried forward his remarkable research from retirement to the end of his life, a few years later. Only much later in life did I come to understand the profound judgment that gesture—moving out of the community where he had spent his active career—represented.

Goodenough certainly excelled all his Yale colleagues in learning, creativity, and accomplishment. That explains why he was marginalized. For the mediocrities will always make up the majority and, where democracy rules, will govern. Universities work best under benign dictatorships, and, as the next decades were to teach me, they fall apart under mob rule, especially that of the common professors. Goodenough's career, begun in the age of academic sloth and aristocracy, prevented me from imagining that the old days ought to be fondly remembered. Universities then were hostile not only to blacks, women, Jews, and other minorities, but also to their best scholars.

Certainly, no one in the study of religion or theology (the Divinity School) at Yale could compete with Goodenough's originality, erudition, solid achievement, or ultimate influence. He defined the issues that would occupy the study of ancient Judaism for two generations: Is there one Judaism or many? And how do we cope with conflicting evidence? It was Goodenough's study of synagogue art that opened all the doors. The conflicts between the data of Judaism emerged when archaeology revealed the use of iconic art that literary evidence had never led anyone to anticipate. Trying as best he could to deal with this evidence, Goodenough postulated not a single Judaism, but two different Judaisms (that was my formulation, not his). One was mystical, represented by the art and its symbolism; the other legal and philosophical, represented by the rabbinic writings on which I was working. Since, at that time, I had never imagined that the Talmud yielded more than secular, historical information, I found surprising the notion that it adumbrated a religious system (again, my formulation, not his), and not just history.

For two years I called on Goodenough from day to day to talk. Serendipitously, I was asked by the then editor of *Conservative Judaism*, Rabbi Samuel Dresner, to write an essay-review of the first eight volumes of Goodenough's *Jewish Symbols in the Graeco-Roman Period*, a monumental work that would reach thirteen volumes of text and illustrations. I had (and retained) the odd habit of actually reading, cover to cover, books I was asked to review. I remember my amazement at finding, even in the opening pages, a challenge to the never-before-examined premises of my work—a single Judaism and the essentially secular character of the rabbinic legal documents. I recall, also, my admiration for his lucid explanation of problems of method and evidence and interpretation. He did not only do the work, he also explained why he did it in one way, and not in some other. His book therefore served as a handbook on how to work on the history of religion.

Goodenough maintained that there was more than a single Judaism, and he insisted that the legal documents took positions on questions of religious interest and framed a particular Judaic religion (I would later invent the language, "religious system" and the use of the plural, Judaisms). In frequent conversations with Goodenough I followed up on what he had left implicit. But from him I learned more than the specifics of my subject. He was certainly the most perpetually curious person I had ever known, the most responsive to ideas and people, the most devoted to learning, and the most courageous.

Paradise at Widener conferred access to all the books I could want to see and two great men whose greatness came to full expression in their scholarship. I began to understand that learning forms a medium of personal expression, a testimony to character. Years of study with rather ordinary minds had left the impression that something more, beyond merely knowing this and that, must await. From surviving boredom to tolerating aimless erudition and now joined to endless self-celebration, I discovered what a life of learning promised in the lives of a Frye and a Goodenough. As the years passed, I realized they exemplified many in the academy.

Not all lessons in Cambridge concerned learning. Besides Frye and Goodenough, a third great man taught me yet another lesson, and that was, the lesson of personal integrity and humility—still more rare than solid accomplishment in the academy of that time, and rarer still in our time. He was Harry A. Wolfson, the historian of philosophy who worked on the continuity of the philosophy of Judaism from Philo to Spinoza and the impact of that perennial philosophy upon Christianity (through the Church Fathers) and Islam (through the Qalam). A legend in his own lifetime, Wolfson had come into my life the week I entered Harvard College in 1950, since he had chosen me as a freshman advisee. I did not know, at that time, that Harvard's great professors did not ordinarily advise freshmen at all. I never knew why I was so fortunate. I never took a course with him, not knowing enough philosophy to grasp what he taught or why it mattered, and he accepted that I was an American history major, destined to become a Reform rabbi.

In my college years I had found him welcoming and wise, although I hardly rose to the task of taking full advantage of the opportunity he accorded—talking as often and as long as I wished with one of the giants of the age. From college years I remember only one piece of advice from the old bachelor, which was: never learn how to cook, because if you learn how to cook, you will never get married. I never learned, and I did get married, so I owe him that. Wolfson was born in Europe and raised in this country; he never lost his Jewish accent. He made his way at a Harvard hostile to assimilated Jews, let alone to a Yiddish-speaking product of a Lithuanian yeshiva, who happened also to have mastered the entire Western philosophical tradition. In his life's work Wolfson formed a theory encompassing the whole of that tradition, beginning to end, and placing philosophy in the context of Graeco-Roman and Judaic thought through the figures of Philo, the Jewish philosopher of Alexandria, at the outset, and Spinoza, the Jewish philosopher of Amsterdam, at the end. The grandeur of his vision, the magnificence of his realization of it—these contrasted with the position Harvard accorded to Wolfson. For there he was isolated: floating in the eddies, but not swimming in the mainstream. He provided the model of scholarship, certainly writing elegant academic prose as a model for the rest of us. But he did not define his university through his presentation of his field, and that is what a mainstream career would accomplish.

From college years I also remember the pessimistic view he took of American Jews. He saw the lights go out saying, "American Jews are like the Hanukkah Menorah in the view of the House of Shammai." Years would have to pass before I grasped the bitter message of that gnomish statement. He was referring to the dispute in rabbinic law on the way in which the candles of the Hanukkah candelabrum are to be lit: from one to eight, or from eight to one? The House of Hillel maintained that on the first night, we light one, on the second, two, and onward to eight. The House of Shammai held that on the first night we light all eight, and then proceed to extinguish the lights, one by one. Wolfson's was a sad, but sound, perspective, as time proved.

Coming back to Cambridge, I called on Wolfson and found him as always hospitable, interesting, wise, and full of sound advice. But he was somewhat taken aback by my enthusiastic response to Goodenough, with whom he had conducted a thirty-year debate. He kept his peace. A few years later, I published an article comparing two scholars' reading of the synagogue art discovered in the early 1930s at Dura Europos. The art was a complete wall made up of highly representational pictures of Moses, Aaron, and other biblical heroes and scenes. The official reading was Carl Kraeling's, published in the Yale report on the archaeological finds at Dura Europos, and the other was that of Goodenough. Until Kraeling's appeared, decades later, in the mid 1950s, Goodenough had been forbidden to write on the subject, so work he had done in the early 1930s had to wait a quarter-century for publication. Goodenough's interest in other synagogues was provoked by his enforced silence on the one at Dura. He addressed the symbols and representations everywhere else in the early volumes of his *Jewish Symbols*, and published his Dura volumes only later in his long series, when he was permitted to do so. In my article I pointed out that Goodenough's reading accorded with the larger cultural realities faced by the Jews in Parthian (and Sasanian) Babylonia and Mesopotamia, and that Kraeling's—presupposing a rigid Orthodox Judaism, governed from the center, fully exposed in the writings of the rabbis in the Mishnah and the Talmud—contradicted those realities. Specifically, I pointed out, the cultural diversity exhibited by the Jews' archaeology corresponded to the very representation of matters by the rabbis of the Talmud themselves, and Goodenough's account more closely replicated the diversity that characterized Judaism in that time. Wolfson figures in this tale for the odd reason that, as it turns out, I did not send him an offprint of the article.

When the article appeared I was at Dartmouth College, but I regularly drove down to Cambridge to use the library and talk with Frye and see Goodenough—and Wolfson. On one such trip, Frye and I went to the Harvard Faculty Club for lunch. Wolfson walked in after we were seated. Rising, Frye invited him to join us, saying in his usual, jovial manner, "And you know this man too, don't you?" Wolfson waved contemptuously with his hand, saying; "Yeah, yeah, I know him, I know him." And he walked by without another word and sat down by himself at another table. Frye was shocked and amazed. By that time I was used to public displays of discourtesy by Jewish scholars of Judaism, so I minimized that one. But I did not forget it, and I never thought to see Wolfson again. Then three years later, when I was at Brown University, I got a postcard, in shaky antique handwriting, from Harry A. Wolfson. The card summoned me to visit him in a convalescent hospital in the Boston area: "I am at the hospital and I would like to see you." I telephoned and asked why. He said, "There is something I wish to say to you. Please come." I drove up on that same Sunday evening.

When I entered the room, I stood some distance from his bed. I gave no greeting, asking only, "Here I am. Why did you want me to come?"

No better at small talk than I, he came straight to the point: "I have had an eye operation and have had to spend weeks without reading. I was like Spinoza's God, engaged in pure thought. So I began in my mind to think through whom, in my entire lifetime, I have treated unfairly. And I can think of only two people, you and one other (whom I will not identify)."

"What did you do to me? For precisely what do you wish to apologize?" By that point in life, I had learned to protect myself, placing suspicion before natural sympathy.

"I remembered when I was rude to you at the Harvard Faculty Club when Dick Frye invited me to have lunch with you."

"So why were you rude to me?"

"Because you didn't send me an offprint of your article on Dura. I thought you didn't send it because you favored Goodenough, so you were afraid for me to see the article and you kept it from me."

"So?"

"So I realize that you are an honest man, and you had no such motive."

Then—and only then—I shook his hand. And with such formality as I could muster, I said, "I do forgive you. Now we can talk."

And we talked. From then on I made the trip to Boston every few months to see both Wolfson and Frye (Goodenough died in the interim). Some time later Wolfson was diagnosed with incurable cancer, and, in his months of dying, I visited that same hospital nearly every Sunday night. At his bedside throughout were his disciple and chosen successor, Isadore Twersky; the Harvard Judaica librarian, Charles Berlin; and I. Others in the field of Jewish history at Harvard did not call, so Wolfson told me, with only a touch of bitterness. Like scholars in general, Wolfson had a devotion to learning which shaded over into narcissism. In the months when I was visiting, he was working on a reply to a criticism of an idea of his by a very junior scholar. He composed his reply from week to week. When I called, he would ask me to read that week's work, which I did. It made for a somewhat impersonal encounter; I found it impossible to get him to talk about himself. The last time I saw him he did not ask me to read his writing to him. He was at the hospital in Cambridge, where he had been brought to die. I came that last Saturday night of his life. He told me, "I could not take another week like this past one." I did not know what to say.

Wolfson accomplished under duress—but never welcomed, understood, or appreciated with an authentic understanding of his accomplishment—what I aspired to achieve as an ordinary person and in the normal course of events. His life in the academy supplied proof that it could be done, a challenge to do in normal times with my lesser resources what he had done under impossible conditions with his abundant ones.

XIV. FINALLY, A REAL JOB . . .

Worried about work beyond the two years on the postdoctoral fellowship, I pursued such possibilities as they came along. I wrote letters of inquiry to presidents, provosts, deans, and department chairmen. In those now inconceivable days, people actually answered their mail. Alas, the common reply was, yes, of course, we do want your subject (whatever it is). Now, if the Jewish community will supply the funds, we shall be happy to appoint you (or anybody else the Jews want). Not one to mince words, in reply I wrote to presidents and deans and department chairmen: you teach French without an endowment from the local French Canadians, and the local Germans and Russians and British do not have to pay for instruction on European history. Correspondence dropped off. The Milwaukee nightmare woke me up from night to night.

To me, mine was a subject like any other, with a rightful place in the academy when the disciplines of religious studies came into play. To them, teaching about Judaism or the history of the Jews represented a case of special pleading: Jews teaching Jews why they should be Jewish. And for that, deans and department chairman did not plan to spend academic money. I did not succeed in persuading anyone that another model than the ethnic one might take shape, so, "If the Jews want it, let them pay for it," ended the transaction. No one was so honest as to add, "Anyhow, they've got plenty of money."

Later on, in the late 1970s and 1980s, Jews did give millions in endowment to universities for the study of the Jews and Judaism. For a while endowing chairs even proved stylish. The mediocrity of the chair holders, in many cases hardly at the level of achievement of others holding endowed chairs in those same universities, provoked a scandal on more than a few campuses. At one campus, a department declined to accept the holder of the endowed chair in the Jewish subset of its discipline, on grounds that the candidate's actual achievements would probably not secure tenure, let alone a full professorship, and certainly not an endowed chair. So he was parked in the department where all the others in "Jewish studies" would sit out their careers, a department not organized around the disciplines of anyone but the specialists in the Jewish subjects. Here, it became clear, the academy would form its own ghetto for the Jews—now paid for by the Jews. That would not define the kind of career that I had in mind, and I was never to sit on a fully endowed chair. For a while, at Brown, I did sit on a stool, that is, an underendowed position ("distinguished scholar of . . ."). When the donor discovered I was to hold the position, she refused to complete the endowment. She waited nearly two decades. Then, when I left Brown, she raised the endowment to enough for a proper professorship.

Nowadays—to move forward for a moment—universities happily accept the ethnic definition of what is to be taught and why and by whom. Those definitions have corrupted black studies and deprived the subject of all academic respectability. But few recognize the same impact on Jewish studies. Professors of Jewish studies complain, as they do in black studies, that students are few, majors fewer still, and students taking more than the obligatory single course in the field rare indeed. The same professors debate in the 1990s issues we settled for ourselves in the 1960s—or so we thought—on whether we represent the academic or the Jewish viewpoint. Most of us (everyone not teaching in a seminary) in those days insisted we practiced a discipline on a subject—in my case, the discipline of the study of religion on the subject Judaism. We settled the question of who might teach: any knowledgeable person, Jew or gentile, male or female, found a welcome. And we took for granted that our classrooms would attract a cross-section of the campus, blacks and whites, Jews, Christians, and atheists and both genders.

One generation settles questions that the next debates as though fresh and new and threatening. Today, on many campuses the professors of the study of Judaism or Jewish (ethnic) studies are assumed to be born Jewish and to be Jews of the prescribed kind (presentable, not too religious, O.K. on Israel). They serve as ethnic cheerleaders (some of them, although lacking much religious conviction, also serve as Jewish chaplains). In such a world, who teaches what to whom is decided by appealing to the ethnic loyalty of professors and students and the use of the subject for ethnic purposes. But the professors of Jewish studies hardly represent an exception. On the tribalized campus, split up among social ghettos, these Jewish professors serve along with the gender and race cheerleaders in charge of the humanities and the easy social sciences (the ones you can do without knowing mathematics and statistics).

In my view, seeking a place in the mainstream, anyone—not only a Jew—could teach about Judaism to whomever it may concern, and that ought to be everybody in the academy with an interest in the human condition. The tribalization of the campus would set aside that insistence on the rules of general intelligibility and governing rationality. But for me, the academy would provide for my subject as it did for any other subject that belonged. And, in those days, that view prevailed.

At that time—we are now in the middle 1960s—the academy still defined its work by appeal to its own intellectual traditions and convictions. That meant, everything was open to everyone who qualified, and strict standards of reason governed all. Evidence competently amassed and accurately described, the give-and-take of argument, disinterested judgment—these would define the discourse of the academy. Special pleading would gain no hearing. True, in practice, these ideals competed with the realities of partisan pleading, political preferment, and practical prejudice. So applied reason and practical logic would have to prevail over the bigotry that on the private and even many state-supported campuses excluded blacks, women, most Jews and others of unsuitable origin from most fields. But for a while, reason did come into play and won more than a few battles, although in the end, one bigotry would take the place of another, and, as everyone knows, the campus would turn itself into the battlefield of conflicting prejudices.

The academic study of religion—a field in which comparison is necessary, and in which what we now call multiculturalism is natural, and in which general education is the ideal—formed the discipline to which I moved. It was not only that departments of history did not appoint specialists in Jewish history. It was that, in response to my encounter with Goodenough and my study of Zoroastrianism with Frye, my own natural interests and sympathies were evolving. I slowly came to perceive that Jewish history and the study of the history of Judaism did not form one and the same subject. Each pursued its own questions, brought to bear upon data of its own choice. One scarcely intersected with the other.

Setting side by side Gershom G. Scholem's *Major Trends in Jewish Mysticism* and Goodenough's *Jewish Symbols*, I could perceive the outlines of a field—the history of Judaism—well situated within the study of religion, with emphasis upon the history and comparison of religions. In my case, it would be the histories and comparisons of Judaisms. In the more narrowly historical field, represented by Scholem's overblown and dull biography of the seventeenth-century Messiah in Judaism, Sabbatai Zevi, or by Baron's vacuous and uncritical *Social and Religious History of the*

Jews, Vol. II, which dealt with the Talmudic period, I saw nothing worth knowing, just a mass of uninterpreted information. And, more to the point, the sources with which I wanted to work my whole life answered questions other than those that occupied historians, such as what happened, and then what happened next.

In that context a phone call in early autumn, 1963, from Professor Fred Berthold, chairman of Dartmouth's Department of Religion, asking me to come to Hanover to discuss a possible appointment, brought the possibility of not only a job, but precisely the right position at the right time. The written offer, for three years, open-ended, generous and made in a welcoming spirit, came soon afterward. At the same time Brown offered a one-year visiting professorship, more money but no future. I chose Dartmouth.

In the same month another phone call came, one with a direct connection to the rest of my life and not only as a scholar. But it came because of something I wrote on a Jewish issue, so it was to be life's richest reward for publishing (too much). Someone had read an article of mine in one or another of the Jewish magazines (we had many in those days). It was Max Richter, of Paterson, New Jersey, whom I had met five years earlier when I had gone out with his daughter, Suzanne. She had been my student in Camp Ramah, a JTSA summer study camp where I had gone to improve my Hebrew in 1956; she was then sixteen, and I was twenty-four. I was enchanted, and, a couple of years later, when the law no longer prohibited it, we kept company for some months. We parted when it was clear that I wanted to get married and she wanted to get her education in liberal arts and in art. After completing her degree and studying art for a year in Paris and in Jerusalem, she had come home to teach art in a school in Paterson. He called to say he liked my article and to ask whether I was married.

I: "What?"

He: "Are you married?"

I: "No, is Suzanne?"

He: "No, and I think she might enjoy hearing from you."

I: "What's the phone number?"

He gave the number and I called that night. We met in New York City at the home of friends of mine. After about fifteen minutes with them, we managed to disappear, for what became that entire afternoon. The rest is history. I commuted to Paterson every weekend from that time on. Two months later, we became engaged, and we married in March, 1964. By early summer we were living in Norwich, Vermont, across the river from Hanover, New Hampshire. Our first child, Samuel (whom we called Shmuel, as an act of ethnic assertion in then-pure-Yankee Vermont) was born in April, 1965, the next, Eli, in February, 1967, and two more children; Noam, in 1969 and Margalit, in 1973.

So for me, life had begun. The Milwaukee nightmares faded. But they were to come back a few years later, when Brown turned glitzy and proud and sour. Providence would bring me back to Milwaukee. But not just yet: Brown when I got there had stars in every department, superstars in some, and the university enjoyed the loyalty of a spirited and proud faculty—men and women who were glad to be where they were and worked to bring distinction to their university. The year or so after I arrived, a professor left Brown for the University of Chicago. I remember many of us wondered why. Myopically, we could see no difference in academic excellence between the two universities. Within a decade, when professors left for universities far lower on the pecking order than the place outsiders accorded to Brown, everyone would say, well, why not. The academy's management, illustrated by Brown's, because of the campus revolution, was falling into the hands of blundering alchemists, who discovered the secret of transforming gold into lead.

XV. ... IN A REAL ACADEMIC FIELD

In the academic study of religion, Judaism found its place in the second phase of the development of the field in general. My career fit naturally into the second stage in the field's growth. First came Christianity, with its ancillary subjects, biblical studies, philosophy of religion, and missiology. Then came a specific religion other than Christianity, and in many colleges and universities from the earliest 1960s it was to be Judaism. Since, at that time, few endowments for the subject were forthcoming, the departments made a solemn commitment of resources. For until universities had concluded that their cultural horizons encompassed the religious activities of humanity, Judaism would hardly present itself as a candidacy for inclusion within the curriculum. Hebrew was fine among languages, since it unlocked ancient Judaic writings or medieval ones for historians of antiquity or the middle ages. But not Judaism, which, after all, found itself represented as a religion that died at Calvary or was superseded with the Quran. And, it must be said, even after the study of religion rested on firm foundations, it was hardly self-evident that Judaism, among religions, would gain the prominent place within the curriculum of departments of religious studies it now enjoys. After all, it is a small religion, scarcely heard when Islam and Christianity raise their voices.

But once the initial appointments had taken shape, deriving their design from the antecedent of Protestant divinity school curriculum—Bible, philosophy of religion, history of Christianity (a.k.a., church history), and history of religion or world religions (a.k.a., missiology)—Judaism came next. One department after another found urgent the addition of a full-time, academic specialist in Judaism as the third or fourth appointment or fifth appointment—after those in the fields just now designated—and even though local rabbis had for a generation given courses on Judaism, now the departments determined that they wished a different kind of instruction in that field to take shape. The aspiration to locate, or even raise a generation of academic specialists instead of believers, native-informants, and rabbis carries us to the late 1950s, and the realization of that aspiration, to the 1960s. My story shows that I was there. So far as I know, I was the first person holding a Ph.D. in religion (Columbia–Union, 1960) to make a career only in the academy and never in institutions of Jewish sponsorship (seminary, Hebrew teachers college, Hillel Foundation, or the pulpit) and to receive a full-time, permanent appointment in the study of Judaism.

If, then, we wish to look back from whence we have come, we must ask ourselves why the founders of the academic study of religion turned to Judaism when they had completed their initial development? First, who were the founders? If we take as our models the exemplary figures of George Thomas at Princeton; Fred Berthold at Dartmouth; J. Alfred Martin at Columbia; William Clebsch at Stanford; and Steven Crary at Brown; Valerie Saiving at Hobart and William Smith, the true founder of the enterprise; Robert Michaelson, then at Iowa but later at University of California at Santa Barbara; and the two figures who brought the field to its institutional maturity in the American Academy of Religion and the Society of Biblical Literature, Robert Funk and Ray Hart—thus spanning the first and second generations of the field, from ca. 1945 to ca. 1975—what do we find? In many cases Protestant clergy moved from the college chaplaincy to chairmanships of academic departments, or did not even move out of the chaplaincy when they took on the work of organizing departments. In others, philosophers of religion broadened their horizons. The founders exemplified the framers of American civilization: white, mostly male Protestants, generally deriving from old American families, many trained in liberal protestant seminaries, who defined the field to accommodate everybody and in theory exclude nobody. They were truly multicultural in sympathy and intent. They knew one another and wrote books for one another. As I said, many met annually at the Week of Work of the National Council for Religion in Higher Education, and, as a Kent Fellow in the late 1950s and early 1960s, I found myself the first Jewish scholar of Judaism among them. For me it was a defining moment.

It is fair to ask in that specific context, precisely why did these framers of a field, influential figures on their own campuses, in many instances founders of their departments, give priority to Judaism in the second stage of the expansion of their departments? It represented difference, but difference near at hand: a religion akin to Christianity, therefore accessible, but not Christianity, so available (as it had been for centuries before) for comparison and contrast.

So, why study a religion other than Christianity? Since we deal with the phenomenon of the 1950s and earlier 1960s, we do well to turn first to the political tasks of the universities of that time, which found definition in the preparation of young Americans for a long twilight struggle against the Soviet Union's quest for world hegemony: to provide the intellectual foundations for this country's encounter with world politics. Isolationist and xenophobic before World War II, Americans had to learn to deal with difference, to negotiate diversity on a world scale. Intellectually quiescent and hardly the leaders of world science and learning before World War II, Americans had to build upon remarkable achievements in natural science and social science, retool in engineering, and reshape the humanities into the medium for our country's encounter with its allies and potential allies throughout the world.

Within that political setting, the academy opened its doors to formerly excluded groups: Jews standing first in line at what they conceived to be the prestigious universities, the private, rich, ancient ones; then Catholics aspiring to draw their parochial system of higher education into the mainstream. In the late 1940s the Ivy League imposed a rigid quota on Jewish applicants and cannot be said to have afforded Catholics a cordial welcome; blacks were scarcely to be seen. By the 1960s, quotas against Jews persisted at only the most stubborn holdouts, Yale and Princeton, for example; Catholics began arriving in numbers; and even professors of Jewish origin could gain tenure in humanities and social science departments (in mathematics and the hardest natural sciences, Jews could always be declared honorary Aryans when they were acutely needed). In the 1940s and 1950s Jews aspiring to doctorates in the culturally determinative fields—American and English literature and American history, for example—were advised to choose other fields; a Jew could no more find a position in American literature than in New Testament studies, and for the same reasons. Now, determining that Jews and Catholics would find a place, the academy under private auspices followed the model of the state-supported schools, which had discriminated only with difficulty against these same and kindred groups.

It follows that when the academic study of religion was taking shape, turning its attention to the world beyond the liberal Protestant seminaries and churches, on the one side, and the West, in general, on the other, sizable numbers of students were arriving on campus who were not liberal Protestant and who came from other places than Britain, Scandinavia, and the Protestant parts of Germany. Choosing between the Catholics and the Jews, the departments opted for courses to address the religious heritage of the Jews. This was probably in the theory that, until the Reformation, the Christians already were amply represented by the Protestant theory of Christianity. Then after the Reformation, the Catholics (from this perspective) scarcely mattered.

These two important changes in the academy, deeply affecting the formative field of religious studies—the new, national task assigned to the universities, the advent of new student populations in the very universities at which the new field was aborning—should not obscure a third formative change in the academic study of religion. That change concerned the very issue at hand: how do we deal with difference? What changed was the very definition of the curriculum, the redefining of who teaches what to whom. Formerly, believers taught their faith to believers. Now something else would be needed.

One model—famous as "the zoo department"—called for rabbis to teach Judaism to Jews, priests to teach Roman Catholic Christianity to Catholics, Buddhist priests to come and mystify everybody, and Protestant ministers (with Ph.D.'s) to teach Protestant religion, commonly in the form of philosophy of religion, to everybody else. Along these same lines, the introductory course would present "the tradition," meaning, in sequence, Judaism–Catholicism–Protestantism (first were the Jews, meaning, the Old Testament; then the early Christians–who were really Catholics–then the Protestants). That represents a massive step beyond the original definition of the field, in which Judaism played no role beyond "the Bible," (itself a category of Christianity), and in which the Catholics scarcely counted. This same model took as its organizing and definitive category not religion but religions, and, within religions, mostly the ideas that these particular religions held. Once more the ever-imperial philosophy of religion defined the categories of the study of religion and religions. Issues other than philosophical gained slight attention.

From the founding generations—the Thomases of the forties and fifties, the Bertholds, Crarys, Funks and Harts of the sixties and early seventies—the call was simple: Come and join us in the mainstream! You have something to teach us, we have something to teach you, let us form a shared conversation concerning common propositions of general intelligibility and great weight. The attitude in drawing in the study of Judaism extended to a matter of cultural policy as well: Jews found a welcome to an undifferentiated community of learning. And that insistence on transcending the barriers of difference through a common, reasoned inquiry into the character of religion as a shared and public activity—no longer "the Jews believe" but now "how does Judaic religion teach or treat . . ."—corresponded to the Jews', and others', own aspiration to find a place in the mainstream. Seeing themselves as a religious group, sharing religion with other religious groups, but adhering to a different religion from others, Jews would find a comfortable place: different, but not so different as to suffer exclusion. That is what brought me to Dartmouth.

3

—

Parrot's Beak

I. The Campus Calamity

For the campus, the climactic decade of the Cold War began in April 29, 1970, when the United States invaded Cambodia, and ended with the inauguration of Ronald Reagan on January 20, 1981. At its heart, the invasion of Cambodia was a military ploy to wipe out Communist bases. But coming on the heels of Nixon's promise to scale back American involvement in the Vietnam War, it was taken as a shift in war policy. All over the United States college students erupted in rioting. Nixon may have anticipated this; in his speech acknowledging the "secret" war in Cambodia, he remarked that American universities were threatened with destruction by the same people who opposed his war policy. In the next weeks, four students were killed on the campus of Kent State University; riots and confrontations were common on almost every major campus. During the following years faculties would take positions on partisan political issues and declare their position on public policy. In spite of being warned by colleagues that it was easier to enter the public arena than to leave it, admonished that partisanship about matters confronting all citizens equally had no place in faculty meetings, and advised to legislate only about matters of the academy, faculties—those, at any rate, with so little to do as to attend faculty meetings or serve in faculty senates—pushed forward their agendas. So they instructed the president first to withdraw from Cambodia, then to desist from bombing Hanoi, and finally to surrender Vietnam. At home, in the meantime, the same professors spawned the most conservative generation of college students in recent memory—the same students who, a decade later, found in Ronald Reagan their envisioned voice of America. Called in Roger Kimball's striking phrase, "tenured radicals," the professors of the 1970s savored their short-lived victory, which, by the late 1980s, turned the entire country against them.

The decade began with rioting on the campus and ended with the conservative revolution in national politics ratified by the election of Ronald Reagan. In that decade the campus parted company with the country. Radical egalitarianism substituted votes on academic matters—those of students, gardeners, assistant football coaches, typists, now became equal to those of professors—for reasoned argument and compelling criticism. The Berkeleys and Browns and Dukes and Stanfords and Yales and their collegiate counterparts, representing (in their minds) the entirety of the complex and diverse academy, had led the campaign to end the war in Vietnam and bring down the president who had presided at the American defeat.

With us out of Vietnam and Richard Nixon out of the White House, the prominent voices of the campus declared that they would dictate policy. Specifically, the plan was for scheduled castes—women, blacks, homosexuals, American Indians, Asian-Americans, and Latino-Americans—to declare who teaches what to whom on campus. Positions defying all reason—whites are racists, but blacks cannot commit racism, for example—would descend from on high and gain acceptance as self-evident, so they dreamed. And the campuses—always a refuge for that genteel liberalism that saw no enemies on the left—were taken over by the radicals. This brings us to Parrot's Beak, the moment at which the elite campuses entered partisan politics—never to leave.

During that interesting time, on the day when the United States invaded Cambodia, I was lecturing out of town. My blind affection for Brown University, to which I had moved in 1968, made me predict to friends that there would be no rioting. Perhaps protests and demonstrations, but civility would reign still. The crisis unfolded: I returned to a campus where no class was disrupted, no book burned, no window broken, nor a dean's office taken over and vandalized. I took pride in Brown's students—they behaved with dignity and restraint.

But why shouldn't they have—when the university was given over into their power anyhow. Brown left the students nothing against which to protest—but left itself no future. For the administration simply sent the students home and left in the hands of professors the decision of how to evaluate student work in the semester that was now aborted. I took the position that I could not certify the value of work I had not seen. I would gladly provide students with ample time to complete their projects and help the students with them. I would then assign grades to the finished work.

Elsewhere professors were instructed by revolutionary committees on what they were to do: give all students A's and demand no work whatsoever. A few bastions of academic integrity stood firm in that fevered season: Chicago, as always, and the more mature state universities; that month, Brown was one of them.

It was not Brown's finest moment, but it would turn out to be Brown's last truly exemplary statement about itself to the American academy. By the late 1960s, after two truly great presidencies, it had emerged a small, carefully crafted research university staffed by teaching scholars, some of them of truly formidable achievement and influence. In its own way, Brown over the next two decades embodied all that was to go wrong in the academy in the 1970s and 1980s. That is why my story relates to not only an unimportant college in a provincial town, but to what was happening throughout the elite campuses and more prestigious state universities. In the decade when the academy repudiated its own traditions, Brown led the way. In the next ten years, a once-ambitious university would dismantle its standards. It set aside its commitment to the education of an intellectual elite in favor of admitting the children of the powerful—Carters, Mondales, Kennedys. It declared first-class research scholarship too expensive and abandoned the high aspiration of placing substantial, publishing scholars in undergraduate classrooms. In July, 1968, I joined the Brown faculty, and in June, 1989, my family and I moved out of Providence, never to return.

II. THE GOLDEN DECADE ENDS

In the 1970s we who had come to the academy when the Cold War was getting underway now were reaching our forties. We did our best to cope and accommodate; we went along hoping to get along. But that represented self-delusion. In fact we had received from our masters universities that were better than those we would hand on to our disciples—they had been, when we arrived, more humane, more intellectual, and of a purer academic character. In the 1970s and 1980s, I would waste much of my life by placing my highest priority upon teaching students and upon engagement with my university. In sustained scholarship, I could have accomplished much more had I understood that what makes a difference to the coming age and ages beyond is only books: there alone, there alone is life. This chapter and the next tell the story of the end of the golden age and the first decades of the tarnished age. But I always believed that scholarship without teaching proved aimless and arid. Only joining teaching to scholarship, and scholarship to teaching, produces learning of worth and substance.

Enticing the academy into the realm of public policy, offering rich rewards for doing the public business, the political establishment accomplished the goals that it had set for itself—arming for the Cold War. But with success came other results, which only a few anticipated. The universities, and later the colleges as well, entered the service of the political community, took up the agenda of public policy and sponsored partisan positions within it. Ultimately they became instruments of public policy, along with primary and secondary schools, prisons, public hospitals, the Department of Defense, and the Forest Service. The prophets who foresaw in the politicization of the campus an acute threat to academic integrity found no hearing; money answered all arguments against involvement with the government. The contract sealed, both sides in due course would perceive its flaws. But for each, the flaws were different.

No reader of these pages needs to be told the price that the academy had to pay for massive government investment. I recall vividly the day that federal agents confronted the chairman of the Department of Religious Studies at Brown and asked why no black professors were employed there. When told that in the past several searches none had applied, the agents wondered, Then why don't you teach subjects that blacks can take to qualify for positions? That came in the early 1970s; by the 1990s some regional accrediting agencies for schools and colleges would instruct colleges that they must achieve "diversity." In one famous instance, the seminary of a Protestant denomination that does not ordain women was required to put women on its board of trustees or lose its accreditation. The political community would dictate who would teach and who would study.

Professors had made our peace with what we should have fought. Many of us from that time onward were to witness in our unfolding careers the transformation of the academic world from its gentle and intellectual character—women and men of curiosity, seeking understanding—to something quite different, rather more political and less engaged by learning and teaching. In the 1970s and 1980s we were to see the presidents and provosts and deans seek success not in education but in public relations, substituting for an academic vision of education an essentially instrumental program of public policy and shaping public opinion. We were to witness the destruction of a beautiful and precious moment in the history of learning. What good has come from the ruin of the old I do not know.

When the universities entered politics, took partisan positions, and promised to solve social problems, then the community beyond took them at their word and recognized their place in partisan contention. The moral authority that accompanied respect for achievement faded. Universities came to be valued as media for social melioration. That came to mean, for the most part, class differentiation. The degree that one got and the prestige associated with the university that granted it—not the education—now made all the difference. But the breakdown of excellence, indifference to achievement, emphasis upon appointments of those who would go along to get along and not embarrass colleagues by publishing too much—these made still more of a difference.

What marked the end of excellence? It was the intrusion, in the making of professorial appointments, of considerations of a nonacademic character. Mathematics, medicine, the sciences, and engineering kept up standards, but the humanities gave them up, and the social sciences ended up somewhere in between. Overall, the best professors in various fields no longer clustered in the best universities—deemed "best" by reason of such objective measures as salaries and number of books in the library. From the 1970s forward, the ranking of a university no longer correlated with the excellence of its various departments of learning. Talent would be found by accident, where talent turns up.

Since then, searching for suitable colleagues, professors, like water, would find their own level, the "best" universities no longer would take pride in appointing the most accomplished scholars. No objective standard pertained any longer, only how people felt about themselves. That explains why now there is no reasonable expectation that just because a professor teaches at a distinguished university, that professor's scholarship will also exhibit the marks of excellence—or even that that professor will produce scholarship of influence at all. The decline of once-influential departments now at once-great universities attests to events that took place and decisions made ten or twenty years earlier. So, it appears, one of the great ages of academic learning—the American moment—waned in the 1970s and concluded in the 1980s.

III. THE OLD ORDER CHANGES: GENERATIONS MOVE ON

We—the professors who completed our education during the first decade of the Cold War and got tenure during the second—would turn out to be the transitional generation. Our teachers had known an academy that, though in straitened circumstances, understood its modest calling. They identified their own faults and corrected them. Our students, however, would take as a given that different world we saw come into being, slowly in the 1970s and at an accelerated pace in the 1980s. It was to become the world of few and easy degree requirements, easy A's, researchers who do not teach, teachers who do not pursue scholarship, and students who grade professors and vote on academic appointments, with affirmative action and political correctness protecting scheduled castes.

We who came to the campuses as students in the 1950s and returned as professors in the earlier 1960s shaped our careers to serve three causes: scholarship, teaching, and collegial citizenship. We deemed success the writing of books, the raising up of a new generation of thoughtful students, and the sharing of common responsibilities in the building of a campus community of intellect and heart. We measured success by our capacity to contribute to knowledge in some specific way, to share knowledge with others, both in writing and in the classroom, and to learn from others and join with others in a common life of intellect. We did not succeed all the time, or even very often. But these formed the golden measure: scholarship and learning, teaching and sharing, citizenship and caring. It was a gracious ideal, which we received from our teachers, a nourishing faith of the academy and in the academy. We kept that faith not only on our own, but we saw it in the generation that had brought us up.

The things we thought mattered when our generation came on the scene—scholarship, publication, teaching as an engagement with students' minds, commitment to excellence in our campus—these no longer would find a place on the campus. The 1970s started the process and the 1980s brought it to a conclusion. Universities have become places of privilege and self-indulgence, in which boredom—the cost of easy tenure based on considerations of politics or racial or gender preferment, not accomplishment—reigns, and energy and commitment to learning defy the norm. Tenure marks not achievement but acceptability, and those who go along get along. The road to success is withdrawal and disengagement. As in prison, so in a professorial career you do your own time. But on the campus we can locate ourselves by choice—because only there can we do things we think worth doing, and for that reason we accept the restrictions of the place. But that may not be so true for our successors as it was for us.

Once upon a time the things that mattered in the university were scholarship, teaching, collegiality. In good-natured conversation, you could argue a point and offer reasons and evidence. Civility overcame the tensions of disagreement. In such a gentle world, those who loved learning found a natural home. If, therefore, you wanted to teach and also to pursue scholarship, you were wise to follow a path to a professorship. You would not get rich, and not much, beyond learning, would ever be at stake. But you would learn and teach and enjoy the satisfactions of accomplishment in teaching others through both classroom engagement and published scholarship, and those accomplishments would be appreciated by colleagues. Today, the gentle virtues of learning give way to more robust values of politics and management. If young people want to teach, there are better places in which to do it than colleges. If they want to pursue scholarship as an exercise in on-going curiosity, there are better opportunities in many fields, and there are more agreeable situations than universities. It comes down to this: if you have to use universities in order to conduct a career of learning, then use them.

Two generations ago universities were not the main or the only medium for scholarship, but they were the best one. In fact many of the great discoveries in the humanities and sciences from the Enlightenment down to our own century did not come from people who held professorships. People drawn by curiosity found ways to make a living—or lived on inherited wealth—and pursued their scholarship. Many of the most important ideas that shape minds now came from people who made their living other than through university teaching—and some of them did not even have doctorates. Yet they made their discoveries and gained a hearing for their ideas. Today, too, universities provide one locus for systematic learning. But few regard them as the ideal place for scholarship. For universities have ceased to be communities, and they are in the main not very academic.

The twenty years after the revolutions of the late 1960s would yield not a single important educational idea, not a single well-crafted curriculum. The curriculum debate at Stanford found contending parties unable to appeal to shared concepts of education; the whole focused around issues of politics, not learning. The universities have simply gone through the motions of a received pattern barely grasped and scarcely understood. We who wish to restore and renew the traditions of learning that made universities important to society have the curriculum pretty much to ourselves.

As opportunities for research expanded but now began to define an unpleasant environment, those for teaching diminished and followed suit. The universities ceased to conduct an ongoing work of self-criticism in assessing their educational work. In the twenty years from 1970 to 1990, not a single important step in improving the curriculum of universities was taken. Brown's famous policy: Do whatever you want. Take this or that or nothing very much, no required courses but only a major. This, too, would lose favor, but in its place came requirements of a rather odd sort, courses of indoctrination in feminist or radical black ideology, for instance. No counterpart to the general education movement of the 1940s and 1950s took place in the 1970s and 1980s.

Taking up our mantra once more: among the three questions: that define the academy, (1) who teaches (2) what (3) to whom? The second would suffer neglect. Twenty years of dismantling the received programs and familiar purposes of colleges and universities focused on politics and personalities, that is, answering questions 1 and 3. The people in control of universities for twenty years—have had slight interest in (2): *what* is taught. That, then, marked their weak point; they know full well whom they want to teach (open admissions) and who is to do the teaching (the right sort of women, blacks, homosexuals, and the like). They cannot explain what is to be taught, or why it is to be taught. And that, we feel, will be future generation's main flank. In a strategy of sustained assault upon the pointless mélange of topics and purposeless information that today stands behind the baccalaureate degree, a new generation will begin the work of reconstruction that is not only urgent, but also timely.

For, after all, ideas are power, and we who value intellect always will value what people think and the reasons why they think it. What that means in concrete terms is that we have to ask the fundamental questions: What do we teach? And why do we teach this subject, not that subject? How is a young person's life enhanced, changed, in particular through learning and through intellectual things? For people send their children to costly universities which give courses and so claim that learning things matters. The degree should be gained not by charm or public service or interesting hobbies, but by solid achievement in the classroom, laboratory, library—achievement tested by examination and critical scrutiny. Then by our own word, we in universities allege that in the maturing of young people what we teach plays a considerable role, one so critical that parents and society should devote scarce resources to our work with students. But if we cannot explain what we teach and why, provide an account of a well-crafted education, then our word is worthless.

IV. TURNING GOLD INTO LEAD

What changed in the 1970s? It was the entire configuration of higher education. In the earlier decades colleges became universities, and universities turned themselves into centers of research. Publication mattered. Tenure came to those who produced. Students studied, scholars taught, knowledge expanded and exploded, higher education in America set the standard for the world, as much as German universities had defined the golden measure a century earlier—and with good reason. From our universities came the science and the scientists, the social science, the humanities revived by fresh questions, the spirit of discovery, the compelling call of vivid curiosity.

What was the promise of the new age, and how was it kept? The promise came forth in a new definition of the calling of higher education that took hold. We were partners, all of us on the campus, in an adventure of learning. That meant that students would study, not merely gain credentials. Scholars would publish, not merely speculate. Teachers would conduct the classroom as a realm of discovery, not merely as a stage for the rehearsal of other peoples' knowledge and the professor's opinions of that knowledge. Knowledge itself—the definition of what is to be learned for the degree of bachelor of arts or of science—vastly changed. Old boundaries gave way. New subjects found entry.

That was the vision. In the trials of social revolution and political crisis, when the campus became the battlefield and the college students the shock-troops, the scholars and the educators folded and were replaced. What most of them could not do, and did not do, was hold the center. They were educators—scholars and teachers—not politicians, not managers, not planners of budgets, and manipulators of women and of men. And others came along—people thought they were needed—who could do those things. We still on the campus pay the price of the campus revolution of the 1960s and 1970s. And why not? Ours was the mistake, for we believed when we should have doubted. We thought that by an act of the faculty senate we could change human nature, reform society, and redeem the world. But we could not even save ourselves and our own ideals when the barbarians came. And come they surely did.

University leadership has now found its definition not in the particular requirements of the tasks of the academy: scholarship and research. Now what the campus needed was what other large institutions also needed. A person with political capacities could move from the cabinet or the House of Representatives to the campus. A general could turn himself into a college president. So could a chief executive officer of a large corporation. So could a fundraiser, a foundation program officer, anybody who had shown capacities to control, manage, administer—and it did not matter what. These new types of academic officeholders were not chosen because of achievement in education and scholarship, and they did not value the skills of teaching and writing—things they had never done and could not do. They were chosen to keep the peace and balance the budget. And that is what they did.

But in the academy's loss of integrity, did the government gain in the prosecution of the Cold War? With the fortunate end of that difficult period, the answer, alas, is final. For the government the politicization of higher education laid the foundations for a lasting, socially disruptive force. Federalizing the universities by making them dependent upon government grants for research support and student funding, the government aroused on campus a special interest in public policy. Granted so large a role in the national interest, faculties and students responded by a palpable shift in focus from the received loci of learning—library, laboratory, for example— to new places altogether: the open spaces of the main campus, ideal venues for the demonstrations and, at the elite schools, the massive riots that were to come. The result, over the next decades, was to turn the academy into a replica of those Latin American universities that set themselves up as fortresses of revolutionary subversion.

The campus, once politicized, joined the political process—more exciting, after all, than the educational and scholarly ones. Faculties debated public policy and voted resolutions to be forwarded to senators and representatives. Students undertook political demonstrations. First came the class disruptions, book burnings, and sit-ins in presidents' offices. Then came the transformation of the campus into a center of political indoctrination, yielding in the 1990s the circus of political correctness, the expulsion of students for crimes of inappropriate speech, the persecution of professors for what they said in the classroom. The outsiders had come in from the cold. In the first phase, students and faculty debated whether or not federal programs might come on campus, and the military's Reserve Officer Training Programs' instructors would be humiliated—where are their Ph.D.'s, where are their publications?!—and ultimately excluded. As a professor at Brown, I admired the students' genius at public relations— but, after all, they had come to the nation's hot school for all the wrong reasons, itself a mark of effective public relations. Opposing defense appropriations one year, they volunteered to bake cakes and sell them to provide an alternative to tax funds for the Department of Defense. That made the requisite fifteen minutes of headlines.

V. THE MAGAZINER REPORT

When I came to the Brown campus in late spring, 1968, I found the place in an uproar. Indeed, I wondered what had happened to that enchanted village of teaching scholars I had projected. Perhaps I had seen *Brigadoon;* perhaps there had never even been such a place. But I found myself in a cold, aggressively hostile community. I arrived in the Department of Religious Studies at one of its many hours of crisis. Faculty offices then were divided among two different buildings, and each of the two parties of the department, housed all by itself, regarded the other with open contempt. The one good scholar of the group, whose office was in the other building, away from mine, left the year I came. He condemned me for having allied myself with the department's venal and sterile politicians against its scholars: "You glommed on to the mediocrities, (Ernest Sunley) Frerichs, (Wendell Spenser) Dietrich, and (Horst Rudolph) Moehring," I remember his saying to me, "and I could never be friendly with you." That formed the only conversation I had the entire year with those in the other building—but not for lack of trying. But their judgment was hardly idiosyncratic. That department was seen by some on campus as professors who, with trivial publication if any to their credit, were not really scholars at all but nonentities, preoccupied with backbiting gossip and intrigue about nothing of much consequence. The lot of them would get more attention from me than a wiser man would ever have paid.

But in retrospect, the petty politics of people I came to regard as never-wases pretending to be has-beens hardly demands attention. The ominous welcome I received scarcely mattered, for Brown rapidly showed me it was quite different from what I had anticipated. It seems that a student movement, organized by a particularly ambitious and forthright figure, had coalesced around a goal, a crisis, and a report. The goal was "educational reform," the crisis was an allegedly failing curriculum, and the report was a massive document spelling out what was wrong and what was to be done. At the fringes of the campus debate, I asked about the issues, and colleagues reported a highly idealistic proposal that came down to the abolition of all grades and requirements.

Instead of such formalities, the student committee declared, Brown was to conduct education in a cooperative and egalitarian manner, with students allowed to do anything their hearts desired, persuaded by reasonable discussions with faculty friends, and guided by an elaborate advising system. Instead of coercing people to do what we thought was right, we professors would persuade them to want to do what students determined was right. Instead of grading them, we would write up little reports about their work. Instead of recording failures, we would wipe them from memory. We would construct an environment for learning that would encourage and nurture, a community that would attract the best and the brightest to be set free to transform themselves into exemplars of the practical intellectual in charge of applied knowledge—able to size up a situation and set forth the logical and rational solution. Brown University was asked to repeal the laws of human nature and to declare the millennium. No one would be lazy again, no one would excel, and everyone's opinion—for himself or herself at least—was right.

Now the presentation of these utopian ideas—they struck me as vague, uncomprehending, and inexperienced—took place in a massive report, covering hundreds of pages. It was available for public inspection in a university office, and I went over to read it. The sign-up sheet showed me that the report was more talked about than read, having found for itself a great many more vocal advocates than actual readers.

To give one example, the report called for the creation in all departments of "modes of thought courses." I quizzed student advocates of the report, "Tell me just what a modes of thought course is? What type of course would not qualify? What is the difference between that and the other?" The best I could get was from a leading student advocate, who happened to take a course of mine.

He said, "Well, I can't tell you in general, but this course [mine] is a modes of thought course."

I: "Well, how might I have changed it so that it would not be a modes of thought course?"

He: "Mr. Neusner, any course *you* give would be a modes of thought course."

That left me puzzled as to the substance of the matter, but clear as to the student's purpose. Charmed and complimented, I once more acknowledged the students' skill at public relations. So I read that student's work with more than an ordinary measure of self-suspicion. He did not rate an A for his written work and did not get one. The work was as imprecise and beguiling as his definition—promising much, delivering platitudes and trivialities. Over the next two decades I was to encounter many students at Brown whose skill at public relations vastly exceeded their intellectual ambition, and even moreso, their achievement. But, I hasten to add, I have never faced a class, in four decades of teaching, where I did not meet at least some students worthy of the best I could offer—and better than that. Nor can I remember many classes that lacked some who made me wonder why they got up that morning, or how they had gotten into college at all. The sole difference between the elite colleges and the mass state universities comes to expression in the attitude of entitlement and self-importance characteristic of students at the one but quite beyond the imagination of the students at the other.

In the end, the report was adopted and defining "modes of thought" courses became a matter of a student-faculty committee's following its unarticulated intuitions. In general, over the next decades, courses met the modes of thought criteria if they were general, not too scholarly, and undemanding. But, in due course, people more or less forgot about the matter altogether, and by the 1980s, modes of thought courses no longer figured on campus. But in the confusion of the moment, I realized, a university that had just celebrated its two hundredth anniversary proposed to abandon its entire educational heritage in favor of a scheme few professors or students actually had examined in detail and none could explain in a concrete way.

And what I found in the actuality of the report positively alarmed me. First, it was ignorant; the sizable literature on the academy, its history, goals, and value, was at best copied down, but not utilized or interpreted for the present context. Second, it was burdened with the typical undergraduate space filler, the usual make-do dishonesty, a pastiche of citations and quotations. Third, the substantive sections were not only drafted in clumsy style, but lacked all signs of concern for accurate and incisive expression. Awkward, often grammatically obtuse sentences trailed off into incoherence. Heavy, leaden prose dragged down such flights of thought as may once have hovered about. Fourth, the practical proposals people discussed turned out to form only the surface, meant to deceive. For underneath, the document completely reconstructed Brown's educational structure, or, more accurately, simply dismantled it.

But the report proposed to put in place a curriculum that was no curriculum and made possible courses consisting of student self-instruction and self-evaluation. Students could organize their own courses, not only in independent study with a professor's help, but entirely beyond professorial supervision, beyond the initial approval of the proposal (and the proposal rightly took for granted a willing professor could always be found for any proposal, however distant from that professor's area of expert knowledge, or, indeed, knowledge at all). So, with nothing required, everything was possible. The corruption of the academy in the name of "reform" would run its course, and, over the next twenty years at Brown, it did. No political will survived to change matters; even two decades later trivial and cosmetic changes masked the status quo of chaos. People would pretty much make things up as they went along and call the result an education.

When it came to Brown's existing educational program, nothing would be left but departments and their majors. No more required courses of any kind, and no pretense at an interest in education in general. Students out of high school, never before exposed to the larger part of the university curriculum, would follow their whims. The report's premise—that adolescents come to college to learn, that they would seek the hard and challenging courses, and that they could put together a balanced and thoughtful curriculum for themselves—contradicted well-grounded knowledge of adolescents. No experienced professor can imagine that most adolescents concentrate for most of their time on their education, which more commonly gets a low priority indeed, well below the consideration of what others think of them and how they feel about themselves. Demolishing the existing requirements that defined the curriculum of a comprehensive education, the students had made for themselves a Garden of Eden, where, wandering where one will, no one would have to eat of any particular tree, or refrain from any for that matter. To every smart but aimless and undirected adolescent in the upper classes of the East Coast aristocracy and its Midwestern imitators, who alone could afford the cost and would spend the money to purchase the prestigious degree of an ancient university, Brown now beckoned.

But the report also missed the reality of professorial self-engagement. Students do not always grasp that professors find their scholarly work engaging and are drawn into it by curiosity. Courses formulated within the frame of general education require professors to move beyond the limits of their concrete, specific knowledge. Few wish to take the risk, let alone undertake the labor of expanding their education outside of their narrow fields. Now, freed of the obligation to formulate courses of general interest beyond the introductory ones, the departments would invest their best energies in those upper level courses open only to their own majors. Just as students would specialize too soon, so the academic departments would build ever-higher structures of courses resting on extensive prerequisites; they would hold their majors and neglect the rest. The faculty had created for itself a paradise for narrow specialists.

The entire spectacle played out on the local stage what would later on became a national drama. In my years at Brown, I remember how George Bortz, a wise and profound economics professor, would find occasion to remark, time and again; "But is this disaster absolutely necessary?" For the university would lurch from one fabricated crisis to the next. The New Curriculum (as it came to be called) grew old, but the way in which its sponsors orchestrated the formulation and adoption of their imposed utopia, would repeat itself time and again over the next decades. And, after the Cold War ended, the country as a whole would become accustomed in the first two years of the Clinton administration to the declaration of a national health care crisis, justifying the formation of a blue-ribbon commission to study the situation, yielding a massive, unread, and unintelligible report that purports to solve the problem, published in an atmosphere of crisis and urgency, bearing a barrage of promises of a final solution and a better world. The United States did not panic and did not cave; too large, protected by too strong a web of checks and balances, the country survived the technique of government through public relations. Brown did not. It was simple in structure—run by an all-powerful president through his omnipotent provost, therefore governed in the end by the politics of the presidency checked only by an absent board of directors (at Brown: "Corporation").

At Brown it was the crisis of curriculum. For the United States it was the crisis of medical coverage. At Brown the solution was to demolish the curriculum, leaving only episodic courses (many of them student-organized and taught, or self-taught) and inchoate, dubious majors. For the United States it was (in the ideal) to demolish the complex structure of institutions of medicine, leaving (in the ideal) a single payer, as in the Canadian model. In reality, the ideal was to federalize medical care one way or the other. So why introduce the latter in the context of accounting for the former? The reason is that the fingerprints are the same, and so too the principal player, Ira C. Magaziner. Brown was ruined by the first Magaziner Report and never recovered. American medicine proved not so readily manipulated, and what is surely, for the nation as a whole, the final Magaziner Report came to a more felicitous end. Those who question the promise of social engineering—not to mention the authentic intelligence of the engineers—to prove their point need only follow Brown's educational decline from the faculty's adoption of the Magaziner Report to the present time.

VI. THE COUNTRY TURNS AGAINST THE ACADEMY

For all the angst shed about the future of college campuses in the late 1960s, the choices made by both faculty, students, and administrators had settled the central issues facing the academy. In a 1973 lecture, Clark Kerr argued that the work of universities had become a national commodity just as important as land, minerals, or labor. And yet, with that new prominence and influence, American universities—which held a near monopoly on the commodity—increasingly rejected the society they served. As such, American universities exposed themselves, not simply the attitudes they harbored, but to the counterreaction of the American public, which provided both the good will and the cash needed to keep universities well-oiled.

David Riesman, who documented the rise of the professorate, noted in 1969 that universities were on a "collision course" with the society that lent its support. He argued that universities would face a difficult future if they continued to beg for national resources with one hand while slapping the nation with the other. Students and faculty had not only become more radical, but more willing to use their position to promote their political agenda. But violence and campus radicalism were, to a certain extent, mere preludes to issues that also changed the standing and excellence of American universities. The economy had changed, the students had changed, the faculty had changed, and the nation's priorities had changed. While a significant trend, the politicization of the campus was not the sole reason for the series of events that we now know marked the beginning of the end of the golden age in American higher education. When students at Kent State and Jackson State lay dead, victims of bullets fired by their fellow countrymen (who perceived themselves protecting important institutions), it became quickly clear that nothing could return American higher education to its former standing. The National Guardsmen were, in fact, protecting an institution which had already changed, and which would continue to change more than most people were willing to accept.

The Carnegie Commission, which surveyed the opinions of 60,000 faculty and 100,000 students between 1969 and 1972, concluded that those who had joined universities in the 1960s, when half of the nation's faculty was recruited, dramatically differed in opinions with their older colleagues. On the issue of whether universities should get involved in political questions, one-third said yes, when a generation before, hardly anyone would have. One-fifth to one-quarter agreed that faculty members should feel free to advocate violent resistance to authority. One-third agreed that meaningful change in American politics could not be achieved through the traditional political process. One-fourth said students should not be expelled or suspended for disrupting the normal functions of a university. There was, at the end of the beginning of the 1970s, a sizable contingent of American intellectuals—many of whom had recently joined the faculties of universities—who agreed with and supported the anti-institutional views of the American Left. Kerr noted that in the twentieth century, intellectuals were generally aligned with the American establishment: for the New Deal, against fascism, against Stalinism. The advent of the Vietnam War, civil rights, and Watergate threw off that traditional alliance and sympathy for better or for worse. "We have a new situation," said Kerr in 1973.[1] Kerr foresaw the dangers in allowing intellectuals to forget their national purpose, since, he argued, that was precisely what predisposed the campus to student rebellions. Kerr predicted the effects of the politicization of the campus, warning against encroachment on the right to dissent; his warning was

1. Clark Kerr, *The Great Transformation in Higher Education, 1960–1980*, p. 194.

made to the Left and not to the Right. In a mere decade, the establishment went from conciliation to toleration. In the one incarnation, administrators and their opinions held for the freedom to keep a university open. In the second incarnation, those administrators and faculty who took control had to be warned of the meaning of free speech at colleges.

VII. Wall Street and Madison Avenue Meet on Campus

That effect was already making itself known on many campuses, both public and private. At the college of City University of New York, one of the nation's foremost examples of effective public colleges, the politicization of the campus encroached not merely on the safety of students and buildings, but on the future of the institution itself. Theodore Gross, who was the college's Dean of Humanities during the school's transformation, documents both the ideology that allowed such changes, and their effects. Gross, an academic liberal, routinely hedges during his 1980 account, *Academic Turmoil*, offering on the one hand ample proof of the school's demise, but on the other hand declining to make the observations that we, in retrospect, cannot avoid.

CUNY, known until the mid 1960s as a preeminent institution both in learning and its capacity to serve a large and diverse immigrant student body, had held a reputation for introducing a vast number of students both to the promise and reality of intellectual life. But, Gross notes, by the late 1960s, school officials had become aware—not necessarily on their own volition—of the dramatic failure of the school to attract black or Hispanic students. A program of affirmative action in admissions was planned, and when installed several years earlier than expected, it quickly turned CUNY's social experiment into an institutional crisis. That experiment, known as open admissions, placed uncommon stresses on the college, not simply in taking in students of even more diverse character, but evidently much more diverse skills. Gross observed that in CUNY's English Department, which had once offered 70 per cent of its courses in literature, the quickly rising demand for courses on basic composition and communication forced the department to offer, within one year's time, 70 per cent of its courses in those areas. By focusing on literacy instead of literature, Gross said the college may have raised its social sights, but the faculty had become terribly demoralized.

Open admissions did more than simply denigrate the standing of professors with advanced knowledge. It also opened up the doors for electives; since a philosophy of inclusion had determined who should get in, the same philosophy dictated what they should learn. Or rather, what they would like to learn. Gross noted how professors once accustomed to worrying about mere learning and teaching faced a sudden jolt when students could suddenly disregard their class altogether. Entire departments found themselves in the crucible of choice, and in reaction to the threatened clipping of certain departmental budgets, professors literally hawked their classes. Gross recalled with great scorn what occurred as a result, particularly in the humanities:

> In desperate measures redolent of Madison Avenue, the faculty created sexy courses to attract students: Gay literature, Jewish fertility. Then they tried to sell the courses with gaudy posters or notices in campus newspapers. In the sweaty gym, during registration, too many faculty were no better than barkers at a circus sideshow. . . .[2]

The results of the selling of the curriculum, Gross said, could hardly be measured from the faculty's point of view. But from the students' perspective, it meant professors who would not only court them, but also reward them with inflated grades, permissiveness for sloppy or late work—giving them a sense that colleges in general would reward them for their mere presence. "College had become a kind of cheap stock market, and teachers were stockbrokers in an inflationary educational economy."[3]

The results of open admissions at CUNY represented merely one stage of the politicization of the campus. When, during the late 1960s, students rebelled against campus authority, they—particularly black and female students—pointed at a curriculum that offered them no classes in their area of interest—ethnic or feminist studies. Liberal administrators, aware of the same fault, were quick to rectify the situation on virtually every major campus in the country. The result—following a pattern set by colleges bent on doubling faculty during the 1960s—was a rush on black faculty, putting a premium on their mere presence at a college. Standards were lowered, with the hope that once in the company of a more qualified faculty, a black professor would meet new challenges. At CUNY, one of the beneficiaries of this policy was Leonard Jeffries, who later took black studies programs and black political issues on the campus to areas no black professor of the 1960s could have imagined.

Support for black studies was not a given, even amongst black faculty. Many cautioned against ethnic cheerleading, proposing that black studies could focus attention on issues forgotten or ignored on most college campuses. They suggested, most of all, that the American black experience could instruct and

---

2. Theodore Gross, *Academic Turmoil*, p. 42.
3. Ibid., p. 43.

elucidate, providing an essential educational function on the campus. Prof. W. Arthur Lewis, an economist at Princeton University, wrote in the *New York Times* in 1969 that the demands by black militants for not only black studies departments, but separate dormitories, separate faculties, and separate classes, would ultimately undermine the very purpose of going to an integrated college in the first place. Lewis said black studies courses should be for white students, and not black, and rejected altogether the idea that black students should attend college to learn more about their heritage.

The crucial issue, however, for blacks was not simply curriculum, but access: like Catholics, Jews, and women one generation before, blacks faced a demographic underrepresentation in colleges. But unlike those other minorities, many blacks had not demonstrated, as part of the routine and objective process of application, the capacity to excel and survive in college. That fact, borne out not simply in test scores but in the high dropout rates of blacks who did attend mostly white colleges in the late 1950s and 1960s, represented a major problem for most campuses. Following the campus riots of the 1960s, minority representation quickly replaced the Vietnam War as one of the unifying ideas of the Left. With no capacity to placate an already upset contingency, university administrators could not use limited programs to bring more black students to the campus. Student groups favoring immediate improvements to the presence of black students repeatedly turned campus meetings into shouting or intimidation matches, even at the expense of alienating liberal or sympathetic faculty members. But colleges faced pressure from the other side, as well. The Nixon administration of the late 1960s and early 1970s notified states that their funding would be cut if they did not comply with federal antidiscrimination laws and submit desegregation plans. Such federal pressure continued throughout the decade.

Significantly, the result was not what either side had hoped for. Not only were standards lowered, but a significant backlash developed. This was particularly true at CUNY, where political pressures of a mayoral race came to bear on the acceptance of the open admissions policy; many felt the loss of standards had hurt the college, and white applicants felt wronged. Moreover, many felt that open admissions (or affirmative action admissions) would have succeeded if universities had retained control over curriculum design. "At the moment when standards had to be perpetuated, they were relaxed," Gross writes.[4] The backlash, not simply among jilted white students but among significant groups of Americans, will be documented later. For now, consider that the campus leaders had now bowed, in one way or another, to the demands or needs of those leftists who once

---

4. Ibid., p. 4.

had to seize control of universities by strikes or shutting down buildings. Not only had they won the battle, they also had won the war.

The concept of a university as even remotely exclusive was held false; open admissions followed at some public universities. At others, standards were lowered or raised based on ethnic or racial identification. The Carnegie study of students and faculty told no lies. Those who staffed and attended universities at the end of the 1960s held starkly different views than the colleagues from the beginning of the decade. And while student rebellions, especially against the war, ended during the summer of 1970, the ideas of those revolts reverberated through academia's halls for decades. We have noted in an earlier chapter that the student revolts of the 1960s appeared not only diffuse, but hardly focused on the vocation of education. That, during the 1970s, could not be such a certainty. A significant effort by leftist faculty and students now shifted attention to what universities do. Who do they teach? Who teaches? And as institutional control shifted to those who had participated or sympathized with the leftist rebellions, those issues not only generated momentum, but took on the same quality as earlier protests: they were heavily infused with political ideology, and arguments were framed in terms of politics, not academics.

When, in earlier decades, some felt the university needed an overhaul, reform often meant looking back for models. The concern over specialization and professionalization had, in the mid 1950s, resulted in a surge of support for liberal arts education and a curriculum which emphasized certain subjects and subject matter—history, philosophy, languages, classics—over others. But in the 1970s, curricular theory, framed largely by the faculty who had come of age in the 1960s push for "relevance," rejected any pretense that a college education should be predetermined. For such theorists, student choice, whether in the form of departmental major or in a slew of electives, promised a far happier college experience. Required courses, viewed as indoctrination, were rejected altogether. Curriculum as a means of establishing institutional purpose or unity was also held false. Students asked for, and received, nearly complete control over their schedules. Some have argued that this was less a result of leftist educational philosophy and more a consequence of weakness within liberal arts itself. Martin Kaplan, a former speechwriter and journalist, argued in 1978 that curriculum requirements were no different than protective tariffs: they protected otherwise weak departments. A liberal arts education, he said, had lost its economic value, and any requirements to uphold courses in philosophy, European languages, and history simply acted in defiance of market truths. As evidence, he said Harvard's top ten most popular courses were mostly professional or preprofessional: premedical, prelaw, accounting, economics, and calculus.

Kaplan argued that any return to requirements in the curriculum must be accompanied by a serious reappraisal of what's worth knowing. However, Kaplan did not shy away from the root force behind the antirequirement movement. He cited the "openness" and "individuality" elective courses would offer students. He further argued that calls for a core curriculum were motivated less by educational need and more by social concerns. When, by the late 1970s, arguments for a "back to basics" approach forced leftist academics to restate their arguments, Kaplan's words contained gems of unlikely candidness. In one instance, he argued that relativism had destroyed any meaning in the humanities. We shall raise this issue later; precisely who was responsible for academic and moral relativism?

By the late 1970s, not only had students been granted partial or full control over their academic schedules, but they had achieved, in certain cases, independent study credits, college credit for social or political projects, classroom democracy on issues of fact or truth, and even alternative universities. The demands for relevance made in the 1960s had come full circle. The relevance asked for in the 1960s became a 1970s rush on preprofessional programs. Schools of medicine and law, judged in teetering financial condition early in the decade, did a robust business by its end. This movement away from requirements challenged those faculty in the humanities and liberal arts to justify their presence on the campus. For them, a college education was not simply a form of vocational training or an appeal to the curiosities of students, but an approach to thinking, a way of looking at events and texts. But sadly, those in the humanities found this decade painful, heralding a still-unbroken journey into marginality. Not only had courses become "relevant," but entire universities, too. So relevant, in fact, that students not adequately prepared for college forced entire departments to deliver the equivalent of college preparation as part of their college education. Gross, in perhaps his most sympathetic observation, argued that his CUNY open admissions students exhibited much greater motivation than their counterparts of ten years before. But, alas, that motivation simply meant more devotion to the task at hand, which was mastery of standard English language, something their predecessors had no trouble comprehending and phrasing.

VIII. LOST FAITH, LOST TRUST

That kind of sympathy did not enjoy great popularity among a growing group of politicians, both state and federal. For one, the revolts on the campuses appeared uncontrolled, and politicians viewed the situation not simply in terms of how students behaved, but how administrators governed. President Richard Nixon's 1970 Commission on Campus Tensions found that the campus's "service" function had been taken too far. The vision of universities assisting the nation in an international struggle no longer carried much weight. Nixon's commission ruled that, to the contrary, universities had put too much work into applied research and social problems—pursuits that took money away from research and teaching. Gov. Ronald Reagan, vilified by the Berkeley campus for his deployment of state National Guardsmen in response to the ongoing revolts on that campus, exemplified the dramatic shift of attitudes of politicians toward college campuses. Suddenly, universities that once enjoyed the reputation of producing both human resources and important research were viewed with skepticism by legislators, governors, and the U.S. president. From 1966–67 to 1969–70, the University of California's operating-budget requests were cut by an average of 8 1/2 percent a year; in 1970, Reagan proposed, and received, a 12 percent cut in the university's budget request. The net effect was the university had to operate at the same budget level as the year before, even though inflation and student enrollment were going up. During the 1969–70 academic year, the California legislature extended a cost-of-living pay raise of 5 percent to every state employee except the faculty members of the California university and college system. A legislative spokesman said, at the time, that the salary freeze was punitive, and that the faculty had to be held accountable for the student revolts following the U.S. invasion of Cambodia in May, 1970. This was not an isolated view; in Michigan, the chairman of the state House of Appropriations said in 1970 he would try to cut university budgets until "these kids decide they want to go to school."[5] Across the nation, state legislatures and governors made a concerted effort to bring universities under centralized control. By 1979, thirty-eight of the nation's state public university systems were controlled not by campus boards of trustees, but by statewide committees. The federal government also extended its oversight in the 1970s, although not always as a result of the student disruptions. By the end of the decade, it was

---

5. Earl Cheit, *The New Depression in Higher Education*, pp. 16–19.

not uncommon for the federal government to oversee and inspect hiring practices, financial management, student rights, and safety.

The public did not become enamored of what had become the institutionalized leftism of the university, especially its proclivity to criticize. Even Clark Kerr, who sympathized with the liberal views of the new professorate, warned against its propensity to silence views it did not agree with. He also said the campus Left had exposed itself to charges of hypocrisy when it criticized the federal government on affirmative action and increasing opportunities to minorities; in reality, the Nixon and Ford administrations led most other national institutions in affirmative action programs and providing more financial aid for low-income students. What was worse, Kerr noted in the behavior of universities in the 1970s that the effort to reform colleges had devolved into an array of enforced bureaucracies and legislative hurdles. The "participatory democracy" imagined at the beginning of the decade had resulted in "more veto groups, less action, more commitment to the status quo . . . " Kerr observed in 1980.[6] The fact that one campus agenda had calcified into institutional policy was not lost on either the governors or the governed.

While Reagan, a future U.S. president, and the California Legislature took an early role of antagonizing and opposing any student protests, California voters demonstrated the same views. In 1970, voters in fifty-five of the state's fifty-eight counties voted down a bond proposal to support the state's medical schools. Kerr's observation that the faculty had, for the first time in the twentieth century, fallen out of step with the society it supposedly served—now had a calculus attached to it. Just as the political support of universities created super centers of research, massive expansion of facilities, and unsurpassed public loyalty and appreciation, the mood and financial reality shifted quickly at the beginning of the 1970s. And most universities were not prepared.

The growth of alternative research institutions (Rand, Brookings), alternative teaching institutions (workplace, technical schools), and alternative advanced consulting networks (private consultants, professional associations) all described the end of the academy's monopoly on its traditional vocations. The period between 1968 and 1972 found academics in a terrible mood, coming off an inspired period of growth and turbulence, and facing another decade of anticipated losses. The OPEC oil crisis, which ballooned energy costs for universities, only exacerbated what was quickly

---

6. Clark Kerr, *The Great Transformation in Higher Education 1960–1980*, p. 155.

becoming a financial nightmare. Federal research support, which served as one of the linchpins of university growth and expansion throughout the 1960s, had begun to trail off by the late 1960s. Increases in federal financial support either froze or dropped off; at the same time, largely because of political pressures, student aid programs grew. Because most universities found that billing students was the only feasible means of bailing themselves out of financial problems, they found themselves in the unlikely—some said hypocritical—position of raising a gate of elitism and wealth in front of their campuses. A popular reaction to this resulted in the student aid programs; it also was demonstrated in an increasingly skeptical attitude toward the pleas of poverty of university administrators.

Federal policy had become very enmeshed in the workings of universities, and not simply those with major research budgets. Catholic colleges benefited greatly from a 1971 U.S. Supreme Court ruling entitling them—under certain conditions—to federal grants and loans. Those conditions precluded the recipients from setting up religious barriers to faculty or students, and also prevented the schools from requiring religious practice or conversion. The power of federal money was such that even though those standards were not requirements, most volunteered to abide by them. At black colleges, too, the full effect of federal legislation was—even after the earth-shattering antidiscrimination court decisions and federal bills—still being felt. The U.S. Congress, sensitive to the concern that blacks needed access to opportunity as much as equal opportunity, created financial incentives to colleges to admit more disadvantaged students. The net effect of this legislation, passed in 1965 and complemented by a U.S. Supreme Court decision in 1977, meant mostly white public colleges and universities had to focus on admitting more black students in order not to be cited for failure to meet federal civil rights laws. The concurrent strain on black colleges to retain their best students and faculty posed yet another challenge. And since more blacks began to attend college at mostly white colleges, but whites did not take much of an interest in black colleges, enrollment declined at the black colleges.[7] But while federal legislation encouraged fuller integration of blacks into previously white universities, court decisions also forced state legislatures to consider the future of their public black colleges. In a newly integrated system, the courts protected black colleges from closing or merging with mostly white colleges. Federal oversight, it seems, provided both a challenge to the long-term success of the

---

7. Julian Roebuck and Komanduri Murty, *Historically Black Colleges and Universities*, p. 41.

institutions, but also a guarantee of institutional survival. This guarantee, for several black colleges, may have prevented their closure; later, in the 1980s, when federal policy again shifted, these colleges enjoyed much greater success in attracting students.

IX. A DEPRESSION? AVERTED, BUT NOT FOREVER

Earl Cheit, a professor of business administration at Berkeley, addressed the new financial reality of American campuses in his 1971 study, *The New Depression in Higher Education*. The title, alarming as it was, hardly promised more than the book delivered. Cheit reviewed financial data and conducted interviews at forty-one campuses, finding that most were concerned about their long-term financial future. He classified many of these campuses—drawn to represent a variety of types of colleges, whether national research or small, urban, junior college—into three categories: those not in financial trouble, those headed for financial trouble and those in financial difficulty. Only one national research university—University of Texas, Austin—was not in trouble or facing it; Harvard, University of Chicago, University of Michigan, and University of Minnesota were looking at long-term troubles; Stanford and Berkeley were already experiencing them. Among his findings, Cheit found that in general costs were rising faster than revenues. But he also found that the financial philosophy of most campuses—the more you earn, the more you spend, therefore the better you are—was just as much a problem as inflation rates. He also found that student disturbances had ballooned insurance and security costs for universities, and as a result, constituted a new charge to campuses. Cheit, based on his studies, said costs from student disturbances constituted about 3 percent of college budgets. As if to underscore this point, Cheit noted that among those colleges that did not suffer major disturbances, it was much more common to find financial stability. He attributed this as much to the financial costs of riots as the lost good-will of politicians and the public following those riots. Why, they were beginning to ask, does State need all this money if all the students do is shut down the university?

Cheit cites 1967–68 as the watershed year for college finances: the year when growth stopped and costs continued to rise. The problem, he noted, was that when colleges added new programs, or attracted federal funds for new buildings, rarely did the universities assure a continual stream of money to support such programs into the future. When buildings went up, long-term maintenance budgets did not necessarily accompany them. Some noted this trend as early as 1967 and individual college presidents rued the coming days of cutbacks. Yet a "boom psychology" pervaded well into the next decade. As colleges and universities attempted to grow out of financial hardship, many would not make necessary cuts for fear of setting off an alarm of failed financial credibility on their campuses. One of the ironies of this crisis, Cheit observed, was that the public doubted this crisis, largely because of the tuitions and trappings of these institutions. Private giving had dropped off, and so did government spending. And as we shall note later, this drop-off had enormous consequences on the structure of university control over research. Cheit's study, however, cemented a truth that few college administrators had not yet understood: the public doubted that universities suffered from any kind of crisis at all.

Cheit, in a supplementary study completed two years later, found that on balance the forty-one colleges had addressed their financial condition with varying degrees of success. But, he said in his 1973 follow-up, external conditions like public attitudes, government support, and inflation had not changed dramatically, leaving most institutions in the hands of powers they could not control. Among these powers, none was more pervasive and acute than the demographic downshift of the end of the baby boom generation's college years. By 1972, college attendance had drifted off its mid 1960s levels. Freeland, in his study of Massachusetts colleges between 1945–70, argued that this drop-off had as much to do with the pattern of college attendance as declining birthrates. Throughout the three decades following the end of World War II, the middle class had pursued college educations for their children as an investment. By the 1970s, most of those who would want to go, and could realistically succeed, were already there. Studies of the nation's economy of that period have ascribed a variety of reasons for the declining value of a college education during the 1970s. Not only had so many students attended college in the 1960s, but many of them stayed on in graduate school, delaying their entry to the economy. During that delay, the nation's growth—particularly in government and education sectors—placed a premium on college degrees, since relatively few were entering the economy. So when, a half-decade later, when a bulge of graduates entered the workforce, economic opportunities did not follow the pattern established in the 1960s.

The situation was felt by graduates who sought to make their lives in the academy, perhaps more than anyone else. In 1973, 1,402 English Ph.D. recipients competed for 139 openings; only one in six Ph.D. recipients found a job that year. Such competition was a boon for a university seeking to upgrade its status. Tenure was granted sparingly, and as qualified faculty sought positions, they were willing to take lesser pay, lesser benefits, and often in a less prestigious location than they might have one decade earlier. The corollary event of this period was the advent of collective bargaining as a legitimate academic force; unionization was not a consideration at most campuses until the 1970s.

X. LOSING LUSTER

By the mid 1970s, both economic reality and the mood of the nation put college at a much lower priority of prestige than it was accustomed to previously. Applications dropped off to the point that in 1973, Massachusetts officials concluded that they had overstated the need for places in their college system in 1980 by 200,000. Moreover, the nation's graduating high-school seniors were not simply dropping-off in number, they were also looking elsewhere for advanced education. In a buyer's market, students for the first time enjoyed the consumerism common to almost every other American industry. The premier national universities no longer framed their institutional or financial challenges in terms of growth. Rather, they struggled with maintaining their size and began, in earnest, to recruit students who had the talent and money to go to any number of other universities. Freeland, in his study of Massachusetts universities, found that Tufts and Brandeis, both of which aspired to join the nation's elite research universities, began to reverse, in their admissions policies, many of the meritocratic gains of the 1960s. At those schools, rising tuitions froze out many of the talented but nonwealthy students who would have attended the schools a mere decade earlier. Both universities found themselves admitting more wealthy, but less qualified students as a result. The pattern, we feel, was carried out on many campuses nationwide.

As it turned out, however, the fear over a major drop-off in enrollment was exaggerated. About 3.5 million more students attended college in 1980 than in 1970; among this group, the largest new subgroups were blacks, women, and older students. The nation's only growth industry in education, it turns out, continued to be the community colleges. There, enrollments grew unabated. From 1970 to 1980, the number of degrees conferred by such institutions increased by nearly 150,000, from 253,635 to 405,378. Enrollment nearly tripled, going from 1.6 million students in 1970 to 4.5 million in 1980. The growth of the two-year college was not found among refugees of the universities' liberal arts programs. Rather, just as in the universities—where liberal arts degrees suffered the scorn of those pushing for relevance, ethnic or interdisciplinary studies, and an economy that didn't need thoughtful but unskilled graduates—community colleges saw their growth largely in preprofessional and occupational programs like those for paralegals, nurses, and other skilled service trades. In years past, especially in the vocationally oriented community colleges, students had resisted taking vocational or preprofessional courses. But in the 1970s, such programs flourished, even as enrollments slid or froze elsewhere. Among community college degrees attained in the 1970s, the percent of students finishing vocational or occupational programs increased from 43 percent to 63 percent. Of course, the vocational interests of students were matched by those in four-year programs; Clark Kerr, in a 1984 article, said that during a six-year period in the 1970s, students majoring in fields outside the arts and sciences went from 38 percent of all students to 58 percent, almost mirroring the same growth in community colleges.

These conflicting trends—a freeze on student enrollment nationwide and especially in the liberal arts while enrollment nearly tripled in community colleges—was accompanied by a series of social changes over which colleges had no control. As we have already noted, the economy had placed less value on a college degree, since so many graduates were available. But at the same time, more adult women, minorities, senior citizens, and part-time students joined the rolls, and they went, with invariable consistency, to community colleges. Community colleges, which had not suffered but also had not dramatically succeeded in the prior two decades, found in the 1970s' economic malaise several unique opportunities. For instance, a February, 1978 study of 1976–77 bachelor's degree graduates found that more than one in five were "underemployed."[8] Such students, community college leaders argued, were strong candidates for their kind of institution. The mood of the nation's political leaders had shifted in the early 1970s, and not coincidentally after the student disturbances of the late 1960s: these leaders, especially federal officials, viewed community colleges as a fruitful area of growth. Consequently, from 1969 to 1973, federal support nearly tripled, from $91 million to $256 million.

And while Cheit found that the depression afflicting many four-year colleges was a function of their lack of vision and planning, community colleges created weekend programs, special senior citizen institutes, workplace study, ties with businesses and student aid programs. For Cubans in Miami, Asian-Americans in California, and Mexican-Americans in the Southwest, the community college became the new entering point into American society. The problem with this, some have argued, was that the growing emphasis on vocational education was accentuated among those

8. Steven Brint and Jerome Karabel, *The Diverted Dream*, p.113.

students who had traditionally not entered four-year colleges, thus exacerbating differences of opportunity between men and women, whites and blacks, and so on. Community colleges once represented a fairly cheap way for states to provide universal opportunity to higher education; by the end of the decade, such colleges offered opportunity, but not necessarily to the four-year degree still viewed as an economic lift for any student.

XI. LEAVING DARTMOUTH

Standing for the integration of the subject, Judaism, into the curriculum, I did not then propose to give up what was most particular and dear to me, which is what made me special and different: Judaism. The tension between my academic commitment to the mainstream and my personal conviction of the truth and value of my faith came to the surface when I contemplated where to spend the twenty years that raising children would require. And making the choice between my academic home and my responsibility to the next generation of my—and my wife's—family, I left Dartmouth, although I took pride in serving on its faculty and had found a home there.

The reason was simple. By 1967 I had two young sons, and my principal concern was their upbringing, from then until they—and the third son and daughter who were to arrive in the next few years—reached maturity. Nothing else mattered to my wife and myself. She pursued her career in art, I mine in scholarship, but together we lived for them. Judaism, beyond ourselves, would form the source of their character, ethics, life's purpose.

Hanover then had no synagogue, no Jewish community, no organized Jewish student life, and few Jews for whom being Jewish mattered as an ethnic engagement, fewer still for whom Judaism made a difference as a religious commitment. I did not conceive that I could give my children that sense of rootedness in Judaism that I wanted for them. I did not want them to imagine they were the only Jews in the world, or that Judaism was the private preference of isolated individuals. And I had an additional requirement in mind. I also looked for a university that formed a community within a larger city, one whose professors saw one another regularly and talked together and worked on common projects. Dartmouth had shown me the intellectual promise of such a community, and I did not propose to give up what I had come to admire.

Here, at this particular moment, I lived out in personal terms the conflict that being Jewish in an open society provoked, between the mainstream and that particular current that was mine. Like the third generation beyond immigration in groups of many origins, European and Asian alike, I wanted to remember what the second generation tried to forget. The former generation wanted to be Jewish, but not so Jewish as to lose a place as an undifferentiated American. For my part, life as an undifferentiated American meant no longer being Jewish at all. For most of the Jews we knew in Hanover, that result posed no problem. Their children would repudiate their Jewish origins, and their grandchildren would not even have to.

For my wife and myself—and four thousand years of family that had come down to us—we chose otherwise. It meant giving up a career where I was wanted, respected, and treated with honor and dignity for two decades in another kind of college, where I would find no home for myself, but a fine place in which to raise my children. To define a suitable place in which to raise them, I gave thought to what seemed to me if not ideal, then suitable circumstances. I had in mind a city much like Hartford when I grew up, with a solid Jewish community well integrated into a diverse community, one with synagogues and other institutions of Jewish community life, and, above all, a Jewish day school of some educational ambition. In those times, it seemed to me, Princeton did not meet these criteria, nor did Palo Alto (Stanford), nor did Durham, North Carolina. Columbia, in that capital of Judaism, New York City, certainly did. But to live in the suburbs and commute did not promise that academic community I had so valued in Hanover.

Not only so, but I had grown used to working at home. That was because I wanted the children to know me and what I did—book writing, for instance—for a living. The children were to grow up in preschool years therefore seeing me almost as much as their mother, since I ate lunch with them, until they went off to school and left us behind. Now, where could I find the Jewish community I had in mind, in a location that was small enough to allow me to spend work time at home, but devote ample time also to the life of the college? Add to those two probably chimerical requirements the third, that (given my fantasy at that time) the prospective university had also to belong to the Ivy League or enjoy comparable status, and you come up with—Brown University. I thought Providence provided for every need—a theological as much as practical judgment. I was right about Providence, but quite wrong about Brown.

XII. THE ETHNICIZATION OF LEARNING

The tensions on the campus—between the new order and a traditional commitment to reasoned argument among persons differentiated not by race, religion, gender, or national origin but only by wit, imagination, and intelligence—in the late 1960s and early 1970s precipitated a crisis not only for the community, but for me personally. For I well understood the feelings of black students who found nothing in the curriculum that spoke to their experience; with women, who maintained that everything was taught from the man's viewpoint; with Catholics, who were taught Western Civilization from a Protestant viewpoint and learned that in leading the Reformation against the Catholic Church, Martin Luther established the right to follow one's conscience and so founded the idea of freedom. At just this time, black studies, long banished to corners of the academy, came to the fore in the foundation of black studies centers, programs, and departments, and so too did Jewish studies, women's studies, and the like. What those of us who favored the new humanities wanted was inclusion, within the range of rational conversation, of formerly excluded subjects. But the real advocacy came from a different motivation altogether, one that took a deeply antiacademic position and imposed it upon the academy.

To tell the story in terms of the study of the Jews and Judaism, the choice is readily spelled out. Does the study of topics concerning the Jews or of Judaism find its place within the established disciplinary departments, e.g., history or religion or literature or sociology? Or does the subject matter serve as an organizing focus, so that whatever concerns the Jews and Judaism—whether history or religion or sociology—will find its home in centers, programs, or departments of Jewish or Judaic studies ("Jewish" standing for the ethnic, "Judaic" for the religious side to things)? In disciplinary departments, the Jewish subjects would receive treatment as part of the normal curriculum, that is, history courses on various territories or groups or periods of time, encompassing Jews' histories. Students in departments of religious studies would routinely take a course on Judaism, and professors would not suppose that students brought along a personal agenda to their classroom. The subject made sense as part of a larger curriculum. The teacher did not address the souls of the students (let alone ask what they had eaten for breakfast or the religion of the person they were thinking of marrying).

A conflicting theory maintained that black studies should convey the ideology and special knowledge that blacks ought to acquire, that Jewish studies should persuade Jewish students to stay Jewish, and so on through the curriculum. Rejected as special pleading by some, this approach to the new humanities and social sciences would demand that professors serve as ethnic cheerleaders (for the Jews) or as exemplars of race pride (for blacks), and so on. In the beginning, as we have seen, scholars of black history and other aspects of African-American culture, like some of us in the study of Judaism, rejected the ethnicization of our subjects and insisted that anyone could study, and anyone could teach, what they knew. But as the 1970s wore on, the ethnic party expanded and the disciplinary one faced a considerable challenge.

What no one anticipated in the 1950s and 1960s, as Judaic studies first made their way into universities was the re-ghettoization of the field. And that development produced a civil war on campus, the forces for a disciplinary approach to the field opposed by the advocates of the ethnic definition. The result came in the complete split between Jewish and gentile scholars of Judaic studies in universities on one side and, on the other side, Jewish scholars of Judaic studies (there are no gentiles to speak of) in institutions under Jewish auspices in the United States and Europe, joined by most Israeli scholars of Judaic studies in the humanistic mode (as distinct from the social scientific). A civil war—fought on uncivil terms, of course—has broken out. By the end of the 1970s, there was no more a single field of Jewish learning, whether called Jewish or Judaic studies. The two theories competed as universities raised huge sums of money for Jewish studies. Most ghettoized the subject, but some insisted that studying the Jews and Judaism was too interesting to allow only or mainly Jews to monopolize the subject.

Two separate academies by 1980 had taken shape, the ethnic and the genuinely academic, and discourse between them is becoming increasingly strained. The one side addresses issues of humanistic learning, engages in no special pleading, and treats the Jewish or the Judaic data as exemplary of broader issues. The other side takes for granted the interest and importance of the Jewish and the Judaic data and regards incremental erudition, whether or not formed for a purpose, as self-evidently interesting. Professor William Scott Green, of the University of Rochester, states matters as follows:

> From the perspective of ethnic Jewish studies, materials are deemed interesting because they are Jewish. This school of thought is marked by a fundamentally romantic view of all things it defines as Jewish. Ethnic scholarship tends to be avenging and celebratory. Ethnic education at whatever level makes learning into a ritual attachment to the heroic people. Ethnic intellectual discourse tends to be restricted . . . and directed primarily to those within the ethnic group or those who share its romantic suppositions. In short, ethnic Jewish Studies is a self-validating enterprise, designed to preserve Jewish distinctiveness. Ethnic Jewish scholarship serves a powerful communal purpose and therefore is highly charged. It aims to teach the Jews about themselves and thereby to create a usable Jewish past, a workable Jewish present, and a viable Jewish future. Within this framework, reasoned intellectual

dissent is all too often ignored or censored, or discounted and dismissed, as a form of disloyalty and disrespect.[9]

In the coming decade, through the 1980s, Judaic studies broke apart into these two essentially irreconcilable camps, with little interchange between them. The size of the two camps is roughly the same in numbers, but the distribution is different. The Jewish ethnic scholars of Judaic Studies are concentrated in a few places—the Jewish seminaries, the Hebrew teachers colleges, yeshivas, and in the State of Israel and its universities. The academic scholars of Judaic studies, both Jewish and otherwise, are widely distributed among universities, with from one to ten at any one place, but with no sizable number anywhere.

They are scattered in a second sense. In their universities, they are not assembled in a single department, but they serve in a variety of disciplines and therefore also disciplinary departments, e.g., as at Brown, history, religion, literature, language, sociology, political science, and the like. In some places there may be a program or center or even an interdisciplinary department. But it is not the same thing as a yeshiva or a seminary or the Hebrew University of Jerusalem and its confreres, in which dozens of scholars, not differentiated as to discipline, form a unified and large cadre in a single school.

But while widely distributed, the academic and discipline-oriented scholars of Judaic studies form a vital consensus on the basic issues of learning. They view the Jews as exemplary, and they address a broad audience of interested but neutral scholars, in a variety of fields, on a common and shared agenda of inquiry. They do not treat the Jews as self-evidently interesting, and the data do not validate themselves without analysis. The academic sector of Judaic studies proves as productive as other parts of the humanities and social sciences; debates go forward; theses are presented and tested; much, for learning, is at stake. Green explains matters in this way:

> Disciplinary Jewish Studies . . . apply to Jewish sources and materials the standardized inquiries, analytical criteria, and . . . skepticism of university studies in the humanities and social sciences. These disciplines attempt to address common questions to various texts, cultures and societies, and thus deny special privilege to any of them. They reject in principle private, self-validating worlds of experience whose meaning is pertinent and can be transmitted only to initiates. Within a disciplinary framework, the study of discrete Jewish materials is shaped by general questions about human imagination and behavior, questions extrinsic to particular Jewish needs, concerns, and preoccupations.

---

9. *Midstream*, October 1986, p. 39

The ethnic or theological or Israeli sector, by contrast, slouches toward a certain aridity in both method and result. While wonderfully erudite—if not original—this sector puts little at stake in debates conducted under the ethnic and theological auspices, and in a broad range of subjects publication is limited. What is more consequential than the absence of publication is the poverty of a scholarly program characteristic of the ethnics, since most of the articles in *Tarbiz* and *Zion* (to take two prominent journals of the ethnics) could have been written a century ago.

Proof of the complete break between the two academies may be adduced from the conduct of the ethnics toward the academics. The former condemn without reading, receive with sedulous silence major statements, and violate the accepted norms of academic debate. As Green, who had studied with me at Dartmouth and come to Brown for his Ph.D., comments:

> Strong criticism of others' work is an academic commonplace. It is the principal form of public intellectual engagement—the way scholars transact their business—and is supposed to promote the understanding of ideas, the assessment of theories, and the advancement of knowledge. When criticism degenerates into mere condemnation and overt insult, the dispute is political or personal, not academic and professional. When criticism aims simply to discredit rather than to discern, the conflicting positions are irreconcilable, perhaps incommensurable.

The mode of criticism of the ethnics is to point to "mistakes," which may or may not be mistakes at all, of which much is made. That is a form of discrediting. To prove plausible, however, lists of mistakes should be joined with lists of nonmistakes. Otherwise the mistakes may prove—if in fact errors at all, and the great authorities pass their opinion on the basis of remarkable disinterest in facts—adventitious. Reviews that list errors but do not list correct statements are invidious and present mere innuendo; they do not persuade anyone who is not already persuaded.

When, again, the ethnics invite the other side to conferences and then rescind the invitation, as was the case for me with the Israel Historical Society and the Jewish Theological Seminary of America in 1984 and 1985, then we stand in the presence of not debate but something else entirely. And the something else, as Green says, has no scholarly or academic interest. That is why the future will witness the fruition of what has already taken place, the complete break between two completely different scholarly camps, both working on the same sources and data, but one ethnic and the other academic, or, as Green says, disciplinary.

What we have now to accept, in my view, is that the world of Jewish learning has broken in half, with a few strong and segregated centers of the ethnic, and many diffused and integrated presences of the disciplinary and academic. The two sides can no longer meet and transact business, because there is no business to be done any more, and, if truth be told, there probably never was. As Green says,

> There is a surrealism to the entire dispute. Ethnic and disciplinary Jewish Studies operate in incongruous worlds, have incompatible motivations, and address disparate constituencies. The dispute between them is bitter because it is pointless. Not enough is shared between them to allow the possibility of communication, much less persuasion.

I find the development of the two worlds of Judaic studies a perfectly natural outcome of that free academy which welcomes Judaic learning on its terms, alongside that Jewish world which nurtures Judaic learning for its purposes. Both are valid terms and purposes. But the absolute and final division between the one and the other has to be recognized now, so that we can get on with our work. What we see is simply the result of the end of a monopoly that held firm through the 1950s and the beginning of competition in the 1960s. What can be wrong with that? I see nothing so healthy as the free marketplace in which ideas compete and in which people make up their own minds. The disciplinary scholars will learn what the ethnics have to teach, when (and that is not often) they come up with new facts. They will not be much affected by the imprecations of the ethnics; they will go on with their work, as they already do. As Green says,

> Ethnic Jewish Studies, which serve communal political needs and have communal support, will continue. But disciplinary Jewish Studies have taken firm root in American universities, and they will endure there. No amount of ethnic resentment, hostility, or anger can change that.

Green is surely right. I am not inclined to regret what has happened. On the contrary, I believe it is healthy for the Jewish people to preserve both kinds of learning, since there is a vital role for each, the one for the inner world, the other for the academy.

XIII. THE NEW EGALITARIANISM ON CAMPUS

And this brings me back to life on the barricades. For, as the years unfolded at Brown, the impact of the Magaziner Report would make itself felt. Dismantling Brown's once high standards took not only student activism but faculty complicity. I quickly found myself a target of both. It was not that I opposed the noble dream of a truly democratic community of learning. It was that, in my actions, I violated the norm.

My department's chairman in the early 1970s—I had declined the post when it was offered—was a German postwar immigrant, a veteran of the Wehrmacht of World War II, named Horst R. Moehring. Good at Greek, Latin, and Josephus studies, he had little use for religion, and when he taught New Testament, he delighted in telling faithful Christian students, "The things that you're liable to read in the Bible—they ain't necessarily so." He treated Christianity with unconcealed contempt, but, like Germans of his generation, dissimulated when it came to Judaism. Within the first year of his chairmanship, he called me by phone, and asked me to come to see him so he could save my career at Brown.

As a tenured full professor, I found his concern odd, but when summoned, I answered his call. His message was, "Your problem is, you do everything too well, you write well, you teach superlatively, you publish a lot, you organize conferences and bring lecturers and generally dominate every room you walk into. In fact, you're a pain for everybody in the department. I want to advise you to be more careful, don't do so much, so you won't get kicked out of Brown. They all want to get rid of you, including your 'friends'" (among whom, he said, he counted himself).

So I had never left Milwaukee after all, and the bad dreams starting come back. I began to wonder whether among the academic freedoms that now had come under attack was the freedom to excel. With no choice and not easily intimidated anyhow, I continued as before and he resigned his chairmanship two years into a five-year term—because he couldn't "control" me. Years later, shortly before his death, he told his principal student, "Jack was right about those people." And he telephoned me shortly afterward and said, "You were right, I was wrong. Dietrich was never a scholar, Frerichs was never to be trusted, the others were worthless. You were right to persist. You did the right thing. You didn't let the bastards wear you down."

I: "I don't know what choices I had anyhow. But thanks for saying so."

Although students took over the curriculum and the mediocre professors—never missing faculty meetings and glad to serve on committees, having nothing else to do—would define campus politics, neither professors nor students in the end would dictate the character of the campus. The administration always does, through policy realized in concrete ways in its choices for support or neglect. The kinds of people chosen for chairmanships, the sorts of activities that a university administration celebrates and those that it denigrates, the departments that are favored and those that are treated as marginal or even closed, and the criteria announced to explain each kind of action—these form concrete expressions of fundamental policy. Administrations that curry favor with average professors and ordinary departments will enjoy broad popularity, for most professors produce little research and less publication. Departments that demand little support for scholarship will ease the life of deans. To reward the productive few for achievement creates jealousy, and for the near-term, bad politics.

At Brown through the 1970s and 1980s I saw, I understood, I registered my protest and proposed a better way and lost. Not consulted, I gave counsel; not attended, I raised alarms. Where I was, like my counterparts in many other universities, I led the contra party even when all alone. Not seldom, and not surprisingly, I found that people who in private agreed with everything I proposed—instructing me to pursue more critical perspectives than I had formed and providing rare intelligence on what was happening in the inaccessible offices of the other side—in public crossed the street when I approached. In the peculiar underground of the campus, talk flowed my way; but when it came to setting off the bombs, no one volunteered to join me in lighting the match. When the bombs went off, no one—where I was, at any rate—stood by me. Now, that set me to thinking, and here are the results.

During those two decades I watched a national treasure waste itself. I fought the good fight, and I lost every battle and, in the end, the war itself. Many groused, but few on the faculty leapt to the barricades, and the majority of the professors—in particular the unaccomplished seven-eighths of the faculty—competed to carry out the administration's bidding. They knew precisely what they were doing, these unaccomplished time-servers. Two incidents capture the result. Both carry us forward into the last stages of the collapse a decade later, but both embody the ethos of the campus in the 1970s as well. When, in the mid 1980s, Brown's administration neglected the great mathematics department built up over generations, the chairman of that time came to see me to ask my advice: "You've been fighting these jerks for years, what do you advise me to do?"

I advised; "There is nothing you can do. Professors do not make or break universities and certainly cannot produce a university better than its president and provost want it to be. Leave."

He did, and so did five others. The next two years saw the departure of all of the department's stars and the end of Brown's best department.

A few years afterward, the director of admissions gave up and took his leave. He addressed the faculty and pointed to a striking phenomenon, a problem that required attention. When Brown competes for students, he said, with Yale and Stanford, it is easy to predict the result. If the student knows what he or she wants to study, the student always chooses Yale or Stanford. If not, the youngster chooses Brown as often as the more prestigious schools, opting for the curriculum without requirements that defined Brown's appeal to lazy, smart rich kids who enjoyed four easy years en route to a degree.

I accomplished my goals in Providence, because my wife and I raised the kind of Jewish Americans and American Jews we aspired to bring up. But, as I shall explain in the next chapter, as soon as our fourth child had gotten whatever she might from an upbringing in Providence's East Side— a part of town where we found much delight, and which we were sorry to leave, among neighbors who turned themselves into friends, then family— we left. Saying good-by to our neighbors on Vassar Avenue proved more painful than I could have anticipated. I cried on the shoulder of one of our dear neighbors, an old Rhode Island Yankee in her eighties, whom I was never again to see in this life, and realized, had I known how difficult it would be to part company, I should never have had the courage to leave.

XIV. TEACHING

As the years at Brown were to lengthen—a long spell of difficult and increasingly gloomy times, at that time—I tried to find a mode of teaching that would make some difference to my students. The story begins in Dartmouth, when, for the first time, I had found the security and confidence to examine critically what I did in the classroom. Looking back, I find no pleasure in memories of the kind of teacher I was when I came to Dartmouth, but then, what professors did, and what many still do, in their role as teacher hardly serves any educational task I can define. What I did was deliver long, enthusiastic monologues, which people called (and call) "lectures." They were formal, elegant, carefully prepared, full of wit, brilliant, insightful, original, and—to the unfortunate students sitting in front of me—simply beyond all comprehension. I taught with my colleagues in a course that met a requirement and attracted hundreds of students: Religion 1—Catholicism, Protestantism, Judaism. Fred Berthold not only chaired the department but ran the course, and he expressed to me only delight at the fine lectures I was giving. He told me how much he learned from them. He did not tell me how little the students were learning, and I knew no better. Other colleagues did much the same.

Berthold was the only exception. His lectures were hardly lectures at all. They were conversational, slightly anecdotal, repetitive, simple, clear, obvious, and addressed to the "you" that was sitting in front of him. One lecture, before a special weekend (one of the regularly scheduled bacchanals that Dartmouth students ran for themselves), always ended with an explanation of Luther's concept of grace: "Sin bravely." Another, on the

Great Awakening in America in the eighteenth century, ended with a reference to the tolling of the bells, at just the moment at which the bell sounded to end class. At first I asked myself why Berthold told the students such obvious and simple things.

Alas, I found out on my own. During colleagues' lectures, I would sit in the back of the lecture room. One day, in my second year at Dartmouth, in the autumn, I overheard a conversation. One student asked the other, "Who's lecturing today?"

The other: "I don't know."

The first: "I hope it's not the babbler."

After a very few more exchanges, I discovered that I was the babbler. And the babbler was the guy who talked at a great pace, mostly to himself, about matters beyond all comprehension—or interest. The study of Judaism not only contributed nothing to the students' study of religion, but also consisted in the rehearsal of gibberish. Even facts failed to register. In those days we gave a multiple-choice exam, just to monitor the basic knowledge students were acquiring. As a joke, we tossed in the choice:

Diaspora

    a.   Abraham's wife

    b.   Solomon's horse

    c.   Jews living outside of the Holy Land

I was not amused to discover that the answers were equally divided among the three proposals. So much for a year and a half of my lectures on Judaism.

I realized that at no point had I succeeded in teaching anyone anything. I was too much interested in pleasing myself, and those unnamed and disembodied judges I invented in my mind for judging my performance. There was no "you" in my lectures, because I was presenting what I conceived to be insights formed of available information to whom it may concern. My theory of the lecture was to put things together. The fact of my lectures was that I never communicated with the actual students sitting in front of me. The reason was not just that I focused on what I was saying to the exclusion of anyone who may have been listening; the entire concept of the lecture rested on the false premise that education takes place when people acquire information, and the equally wrong concept that people acquire information best by being told facts.

After decades of effective teaching, Berthold knew better. He taught; I babbled. Years would pass—years of frustration and failure—before I came to the conclusion that my basic theory of education (not mine alone to be sure) missed the mark. People learn not when they are told things but when they make discoveries. Early in my years at Brown, I determined never again to present formal lectures. Rather, I would organize my propositions into an outline, which I would memorize. In class, I would spend all my time exploring one main point, and the mark of success, if I succeeded, would come when students at the end of class could make explicit; "This is what I learned today." I would accomplish my goals through questions and by indirection, hoping to lead students to discover on their own the point I wished to make, guiding them to their own explorations into the unknown. At Dartmouth I did not learn how to teach—I cannot claim ever to have learned that lesson—but I learned how not to teach. That is what I carried with me to Brown, where, after a brief period, I jettisoned the lecture-system altogether and conducted every class, large and small, as a seminar, finding its dynamism in the dialogue of questions and answers.

XV. SCHOLARSHIP

At this point in the narrative, let me set forth in a few paragraphs the scholarly work that I undertook at this time—when my doctoral dissertation was complete—and have pursued ever since. The story is a continuous one and is best told all together. Since this chapter and the next retell my decades at Brown, let me stop and briefly account for how I spent most of my time: studying, learning, and reading and writing books.

My work for the past four decades has pursued a single problem: to explain how Judaism as we know it came into being. I have wanted to account for its success, when and where it succeeded in its social goals, and to explain the conditions of its failure. While a field-theory of the history of Judaism has emerged, my principal interest all along has been in the formative age, the first seven centuries A.D. At that period, the books came to closure that with Scripture ("the Old Testament") form the definitive canon of Judaism as we know it. The canon set forth in written form the Judaic way of life, world-view, and theory of the social entity that it called "Israel," this last a theological theory of the social order corresponding to Christianity's "mystical body of Christ." The work of description, analysis, and interpretation has carried me across four academic disciplines within the study of religion, in an overlapping sequence of approximately a decade each: history, literature, history of religions, and theology. I conceive religion to be accessible to study when it is viewed as an account of the social order and the statement of a cultural system, and the problem of studying religion in my view is to explain the relationship between the religious ideas that people hold and the social world that they create for themselves.

To do this work, I have translated Judaism's canonical books into English, many for the first time, some for the second: the Mishnah, Tosefta, Talmud of the Land of Israel, Talmud of Babylonia, and all of the score of compilations of scriptural exegesis called Midrashim that came to closure in late antiquity, down to the advent of Islam in the seventh century A.D. My translations have provided for these documents their first sequential reference system (equivalent to Scripture's chapter and verse), so that form-analytical studies of the way in which the documents make their statement could get underway. I have further read each document as a coherent statement of a theory of (its) Israel's social order (I called it "system"). I then asked about the world-view, way of life, and theory of the social entity, that each writing set forth. Finally, I have provided a systematic account of the formative history of Judaism as a problem in the history of religions, specifically, the problem of how the religion that people practice together relates to the world in which they live.

Four periods over these forty years mark the divisions of this single project of mine.

In the first, 1954–64, I completed my formal education and postdoctoral studies in cognate subjects, besides the Judaic ones, in ancient history: Roman, Iranian, early Christian, Zoroastrian, Syriac, and Armenian.

In the second, overlapping period, 1960–70, I thought of myself as a historian and wrote mainly history. During that time I called into question the validity of using of the Judaic religious sources for answering the kind of questions historians asked. Further, I came to the realization that the Judaic system behind the writings I studied answered questions other than historical ones. Trying to find out precisely what questions the sources addressed, I moved from the study of history to the literary analysis of the forms and structure of documents.

From 1970 to 1980, I invented form-analysis and the form-analytical translation and commenced to carry out in my translations the form-analysis of rabbinic literature. This period produced the first of my explanations of those writings. The third, also overlapping period, 1975–90, marked the transition from historical and literary study to the study of the history of the religion, inclusive of its ideas. As I grasped the literary structure and conceptual system of documents and began to see how one document related to others, I formed a theory of the character of the Judaism that the documents, each in its way, addressed or represented in context. My work in the history of religion with special emphasis upon formative Judaism required me to set into history other Judaic systems—besides the rabbinic one that has predominated. That effort did yield the field theory of the history of Judaism that I had hoped to formulate.

But, by now, the third period also contained within itself the beginnings of a fourth. From 1989 to the present, I have devoted myself to hermeneutics and shaded over, in due course, into theology. From the late 1980s to the present, I have shaped a set of inquiries into the hermeneutics of the two Talmuds in particular. I furthermore keep in view a broader, now systematic theological interest; but concrete work is not yet underway. What I now want to know through the detailed examination of problems of structure and system—hermeneutics of a concrete order—is how the intellects whose writings I study made connections and drew conclusions, what theory told them what they wished to know and how to find it out. In this quest for an explanation of the principles of self-evidence that govern in Judaism, I am working on a commentary to both Talmuds, along the way also revising my prior translations. For a religious system works out, in vast detail, a few simple ideas. In the principles of selection and exegesis—the making of connections and drawing of conclusions that, in the case of Judaism, embody the faith's applied logic and practical reason—God lives. The fifth period, if there is one, will move from the results of this rather sizable project in hermeneutics to take up for not only constructive but also systematic theological purposes the results of this study of intellectual problems.

What do I think I have changed through my decades of research? To answer that question, let me specify where we stood when I started work and where, in my view, we stand today, in the study of Judaism in the period in which Christianity came into being, the period on which I work. In 1950 everybody assumed that, in the first seven centuries A.D., there was a single Judaism, corresponding to a single Christianity. That Judaism was a linear continuation of the Hebrew Scriptures ("Old Testament"), the original intent and meaning of which that Judaism carried forward. That same Judaism was normative, everywhere authoritative, and accepted. Its canon was so uniform that any holy book, whenever edited, testified equally as any other book to the theological or normative position of that single, unitary Judaism. The allegations of the canonical documents about things people said or did were in general accurate, or had to be assumed to be accurate unless proved otherwise. True, a rational, skeptical attitude treated with caution obviously miraculous or otherwise "impossible" allegations, such as the tales of rabbis turning people into cows or dust into gold. But, in general, the canonical writings defined Judaism, and, as a matter of fact, Judaism dealt with historical facts. It was true, because its facts were true, and its representation of the meaning of Scripture accorded with the original intent and sense of the authors of Scripture as well. Today, not a single one of these principles of scholarship stands.

But for most of this century, New Testament scholarship in quest of the "Jewish background" or "the Jewish roots of Christianity" thought it could rely upon this literature of the one and only Judaism to tell them about that single, uniform Judaism to which earliest Christianity referred. If a sentence, taken out of context, in a seventh-century writing seemed to intersect, or even say the same thing, as a statement of Paul, then Paul could be assumed to have drawn upon "his Judaism," in making the statement that he did. And if people wanted to know the meaning of what Jesus said and could locate a pertinent statement from a fourth century Babylonian rabbi's mouth, well, then, that tells us what "Rabbi Jesus" had in mind.

It is no surprise, therefore, that people commonly interpreted a passage of the New Testament by appeal to what that "single Judaism" taught. The holy books of that single Judaism, whenever and wherever they reached closure, told us what that one, unitary, harmonious Judaism had to say. So we could cite as evidence of opinions held in the first century writings edited in the sixth—a longer span of time than separates us from Columbus! Not only so, but everybody assumed that all Jews, except a few cranks or heretics, believed and practiced this single, unitary Judaism, which therefore was not only normal but normative. In such a world, the Judaism of Jesus, in A.D. 30, was pretty much the same as the Judaism of Ezra, 450 B.C., and of Aqiba, in A.D. 130. So, too, was the Judaism of the Land of Israel (a.k.a. "Palestine") of the first century was the same as the Judaism of the Greek-speaking Jews of Alexandria at that same time or of the Aramaic-speaking Jews of Babylonia five hundred years later.

What then did we know and how did we know it? In 1950 we knew pretty much what people said, thought, and did. We knew it because the rabbinic sources reported what they said and did. If sources were not redacted or edited until much after the event, well, then, people had access to oral traditions, which they preserved word-for-word and handed on until they were written down wherever and whenever (and it did not matter). And since we knew lots of historical facts, we could write history in the way that people assumed history should be written: the story of what happened, in order and sequence, beginning to end; essentially the tale of what great men (rarely women) taught.

Scholarship then consisted mainly of the study of the meanings of words or phrases or sentences. If we knew the meaning of a sentence, then we also presumed we knew what the person to whom that sentence was attributed really said and thought; and since everybody was assumed to hold the same views, or at least, talk about the same things, we could then write what "Judaism" taught about this or that. What happened if the text had an unclear reading? One would then have to consult manuscripts—written a thousand years later to be sure—and these would answer one's question and make the history possible. So these three issues predominated: the study of the critical reading of a passage, the inquiry into the critical philology or the meaning of words, and the critical exegesis, or the meaning of sentences, all done against the background of the preparation of critical texts. To dismiss a person who disagreed with one's own view, the scholar would call him or her (and there were very few women!) either uncritical or, better still, ignorant. Scholarly debate then was meant to discredit the other person, not to disprove a position contrary to one's own or even to help solve a problem held in common. Scholarship served as a blood sport for sedentary solitaries.

Today few scholars ignore or neglect the results of the century of work on text-criticism, philology, and exegesis. We still need well-crafted versions of documents, formed out of the broad array of manuscript-evidence, thoughtfully reworked. True, the century that closed in 1950 never witnessed the preparation of the required critical texts for most of the documents of the Judaic canon; but scholars were working on it. We of course need our dictionaries, and if the entire span of positivist study of Judaism failed to yield a decent Aramaic dictionary, even now one is coming. So the report card of the hundred years of positivist historicism shows many incompletes.

But in 1950 people took for granted that same evaluation would contain unquestioned judgments in favor of excellence. For however partial the fulfillment of the great tasks—no definitive dictionaries, no critical texts for the most important writings—still, there were the achievements in critical history. After all, people contended, we no longer believe all those fables; now we bring to the documents' allegations a thoroughly critical spirit. In context, people were entirely right. For they looked back on the age prior to their own—just as we do—and where they remembered credulity, they now discerned honest independence of spirit, and a critical eye examined all claims. But the premises of the long period of historical-critical scholarship corresponded, in their way, to the foundations of the age of faith: these documents yield history, meaning, an accurate picture of what pretty much everybody was thinking, saying, and doing. So when the reader has done his work—established a critical text, determined a critical definition of the meanings of words, phrases, sentences, examined the appropriate "parallels," other presentations of pretty much the same theme—then the reader could say what the text meant. And that statement took the form of history writing: what people said and did and thought at that time. That premise explains the questions people asked: how they defined what they wished to know. To put matters in a plain way: they wanted to know what they thought they already knew—only better.

What called into question the fundamental positive-historical suppositions about the character of the literary evidence could have been the discovery of other literary evidence, e.g., the Dead Sea Scrolls or the Nag Hammadi library. The Dead Sea Scrolls presented us with the writings of a Judaic religious community possibly identified with the Essenes; but prior to the discovery of the library of the community, we had no writings of that group. Nag Hammadi, in Egypt, yielded a vast library in Coptic of Gnostic Christianity, of which, beforehand, we had scarcely a hint. But in the end, these did not form the truest challenge. Literary evidence of one kind could readily be accommodated with literary evidence of some other kind. Nobody in the decade after the discoveries at the Dead Sea and in Nag Hammadi called into question the accepted consensus concerning the character of the literary evidence overall—there was only one Judaism, the one about which the rabbinic canon informs us; the scrolls at Qumran simply showed us a heretical sect. What really shook the foundations was the accumulation of evidence that there really was not a single Orthodox Judaism at all, only diverse Judaisms. And that evidence derived not from writing but from material and concrete data: archaeology.

Specifically, most synagogues built from the third to the seventh century, both in the land of Israel and abroad, had decorated floors or walls. Some symbols out of the religious life of Judaism or of Greco-Roman piety occur nearly everywhere. These include the symbols for the Festival of Tabernacles. Other symbols, available, for example, from the repertoire of items mentioned in Scripture, or from the Greco-Roman world, never make an appearance at all. The symbols of Pentecost, for instance, are rare indeed. A *shofar*, a *lulab* and *ethrog*, a *menorah*, all of them Jewish in origin, but also such pagan symbols as a zodiac, with symbols difficult to find in Judaic written sources – all of these form part of the absolutely fixed symbolic vocabulary of the synagogues of late antiquity. By contrast, symbols of other elements of the calendar year, at least as important as those that we do find, turn out never to make an appearance. And, obviously, a vast number of pagan symbols proved useless to Judaic synagogue artists. It follows that the artists of the synagogues spoke through a certain set of symbols and ignored other available ones. That simple fact makes it highly likely that the symbols they did use meant something to them, and delivered a message important to the people who worshiped in those synagogues.

Because the second commandment forbids the making of graven images of God, however, people have long taken for granted that Judaism should not produce an artistic tradition. Or, if it does, it should be essentially abstract and nonrepresentational, much like the rich decorative tradition of Islam. But from the beginning of the twentieth century, archaeologists began to uncover in the Middle East, North Africa, the Balkans, and the Italian peninsula, synagogues of late antiquity richly decorated in representational art. For a long time historians of Judaism did not find it possible to accommodate the newly discovered evidence of an ongoing artistic tradition. They did not explain that art, they explained it away. One favorite explanation was that "the people" produced the art, but "the rabbis"—that is, the religious authorities—did not approve it or at best merely tolerated it. That explanation rested on two premises. First, because Talmudic literature—the writings of the ancient rabbis over the first seven centuries of the common era—made no provision for representational art, representational art was subterranean and "unofficial." Second, rabbis are supposed to have ruled everywhere, so the presence of iconic art had to indicate the absence of rabbinic authority.

Aware of the existence of sources which did not quite fit into the picture that emerged from Talmudic literature as it was understood in those years or which did not serve the partly apologetic purposes of their studies, scholars such as George Foot Moore in his *Judaism: The Age of the Tannaim*[10] posited the existence of "normative Judaism," which is to be described by reference to Talmudic literature and distinguished from "heretical" or "sectarian" or simply "non-normative" Judaism of "fringe sects." Normative Judaism, expounded so systematically and with such certainty in Moore's *Judaism*, found no place for synagogue art, with its overtones of mysticism (except "normal mysticism"), let alone magic, salvific, or eschatological themes except within a rigidly reasonable and mainly ethical framework. Nor did Judaism as these scholars understood it make use of the religious symbolism or ideas of the Hellenistic world, in which it existed essentially apart and at variance. Today no informed student of Judaism in late antiquity works within the framework of such a synthesis, for this old way is no longer valid. The testimony of archaeology, especially of the art of the synagogues of antiquity, now finds a full and ample hearing.

---

10. Cambridge: Harvard University Press, 1927.

At stake was the conviction that the rabbinic canon was normative and tells us how things were everywhere. Once the archaeological evidence had made its impact, however, people came to recognize diversity where they had assumed uniformity and harmony. Then the conception of a single, normative Judaism, the same through five hundred years, uniform wherever Jews lived, and broadly confessed by almost all Jews almost everywhere, collapsed from its own weight. Scientific studies on "Talmudic Judaism," which had begun about a century ago, had rested on the presupposition that Talmudic literature might by itself yield a whole and accurate view of Judaism in the early centuries of the common era. Iconic evidence was simply ignored.

My work systematically has advanced the theses that today predominate. I insisted, for reading the rabbinic documents, upon the critical principles that govern in the study of the Bible. It was Goodenough who first took seriously the diversity of Judaisms in antiquity. I carried his view to its logical conclusion. And this changed the way in which we speak about Judaism in late antiquity. When the diversity of Jews in antiquity came to be recognized, then the other premises of the received tradition of learning lost the standing of self-evident truths. If there was no single, unitary, harmonious Judaism, then (1) the sources that portrayed that picture could not longer be taken at face value. If the sources stood only for their authors' opinions, not for broadly held norms, then (2) we could no longer assume that all sources everywhere, without regard to when they were redacted, attested to that same, single Judaism.

And if people differentiated between a given document and the worldview and way of life of the Jews everywhere and through a half-millennium or more, then (3) they had also to differentiate among the documents themselves. These three challenges to scholarship today not only outline what we now do not think we know, but also point toward what we think we know and how we think we know it; they account for the kinds of questions we now investigate. Seeing the different texts of ancient Judaism, each on its own, has occupied me from the beginning of the 1970s forward. In time that premise has come to define that documentary approach to the history of formative Judaism that today defines research.

XVI. DEFENDER OF THE FAITH

The shaping of that scholarly program responded to the issues that engaged humanistic learning in the American setting. The possibility of pursuing that program, as I have explained, came about only because of the peculiar circumstances that prevailed at that time in the American academy. Earlier opportunity did not exist for an independent reading of matters, and later a different emphasis from the academic and rational one would gain preferment. Mine then was, and still is, a faith in the worth of the academy, an affirmation of its deepest commitment to a single standard of reason and a uniform rationale of skepticism and self-criticism for all. I like to think that I was an equal-opportunity critic, so that one did not have to be an anti-Semite to dislike me quite uncordially.

But another crisis, at the end of the decade, captures the struggle for the academic and disciplinary definition of the curriculum and against the competing one. I found that the professors who should have supported my position lined up against it. It was then that I determined to leave Brown when my children had completed their growing up, some ten years before I actually did so.

Toward the end of a semester, a student writing an undergraduate honors thesis with me came by to ask whether I would come and hear his paper, and also, did I mind his giving it? It quickly became clear that he was going to read his paper not to the department—professors and students sharing his work—but elsewhere on campus, in a non-academic setting. It was, in fact, part of a presentation of the Hillel Foundation director, Rabbi Richard Marker, to his board of directors. He had organized a program consisting of presentations of three honors theses, two of them directed by me. This would show his board what was happening on campus, how Judaism was making its way.

I answered the student in these terms: "No, not now, for two reasons. (1) The thesis is not done, and you may not have my agreement to present work that is not yet the best that you with my help can produce. (2) The thesis also has not yet been received by the academic department for which it is being prepared; it is not a theological demonstration about religious norms but an analytical and descriptive problem about the character of religion in society (it had to do with American Judaism). But afterward, yes: that is, once the department has received the thesis and given you its criticism and you have revised and completed it, you are free to do as you like with it; it is no longer our business."

He: "Then you don't want me to read it for the Hillel board?"

I: "No, that would bear the false implication that work within the curriculum and activities of the Jewish community on campus are interchangeable. But they're not. What you do in the academic study of religion answers one set of questions, and how you pursue learning for the purpose of religious quest and expression responds to a different set of questions.

Neither is better than the other, but they are different and, for substantive, intellectual reasons, should not be confused."

In so stating, I thought I was defending the faith of the field of the academic study of religion: not ethnic, not special pleading, not in the service of church or synagogue (also not in the service of their enemies), but an entirely autonomous, freestanding, academic venture—so much for the faith. But I turned out to be the sole purist. When I called to the attention of my chairman and colleagues in religious studies the intrusion of the chaplaincy into my teaching relationships with my students, I found no one impressed by the confusion of the academy and the ethnic-religious community.

When I pointed out that the Hillel rabbi had issued such an invitation without consulting me (as in, "Are the students ready to report their results?") and indeed without even paying me the courtesy of inviting me to his event (he claimed that a printed invitation would suffice, but hadn't yet gotten around to mailing it), my colleagues did not share my indignation. Lest I miss the intent, the same Hillel rabbi had asked an assistant professor in the area of Judaism, who had nothing to do with the theses, to chair the event. So much for collegiality at Brown's Department of Religious Studies. That assistant professor agreed to chair the presentation of my students' work, never informing me of what was coming. I pointed out that had I done such a thing to offend him, I would have been universally condemned—and rightly so.

Without support from my chairman and colleagues, I turned to the provost of that time, an engineer who also was a Jew and a member of the Hillel board. He did not share my conviction about the importance of preserving the academic integrity of the study of Judaism at Brown. Everything was the same as everything else, so far as he was concerned. He saw no problem at all—except for my insistence that it was a problem. He did not express concern that students would present work that was hardly finished (or, in my judgment, even terribly good); such standards did not register. And he was not impressed that the academic purpose of the work had not yet been accomplished. Those who should have joined in the defense of the academic faith did not perceive the offense done to it.

Over the next months, from May through November, I persisted in registering my protest against confusing the academic study of Judaism with the religious and ethnic practice of Judaism. In the interim I declined to give further time and effort to undergraduate honors theses, on the grounds that I could not guarantee the academic integrity of the result. I set forth to the Hillel board and to its national commission the dangers I saw in the intrusion of Hillel, a sectarian Jewish community agency, into the work of the academy. No one thought it necessary to answer my complaints, not the Hillel board, not the Brown administration, not the local Jewish community that financed the agency. Finally, weary of the controversy, an associate provost of that time, Mark Schupack, called me to negotiate a conclusion to the controversy. His first words were, "But surely you realize, Jack, that your colleagues do not agree with you and do not support you."

I: "So?"

He: "So what's the point."

I: "So the point is, the academic study of Judaism possesses its own integrity and cannot be turned into a chapter in Jewish students' Jewish religious education. Nor are we going to serve as ethnic cheerleaders."

I spelled out the issue, the separation of the academy from all outside agencies and special interest groups, the presentation of our various subjects in a way that avoided special interests and special pleading and that, above all, left students free to respond in whatever way they chose to the imperatives of the subjects that they studied. I underscored that I could not tolerate Hillel's intrusion in my teaching relationships with my students—they had told me to go to hell and had read their papers to the Hillel board, and I had resigned as their adviser for the projects.

At that time the Hillel rabbi also was proposing to give courses not on how and why to practice Judaism—which as leader of the faithful he should offer—but on the history of Judaism, such as the curriculum afforded. Lacking a Ph.D., he did not have the scholarly qualifications to teach such courses. This, I maintained, in effect lowered the standards that governed the presentation of the academic subject in academic terms.

The associate provost drew up a written agreement, which was reviewed by the Hillel rabbi and his board. They conceded every point. It was—of course—an empty victory; not a long time later, after that Hillel rabbi had left and someone else had taken his place, I was told that the agreement was supposed to be valid for one year only, or for that regime only, and did not apply any more. He gave the course, but not for credit—which was all that mattered. The new fellow could and would do whatever he felt like doing. And no one would object. But by then I was biding my time. I had come to raise my children in Providence; they were coming along. Then I would leave. So the 1980s would be a time of watching and waiting. But they began with an explosion, which destroyed my career at Brown, leaving me only a marvelous job for as long as I could endure the life of a well-paid, privileged pariah. I left on my terms, when I chose to leave for a superior situation. But in the interim came times of testing and trouble.

4

THE GREAT
TRADITION DIES

I. THE CAMPUS AND THE COUNTRY PART COMPANY

The campus in the 1980s split, with students favoring President Reagan, professors in the aggregate despising him. True, on the fringes of the campus, in economics departments, and medical, law, business and engineering faculties for instance, opinion varied. But in the colleges of liberal arts, in the humanities and the stupid social-sciences (the ones not requiring statistics and mathematics), opinion contradicted the national electoral consensus. The radicals of the 1960s and 1970s had gone off to get Ph.D.'s, and by the 1980s they formed the critical mass of the campus opinion that got attention, particularly at the headline-grabbing campuses. Whole academic fields fell into the hands of the radicals—the social sciences that did not require statistics and nearly the entirety of the humanities. Literature, philosophy, history, the study of religion—all substituted left-wing ideology for the received tradition of liberal learning. So while the country rearmed, the elite university faculties opted for isolationist pacifism. Reagan led the country to a confrontation with Communism and denounced "the Evil Empire" and planned to destroy it. But the elite campuses chanted, "Better Red than dead."

The country in 1980 affirmed what became twelve years of government restraint. The elite campuses put forth new initiatives in social engineering. The country admired the Polish anti-Communists, cheering on Lech Walesa, and armed the Afghan rebels. The radical campuses produced book after book to demonstrate that the United States and the Soviet Union compared on equal terms and were really not all that different. The great traditions of academia died within the campus walls as radical campus departments of literature, history, and philosophy had opted for postmodernism in its vulgar form ("there is no such thing as truth, just power"); and fascist feminism (female hegemonism); and black racism (it's O.K. if we hate, but no one can hate us). As the professors saw the United States and the Soviet Union as pretty much the same, so they claimed to find no reason to discriminate true from untrue, right from wrong, good from evil in matters of intellect and learning. In their view, anyone's opinion is as good as everyone else's and anything goes.

The campuses, deeply political for more than a decade, now declared themselves bastions of participatory democracy. If opinion mattered most, then popularity with the voters (formerly students) would make all the difference. Instead of teaching them, professors would aim at pleasing them. Winning their approbation demanded little—easy assignments, entertaining lectures, high grades, and no criticism. Those of us who had framed another theory of education, conservative in its values, observed a curious development. Some people, allied in overthrowing snobbery and privilege, placed in their stead a new formalism. If grades preserve "elitism," then no evaluation matters. No student can fail—on principle. Therefore, went the argument, the registrar should obliterate the record of failure and not record F's. Since everybody is as good as everybody else, schools should accept applications by random lottery (a proposal seriously presented at a Brown faculty meeting and debated in my time). Open admission for all who qualify was taken to mean no one needs qualifications. Since anyone's opinion is as good as everyone else's, no one needs to reason with the other. Everything is settled with smiles.

II. "A COMMENCEMENT SPEECH YOU'LL NEVER HEAR" THAT THE WHOLE WORLD HEARD

My own career at Brown came to an end at the beginning of the 1980s, when I responded to the dumbing down of the universities by the changes of the 1970s. In an op-ed piece, printed in the student paper in May, 1981, I took the view that the students should face challenges and encounter rigorous standards, applied first by their teachers to themselves, and then to the students' education as well. Maintaining that students gain most from the teachers who demand most, I wished to say that the indulgent professors, like indulgent parents, in the end traded evanescent popularity for long-term intellectual and even moral failings in the students' lives. My professors who demanded the most and offered the most challenging courses intellectually also imparted the lasting lessons, and some had even changed me. The ones who gave easy A's left nothing in consequence except contempt and disappointment.

Why was I printing my pieces for the student paper as often as for the *New York Times* or *Washington Post* or *Newsday,* as I would from time to time as well? In those days, as part of my teaching office, I would engage students in any forum the university offered. I would call my students to suppers with the university's president or provost or dean and ask them to talk together about substantive matters of student life. I would invite students to my home every Friday night through the semesters (my heroic wife became adept at serving dinner to the six of us plus three or four students each week). Every festival occasion within Judaism found both Jewish and gentile students at our table.

In these and other ways I tried to show that the demanding teacher that I meant to be also cared for and sympathized with the students and wanted them to achieve. Sometimes it helped, but often it did not. I erred in thinking the students cared as much as I did that they learn and grow in intellectual power. But the effort at intellectual empowerment went forward, term after term, year after year. I was a university professor. Stupidly, I thought that meant, address the university. So I did.

As part of this ongoing participation in campus life, I wrote regularly for the student paper, the *Brown Daily Herald*. In quality and character the paper fluctuated wildly and rapidly—one year being sophisticated and capable of shaping public discourse; another year, sophistical, jejune, and childish. Sometimes the paper published only fair-minded and adult debate about substantive campus issues. At other times the editors gladly printed vile personal attacks, students upon students, or students upon professors. It came to the logical nadir in the mid 1980s with attacks by professors upon professors. In one pathetic instance, a popular professor of the crowd-pleasing, nonpublishing category, Edward Beiser in political science, declared his opinion that, for my having criticized the then president, I was insane and should leave Brown.

Regnant opinion at Brown—and not there alone—then held that the easy-going, sandal-clad, untrimmed, and unkempt but above all the undemanding professor, was the one to celebrate. Easy assignments, easy praise, easy A's—these formed the stock in trade of more than a few of my colleagues at Brown. Their classes were jammed. For what they sold found a huge market. Today their counterparts flourish. The kind of education they offer naturally conforms to the psychological problems of adolescents.

In those days—the turn of the 1980s—Brown's New Curriculum, now more than a decade old and self-evidently a failure, validated the easy trade-off, which made students complicit in the professors' patent fraud: an easy education for nothing in particular, sold at a premium tuition.

There in spring of 1981, a low-key debate was underway on how many courses should be required for a degree. The New Curriculum, scarcely examined since its adoption, attracted a renewed measure of interest. Some wondered whether Brown maintained any standards or ever demanded excellence. Others wondered what a degree divorced from all requirements, except a major, might actually represent in solid education. Still others called into question the minimal degree requirements and pointed out that Brown had become a hot school for all the wrong reasons. The campus conservatives—the nonperforming professors—defended the status quo and we radicals took the critical, but unpopular position. The administration wanted nothing less than to give up the charter that made Brown the hot school it then was. They aimed at keeping Brown sizzling, but forgot the steak.

With the op-ed piece, I forced the issue. I wanted to point out to students that those who really loved them offered "tough love." Those who really cared for students would listen to them thoughtfully, but then respond vigorously to the point. To join the discussion, I made up an imaginary speech, one that no one would ever give. It was to be an imagined commencement speech and readers who followed campus life in 1981 may remember hearing about it. For some months in that year I felt nearly everybody in the world had listened.

Brown students certainly got a message, if not exactly the one I had sent forth. On a Friday it was printed in the student paper. Over the weekend five thousand undergraduates in my university read it as a personal letter from me to them, individually. From Monday forward, for several weeks, scores of students, including the graduating seniors *en masse*, replied in angry letters. Proof that the students' education had failed them came from their response. The letters' brutality hardly mattered, but the inelegance of the insults—the "drop dead, you boob" writing—made one wonder what marked the educated mind, if not the power to deliver a cutting insult. Unable to perceive irony, the students took umbrage. The immediate and violent response made me worry that I was more right than I had wanted to be. This is what I printed:

A COMMENCEMENT SPEECH YOU'LL NEVER HEAR

"We the faculty take no pride in our educational achievements with you. We have prepared you for a world that does not exist, indeed, that cannot exist. You have spent four years supposing that failure leaves no record. You have learned at Brown that when your work goes poorly, the painless solution is to drop out. But starting now, in the work to which you go, failure marks you. Confronting difficulty by quitting leaves you changed. Outside Brown, quitters are no heroes.

"With us you could argue about why your errors were not errors, why mediocre work really was excellent, why you could take pride in routine and slipshod presentation. Most of you, after all, can look back on honor grades for most of what you have done. So here grades can have meant little in distinguishing the excellent from the ordinary. But tomorrow, in the world to which you go, you had best not defend errors but learn from them. You will be ill-advised to demand praise for what does not deserve it, and to abuse those who do not give it.

"For four years we created an altogether forgiving world, in which whatever slight effort you gave was all that was demanded. When you did not keep appointments, we made new ones. When you were late to class, we ignored it. When your work came in beyond the deadline, we pretended not to care. Worse still, when you were boring, we acted as if you were saying something important. When you were garrulous and talked to hear yourself talk, we listened as if it mattered. When you tossed on our desks writing upon which you had not labored, we read it and even responded, as though you earned a response. When you were dull, we pretended you were smart. When you were predictable, unimaginative, and routine, we listened as if to new and wonderful things. When you demanded free lunch, we served it. And all this why? Despite your fantasies, it was not to be bothered, and the easy way out was pretense: smiles and easy B's.

"It is conventional to quote in addresses such as these. Let me quote someone you've never heard of, Professor Carter A. Daniel, Rutgers University, in the *Chronicle of Higher Education*: 'College has spoiled you by reading papers that don't deserve to be read, listening to comments that don't deserve a hearing, paying attention even to the lazy, ill-informed, and rude. We had to do it, for the sake of education. But nobody will ever do it again. College has deprived you of adequate preparation for the next fifty years. It has failed you by being easy, free, forgiving, attentive, comfortable, interesting, challenging, fun. Good luck tomorrow.'

"That is why, on this commencement day, we have nothing in which to take much pride.

"Oh yes, there is one more thing. Try not to act toward your co-workers and bosses as you have acted toward us. I mean, when they do not give you what you want but have not earned, don't abuse them, insult them, act out with them your parlous relationships with your parents. This, too, we have tolerated. It was, as I said, not to be liked.

Few professors actually care whether or not they are liked by peer-paralyzed adolescents, fools so shallow as to imagine professors care not about education but about popularity. It was, again, to be rid of you. So go, unlearn the lies we taught you. To life!"

With this little piece of 580 words, I turned myself into a pariah. My career at Brown was over. What I had left, solely because of the protection of tenure, was a job. The hot college got headlines that concerned educational values, commitment to students' intellectual and personal maturing—that, and not headlines about the super-rich your kid will get to go to school with at Brown. It was not exactly what Brown wanted. The message—higher education requires reform and renewal because it has gone wrong—is not what any elite college had in mind.

"The speech you'll never hear" got heard round the world. Students heard a dismissal of their studies and their degrees. They were not wrong. In the aftermath of Magaziner's revolution, Brown required nothing in particular, so its degree stood for anything at all, but little of consequence. Students could get degrees for taking twenty-eight courses, while Yale required thirty-six, and many state universities, forty (120 hours). Brown students could get degrees without taking a foreign language, an English course, a science course, a mathematics course—anything difficult. They could get degrees whether or not they could write, whether or not they could construct a cogent argument, whether or not they knew how to listen thoughtfully, respond to the point, formulate their ideas reasonably and accurately, and set forth their case in a persuasive manner.

But there was worse. Brown students could get degree credit by taking courses of "independent study" involving self-instruction only. They could organize courses taught solely by students with minimal, if any, professorial supervision. Their failing grades were not recorded. They filled up transcripts with not grades at all but elaborate love-letters from fundamentally indifferent professors. Brown students had many lies to unlearn. And, across the country, many others did too; Brown stood for the extreme end of a quite commonplace downward curve in learning.

Above all, they emerged with the lesson that everything was personal and private, so one person's opinion weighed as much as the next person's, with evidence, argument, reason bearing no compelling weight at all. So, in matters of intellect, nothing mattered very much. "Well, that's my opinion" counted heavily in argument, and no one was supposed to try to persuade or through reason to compel another to change his mind. In that atmosphere of intellectual decay and academic atrophy, I set forth a protest, not so much against the students as against the professors. After all, the students had accepted the easy deal, but it was the professors who had offered it.

From adolescents no more could be expected. But professors, holding doctorates, paid to pursue scholarship and teach, owed judgment. Thinking of a colleague who gave trivial assignments and lots of A's, I issued my warning. The "nice guy" professors, of whom there are too many, cynically avoid responsibilities of conscience and commitment. They ask too little, so they teach all the wrong lessons. My target was professors. My arrow hit students, too—right on target for both. That message seemed to me self-evident. To me it was so obvious, so good-hearted, that when I printed it in the student paper, I made a bet with a close friend that the paper would receive not a single response. I thought what I said was commonplace, but amusing. It was neither.

The paper got something on the order of 250 letters in the next five days, 199 of them declaring me "insane and incompetent," "to be fired from Brown" (at least), and "locked up in an asylum for the criminally insane." Those were the nice letters. I personally got many more. And that is not to count the anonymous phone calls in the middle of the night from angry Brown students who couldn't wait until dawn to tell me so. We had to get an unlisted phone number. And as I said, the world took note, for the paradox caught people's imagination, generating just the story the generalists needed for graduation season in place of cliches on the "bright college years:" *Students Lynch Mean Professor. Professor Tells Graduating Students They Have Not Learned Much. Students Tell Professor He's a Fraud.* It was not one of my everyday exchanges, but it did capture the world's imagination in that graduation season.

From the day on which I printed that little op-ed piece in the *Brown Daily Herald* in early May, 1981, my career there ended; as I said, out of the disaster all I had left was a job. Tenure really does protect the few who need it. Would I do it over? Without tenure, no. I would have been fired as soon as it was legally possible, and I had a family to support and by that point in life knew only one craft that I valued. So it would not have been worthwhile to sacrifice family, life, and learning, to issue such a warning. But with tenure, certainly—why not? It cost nothing worth anything.

To be sure, not only the right, but also the wrong people agreed with me. On the one side I got love-letters from assistant professors all over the country, telling me I spoke for them. The junior faculty in an English department wrote to tell me they had gone out and toasted me in beer the day they read my piece. But I also got a lot of mail from misanthropes, people habitually angry at the younger generation. I have never felt anything but affection for students—although I hid it behind ever-more rigorous demands. From those I most respected, I asked the most. My praise took the form of new demands. But I gave praise lavishly—when it was earned—as well as criticism.

My abiding fear then and always has been to ask too little of a student of intellect and ability, not to ask too much of a student of lesser talent. The latter would find plenty of praise and encouragement elsewhere. The former needed slight provocation to rise up and surpass himself or herself. A long and boring education had framed for me the ideal of giving what few had offered me: an education of continuing intellectual engagement. So I do like students, without regard to native ability, but with much regard to their will and capacity to change and grow.

As I look back, I understand that in the op-ed piece I was creating a kind of "persona," the way a playwright does, or a novelist: "What would I say if I were . . . ?" "What would life be like if . . . ?" My invented persona took up the question; "How would I address a graduating class in a memorable way? "I" was not this writer in particular; it was an imaginary "I—"an "I" out there. But quite fairly and correctly, people ignored the headline I gave the little essay, "A Commencement Address You'll Never Hear" (I might have added, " . . . and One I'll Never Give"). They saw my name, and then the message: Boom! Zounds! Pow!

Was it a mistake? No, it was no mistake to tell the students that we professors really settle for too little and demand not enough. And it was a public service to remind students that the best professors also demand the most and draw the highest achievement from capable students. But I should have said something like this: "Like everyone else, I make my mistakes in teaching. And you will make your mistakes in learning. But if I have to choose between asking of a student too little or too much, let me err by always asking too much. At least it shows belief and hope." That is what I meant by the ending; "To Life!" That is the goal and purpose of college education: to bring students to life.

III. THE DUMBING DOWN OF THE UNIVERSITIES

What I saw at Brown was happening at all the colleges and universities which claimed leadership of higher education. The professors, with numerous brave exceptions, cared more for popularity than for education. Pandering to late adolescents' fantasy that they can manipulate the world by giving or withholding approbation, the professors gave infantile assignments, asked for little work but bestowed much praise, passed out A's for class attendance, and, above all, withheld the criticism they ought to have contributed. Most students, placing low priority upon education and intellectual maturity, flooded the classrooms of those professors who unashamedly gave easy and entertaining courses.

With existing demands perceived as excessive, the humanities lowered standards to attract students. For example, majors that required general exams and theses and even the qualification of a foreign language came to redefinition: no exams, no theses, no languages, just the requisite number of courses. My department at Brown, religious studies, exemplified the trend, having reduced the major in rigor and scaled down its intellectual substance. But established subjects spawned new ones, with English departments metastasizing into English, semiotics, modern media, and on and on.

The dumbing down of the universities shaded over into complete intellectual capitulation. Professors of literature refused to tell students the difference between good and bad writing. Indeed, students were taught that bad writing was good. When I told a student of mine who was a literature major just back from France that he was writing gibberish, he replied; "But in France I learned that good writing imposes burdens on the reader to find all the layers of meaning . . . ." He went on to spell out more gibberish he had learned that day up the street in Brown's modern media and semiotics courses. No wonder, then, that professors of poetry announced that "great" poetry and doggerel could not be distinguished. Historians announced the end of narrative history, history as literature, and, with it, they declared that history teaches no lessons worth learning. The ethnic subjects, which always tempted to substitute special pleading for discourse of general intelligibility and interest, shamelessly introduced into the campus a wholly political agendum. Led by Jewish studies, black studies, and women's studies, once intellectually vital subjects transformed themselves into sources of aggression: the nurture of ill-will against outsiders (gentiles, whites, men).

A sign of this change would come only later in the 1980s and reach its full exposure in the 1990s, with the naturalization of bigotry leading even to open anti-Semitism on the campus under the auspices of black studies. Like the Weimar universities of the late 1920s and the Nazified universities of the 1930s, schools such as Howard University sponsored anti-Semitic events. Alongside, books and student newspapers were burned and suppressed, free speech penalized, and strict rules enforced about what might and might not be said—anything lunatic about the Jews and the Pope, but nothing that radical feminists or blacks would find "insensitive."

Including black studies in universities now requires provisions for blacks-only studies and facilities, excluding nonblack professors and nonblack students. A once-respectable academic field sponsors racism and bigotry of a vicious character never before seen in so vast a sector of the American academy. Ceasing to exclude blacks from tax-supported activities, the promise of the 1960s, has now imposed upon universities the requirement to finance black bigotry wherever black students and professors wish to assert themselves. Special pleading replaces learning, politically correct opinions substitute for free debate in reasoned arguments, proscribed attitudes substitute for free inquiry, and a reign of intellectual terror has descended on many, particularly the most advanced and most liberal universities. Indeed, the higher on the scale of the elite universities, the more restrictive and dictatorial the racist regime. Consequently, what began as an effort to improve the curriculum for all by making a place for African-American history, literature, and culture has now shaded over into a sustained campaign of black racism against whites in general, and Catholics and Jews in particular. No one has yet calculated the loss of moral authority that has accrued to black America.

The bankruptcy of the humanities and social sciences would break into public only later in the 1980s. But early on, as changes, dubbed "reforms," of the late 1960s and earliest 1970s began to take effect, some of us began to realize what had happened. In legislating utopia, the academy had abandoned all standards of excellence. In introducing democratic principles into the governance of academic subjects and the conduct of academic business, the universities had repealed human nature—or tried to. With students on all manner of committees, the qualification for making decisions found definition in mere personal opinion, then prejudice, and finally bigotry.

The ideal that I sought in the classroom, throughout the 1960s and the 1970s, from the day I discovered I did not teach but only babbled, expressed a dream of education through discovery and growth through individual initiative. But the reality of the revolution proved to be different. While many of us dreamed of intellectual encounter, some professors translated the quest for a new relationship with the students into the search to be liked. Some felt that the good teacher would be the one students liked, the great teacher would be known by jokes and "being with it." These teachers were around before the revolution and were among the many who scarcely grasped its issues. Indeed, the revolution presented an opportunity in its turmoil not to radically revise the processes of higher education but to conveniently exploit them for personal ends, such as a comfortable career. Thus, there were two revolutions, the one in education and another one, larger and better documented. This larger and more popular revolution aimed at loosing bonds of discipline and making education appear easier and therefore more equal. I know of no campus in which the other revolution—the one now rightly under attack for its degradation of higher education, its loosening of discipline and rejection of rigor—did not demoralize the best and the brightest. For if student response to teaching became a critical issue in tenure decisions (and I believe it should), then who would not want to have popularity among students (and that not necessarily through good teaching at all)?

IV. REAGAN'S REVENGE

The sea-change in ideology among faculty hired in the 1960s and 1970s— more willing to use academics for political ends, more antagonistic to national goals—inspired, in the 1980s and 1990s, a counterreaction from the Right. Looking from the outside in, the campus appeared to incubate a cast that would produce one outrage after another. While not on the same scale as the riotous protests of the 1960s, these outrages constructed an indelible impression that university professors respected only their own freedom of speech and not others, withstood criticism from no one except those on the Left, taught and studied inconsequential things and generally epitomized the very worst of protected laziness.

By the 1980s, as the country voted Republican in presidential elections three times in a row, the campus appeared a strange exception to the rule. And people took notice. Examples of stamped-on free speech and Orwellian rules of student code and conduct (the college gives out free condoms, but enforces strict codes of sexual puritanism) filled the nation's newspages for years. The term "political correctness"—a hodgepodge of enforced sympathy for historical victims of economic, visual, racial or sexual oppression—was a joke anywhere but on the campus.[1]

But unlike the counterreaction of the late 1960s, academics on the Right did not find solace in simple nay-saying. A group of politicians, writers, and some professors described an alternative vision of what a college should be. And while that vision remains elusive, it defined, in many ways, the debate over the adequacy of America's colleges and universities. The political wing of this counterattack was led ideologically by Ronald Reagan and practically by his Secretary of Education, William Bennett, both politicians. Reagan, who exasperated student leftists at Berkeley, did not face the same kind of challenges from college campuses.

---

1. As we noted in the introduction, we take for granted the wide exposure given to previous charges of liberal orthodoxy on America's college campuses. For extensive examples, see D'Souza, Kimball, Sykes, and Bloom.

206 • THE PRICE OF EXCELLENCE

Rather, he enjoyed strong popularity among students, and save for a few pockets of protest, did not face challenges to federal policy from students. Federal support for military research went relatively unchallenged, and university administrators did not, in general, capitulate to the demands of some students to ban weapons research or armed forces recruitment. Rather than react to these relatively minor controversies, whenever or wherever they existed, Bennett pursued an agenda of realigning the curriculum. Joined by Allan Bloom, the University of Chicago professor whose 1987 *The Closing of the American Mind* remarked on the absence of literacy on Western history, culture, language, and philosophy, Bennett pushed for the kind of education envisioned by Columbia and Chicago's administrators decades earlier. The reaction against reduced requirements, lax scheduling and teaching, and lower student achievement may have been grounded in educational theory. But political ideology never left this counterreaction. It enjoyed support on the Right, which had for the first time since the 1960s, begun to frame a cultural agenda apart from being simply reactionary. This rightward push came as most prestigious universities had shifted attention away from general education to particularized and segmented curricula. Throughout the period of the counterrevolution, colleges merged diverse and occasionally mismatched subjects; anthropology borrowed from literary theory, economics from cognitive psychology, and political science from mathematics. At the same time, traditional subjects like classics and foreign languages lost their edge to the emerging hot topics.

The conservative counterreaction partly cited this trend, arguing that common standards in teaching Western philosophy and history needed to be established on the campus. When, in 1987–88, some students at Stanford University rejected the college's required course on Western philosophy and civilization as the summation of thousands of years of white, male domination over women, other races and cultures, Bennett responded with a simple rejoinder: West is best. But just as Bennett retorted with an educational idea wrapped in political rhetoric, the other side was not much better. The difference between an academic issue and a political one was immeasurably blurred by protesters who argued, essentially, that the inherited tradition of the West was undeniably racist, among other things. "There is something inherently anti-intellectual about the notion of an educational institution establishing a canon," said Clayborne Carson, a professor at Stanford and a proponent of the alternative world cultures and values course, which was adopted in 1989.[2] The debate over general education, once framed in terms of establishing

2. Dinesh D'Souza, *Illiberal Education*, p. 62.

set guidelines for a student's entire education, now could hardly hold sway in a campus environment where even a single required course drove debate for three years.

V. DEAD, WHITE, MALE, AND PROUD OF IT

The counterreaction to the criticism of "dead white male" curricula appeared to enjoy wide popularity, and not simply on theoretical grounds. Attacks on Western civilization, in an age when Western forms of democracy and theology were enjoying widespread popularity everywhere on the globe—including former enemies Russia and China—appeared to many the work of self-loathing intellectuals. After all, as American-born students were departing the departments of science and engineering, foreign-born students were jumping at the opportunities. In 1993, about half of the country's post-doctoral fellows in science and engineering were foreigners, and American colleges were quickly becoming a rite-of-passage for foreign students who would return to their home country after graduation to serve in leadership positions. And conservatives parleyed this sentiment into a string of successful attacks, including Dinesh D'Souza's *Illiberal Education* (1991), a full frontal offensive on, among other things, force-fed ideology in America's college classrooms. Taking on the logic of academic feminism, which promoted androgyny; race studies, which supported segregationism; and academic governance, which trampled the freedom of faculty or students to differ with leftist notions, D'Souza, joined by another critic from the right, Roger Kimball, pointed out that many of America's colleges gave refuge to a group of faculty who could not play in Peoria. In describing "tenured radicals," Kimball gave witness to the accumulated experience of American colleges since the mid 1960s when, as we have noted before, the new professorate began to dismantle the academy's traditional relationship with American society. And not just professors; academic governing bodies like the Modern Language Association and accrediting bodies like the Middle States Association of Colleges earned a heaping of scorn from the Right. The associations tended to block out dissenting opinions in important fields like literature, prompting the founding of alternative associations such as the American Academy for Liberal Education. And MSAC, together with the Western Association of Schools and Colleges, got some unexpected attention when both bodies, generally trusted to accredit schools on the basis of facilities, finance, and faculty credentials, sought to remove accreditation from colleges that did not meet some predetermined level of diversity.

Another author, Charles Sykes, attacked not only the politically correct, but the professorate as a whole. While drawing amply from a pool of outrages dispersed by leftist professors, Sykes' two works, *Profscam* (1988) and *The Hollow Men* (1990), dovetailed with a nationally phrased question: just what is the nation getting from higher education? Sykes' argument—that professors have pulled a con job on the country—could never have been made two decades earlier. With billions of dollars pouring into college budgets, either from governments or parents, these institutions suffered through an onslaught of microscopic interest in professorial responsibilities, financial management, and institutional philosophy and morality; attacks like that of Sykes were basically ignored. But now things began to change. A Congressional committee, convened by Rep. John Dingell in 1991, found that academic overcharges to the federal government for research projects were commonplace. Stanford University, for example, was found using federal money for lavish parties, shopping mall trips, and as compensation for the depreciated value of a university yacht. Another investigation found that the Ivy League schools and M.I.T. had conspired to fix financial aid packages for incoming students. Such investigations brough harsh recriminations, apologies, and some refunds, and perhaps more than ever put the major universities on the defensive in acquiring the huge federal grants that had remained their province for four decades. But while Dingell's search proved interesting in certain cases, Sykes attack on the professorate proved systematic.

Sykes' wide-ranging criticism took on not only professors, but the official and institutional world they had created. The peer review boards, the journals, the university presses, sabbaticals, and faculty governance all received a heavy dose of scorn and criticism from the self-described muckraker. He saved most of his attack for tenure, which, he argued, protected not those professors who said and did unusual things, but professors who did nothing.

His summary, both anecdotal and statistical, is unremitting and scathing. He notes with disdain those professors who used tenure and academic freedom to stamp on the rights of those who disagreed with conventional liberal ideas. And he also notes those legions of professors who, tucked away in a comfortable niche in the academy, rarely teach a course students might want to take, rarely write an article or a book colleagues might want to read, and rarely say anything controversial for fear of earning the wrath of a system where nonconformity to accepted academic truths was tantamount to career suicide, if not institutional treason. Tenure, Sykes notes unflinchingly, is less a product of an academic's success than his ability to get along.

"It is, moreover, the academic culture's ultimate control mechanism to weed out the idiosyncratic, the creative, the nonconformist," he writes.[3] He recommends, in tenure's place, renewable contracts, requirements to teach at least nine hours a week each semester; not only to increase a professor's utility, but to lower class size, which Sykes argues had become one of the main scams of the academy. He cites cattle-call classes, where lecturers orated to hundreds, if not thousands of students. He documented with alarming consistency the routine sloughing off of faculty responsibilities like student guidance, reading student papers, leading class discussions, to poorly paid graduate students or part-time faculty.

Sykes was joined, in short order, by a host of journalists and academics. They argued that the standards for tenure—five or so years of relatively solid work in the classroom and some publishing of arcane research—proved a low standard for a lifetime contract. One reporter remarked that tenure, designed to protect academic freedom, "guards little more than the professors' paychecks."[4] And with few professors, no more than fifty in a typical year, getting fired, one couldn't argue with such an assessment. One university president, who remarked that a cost-cutting measure to dismiss 100 tenured faculty died at his school because, "It's not your university, it's the faculty's university."

And while faculty unions defended tenure as a shield against undue influence or stress on either research or academic freedom, the curious case of Tzvee Zahavy illustrated that, even in 1993, a professor with tenure could do more than the university itself wanted. Zahavy held two posts at once, meeting all the obligations of a full faculty member at both schools. When it was discovered that he was double-dipping, he was unfairly dismissed from both posts, although both universities that had him on the payroll—University of Minnesota and University of North Carolina at Charlotte—suffered, too, since the public had evidence that they asked so little of their other faculty.

VI. TURNING INWARD

The demand for relevance, demanded by students in the 1960s, was restated as a demand for relevance to the students' particularities. Enrollment and applications for women's colleges and historically black colleges and universities surged during the 1980s, when, some argued, such students felt rejected by racism or boorishness at the prestigious state and private

3. Charles Sykes, *Profscam*, p. 258.
4. *New York Times*, Dec. 12, 1993.

210 • THE PRICE OF EXCELLENCE

universities, particularly those in the Northeast. Among black students, such sentiment enjoyed wide popularity, and despite clear signs that white and black college administrators sympathized with them, they found the world created by black colleges more appealing. From 1986 to 1994, applications to the United Negro College Fund member schools increased by 20,000; enrollment at historically black colleges went up 16 percent from 1976 to 1990, with most gains made in the late 1980s. Surveys and anecdotal accounts supported the the simple thesis that black students found black colleges a less stressful, more accomodating place to learn. And federal policy under Presidents Reagan and George Bush encouraged the continued support of black colleges, not only through direct grants, but by involving such colleges in more federal research projects. Although these efforts represented an improvement over past federal policies, presidents of such colleges expressed concern that they would become segmented into wealthy and poor sectors, much like the nation's other universities, by the sheer largess of federal grants. In one instance, Morris Brown College in Atlanta faced a $10 million deficit, prompting some observers to criticize the financial gap between those black colleges with some degree of wealth and those barely struggling to survive. We regard this, however, as a sign that black colleges, not unlike their mostly white counterparts, derive the same successes and failures from efforts to woo research and strong faculty to their campuses.

The strong support black colleges enjoyed from politicians may yet be undermined by a undercurrent of racism and anti-Semitism among both students and faculty. Well-documented incidents of militant black speakers coming to campuses to espouse not only self-segregation, but dubious theories about Jews, inherent qualities of races, and the history of slavery, threaten to undermine the work of the many black students and faculty who strive to earn academic respectability. Already, the once respected name of Howard University has been sullied by an April 19, 1994 incident where black students entered an anti-Semitic rejoinder with a speaker. The university's reputation did not improve when the Jewish reporter who wrote about the speech was attacked verbally by university administrators, faculty, and students. Coming as it does in the nation's capital, the incident at Howard University garnered more headlines than perhaps ordinary; the university faces a crisis of confidence nonetheless. After the Howard speech, letters of protest and cancelled contributions rolled into the offices of the United Negro College Fund, of which Howard is not a member. "We have received letters that have attacked black colleges and have basically said they are breeding grounds for anti-Semitism," fund director William Gray said.[5]

When, for example, colleges allow blacks to segregate themselves in separate hallways at diverse campuses—and make the same concessions for Asians, Hispanics, Slavs, Germans and so on, as is the case now at Brown University—it raises crucial questions about whether such a college recognizes what the rest of the nation has achieved. But some, like Gray, president of the United Negro College Fund, argued that black students, as well as others, are simply seeking some collegiality. "We say it's acceptable to have a Hillel House, a Newman House and Lutheran House," he told the *Washington Post*. "But as soon as we have a Harambee (pan-African) House, it's bad. Instead of asking why are black students separating from whites at white college campuses, we should be asking what is wrong with white America and its institutions that blacks don't feel welcome."[6]

Similarly, women's colleges have allowed themselves to slide perilously close to intellectual domination by ideologues. But their appeal, to the growing number of female students who attend them, appears to be less ideologically connected to feminism. Applications to eighty-four women's colleges in 1994 were up 14 percent since 1991; enrollment, at 98,000 students, was at a fourteen-year high. Students at these colleges say they are attracted to campus life redeemed from the pressures to deal with men, who are apparently viewed as a threat, sexually and academically, to women. At the same time, the same students say they feel no aggression toward men and seek out their company when they see fit. "I think this is a place to get a better education for women," one student told the *Philadelphia Inquirer*. "In an all-women's environment you're more likely to receive more attention, to be able to do things you might not do if men are around."[7] This may appear to some as a happy medium between militant feminism and more circumspect attitudes. Others argue that the growth in applications to women's colleges are unrelated to feelings about men; the presence of an assertive Hillary Clinton, and a Wellesley graduate at that, in the White House has supposedly inspired a new interest in women's colleges as an ample training ground for women seeking professional, academic, and social growth.

However, the fact that schools appealing to the particularities of students suddenly enjoyed wider popularity also indicates something else.

5. *New York Times*, May 4, 1994.
6. *Washington Post*, March 13, 1994.
7. *Philadelphia Inquirer*, September 4, 1994.

Clark Kerr's multiversity, a collection of different interests and institutions under one nameplate, had not succeeded in its most liberal goal: to make available and comfortable the riches of a college education to all groups. Women, blacks, and other statistical minorities felt excluded from this promise, and while some did not reject the institution of higher education, those who did recreated the world not of their mothers and fathers, but of their grandmothers and grandfathers.

VII. FALLING BEHIND

Among the subspecialties of colleges, only community colleges had shown a vibrant ability to grow, during the economic or demographic downturns in the 1970s. But during the 1980s, community colleges recognized that their earlier success would exact a heavy cost. The once politically popular option of the community college—to pay less for two years for what you'd get in a state university, and then transfer with credits earned—increasingly faced statistical challenges. For one, students who entered community colleges were less likely to eventually receive a bachelor's degree at any time. Compounding this obvious shortfall in mission, many of those students served by community colleges—blacks, Hispanics, part-time adult students—were getting diverted away from a full college education by the community college system. In a 1982 study, less than 6 percent of students enrolled in two-year colleges in New York, Illinois, and Washington transferred to a four-year college in a given year. And while community colleges had shown a remarkable level of adaptation in attracting adult students to their campuses throughout the 1970s, that talent withered in the 1980s. Legislators, looking for ways to force community colleges to improve either vocational or transfer-track programs, increasingly questioned the wisdom of classes on hobbies, folklore, and personal development. Two researchers remarked that many community college students were not only avoiding any requirements toward a bachelor's degree, but an associate's as well. "Students are taking the 'transfer' course in photography to gain access to the darkroom, the 'transfer' course in arts to have their paintings criticized, the 'transfer' course in a language so that they can travel abroad."[8] And while community colleges had always had supporters who favored a big tent curriculum, fewer leaders of the colleges could sanction remaining an advanced clearinghouse for disparate information. And yet, when posed with this challenge, many community colleges retreated

---

8. Arthur M. Cohen and John Lombardi, "Can the Community College Survive Success?" *Change*, 1979, p. 26.

to the same ideals which had shaped their success in the 1970s. They strengthened their ties to businesses, creating courses specifically for certain industries, and in certain cases, certain companies. One school in Boston offered classes on commuter trains; another, in Minnesota, offered them in a big shopping mall. By the end of the 1980s, it was not uncommon for community colleges to boast healthy vocational programs, but virtually no courses in the humanities. The vocational track could be defended with clear economic arguments; nevertheless, community colleges face a future of increasing criticism for limiting the educational horizons of their students. And with state universities beginning to catch onto the vocational curriculum offerings, bringing them into direct competition with the two-year colleges, the future of the community colleges clearly is in doubt. In a nationwide surplus of college talent, the community colleges blossomed. But in the 1980s, the economy not only devalued the associate's degree; it devalued the bachelor's. In 1994, the average salary of a recent college graduate, for the first time in fifteen years, went down. But with a college degree needed to simply get in the door of some corporate recruiters, community colleges faced what Karabel and Brint called "one of the great ironies" of their success: they had made college such an opportunity that too many students were attending college. Will they, as is the case on several of the campuses in Florida, remain a poor way-station for students lacking the money to pay for four years at the state college? Or, will they promise both immediate career education and an adequate way to proceed to a bachelor's degree?

VIII. THE CONSUMER IS ALWAYS RIGHT

For all the criticism of tenure and the lamentations that universities were run by faculty, the true power in American colleges and universities had shifted from professors to students. One of the hallmarks of the golden age, selectivity, was a shadow of itself by the 1980s. Demographic shifts reduced the total pool of students, pushing many private colleges to a virtually open admissions policy. From 1980 to 1992, the pool of available college enrollment remained nearly static, and without an upsurge in the rate of college attendance, colleges surely would have lost students. And not only so: many such private colleges, particularly those that had relied on a steady stream of students that had eroded, simply removed all requirements in the curriculum and created, in Riesman's terms, a gentlemen's agreement with its students that if they could pay the tuition and collect a reasonable semblance of credits, a degree would be awarded.

Riesman, who noted with acuity the rise of the professorate in the golden age, argued that student consumerism produced major changes in American colleges, and not simply in admissions policies. He attributed, in his 1980 book *On Higher Education*, the rise of the studies of ethnic issues, women's studies, and the arts to student demands. But these positive changes were accompanied by other, less positive developments. As a higher percentage of qualified students attended college—and at the same time less of these students were available—public universities took advantage of their position as a subsidized source of a college diploma. Recognizing the threat to their enrollments, private colleges resorted to nationwide marketing and fundraising campaigns. Largely, these campaigns failed, costing far too much to make the return on investment worthwhile. Riesman argued that students, even though they were in high demand, wanted to feel selected. Thus, he wryly noted the "Groucho Marx syndrome": a student who is pursued by a college may reject the college altogether, simply because "they prefer to believe that they have been selected, not that they are just one more body to be counted in a formula or for the student grants they can bring with them."[9]

Partly as a result of this false sense of selectivity, American teens built an industry of standardized test preparation schools and college guides and rankings. One estimate of the value of that industry—$100 million—indicates only a portion of the adolescent rage among the upwardly mobile middle class. One preparatory class attracted 80,000 students, who each paid $700 for 13 sessions. Criticism of the main arbiter of establishing excellence—the Scholastic Aptitude Test—grew during the 1980s, partly because of concerns that the test measured cultural intelligence more than raw skills. But, as Riesman noted, the criticism was fairly misguided. Most college applications officials did not use the test exclusively or even as a primary guide. Moreover, only a small percentage of colleges did use the test in any meaningful way. These, not surprisingly, were those that enjoyed the highest prestige.

Prestige, which two decades earlier dictated how colleges received federal research money, appeared to indicate whether they would receive the country's finest students. High school counselors bemoaned the pervasive element of prestige. Students who would be best served by attending a small liberal arts college would find, because of a college ranking, that their choice was no good. The standards of this prestige, however, were elusive and ill-defined. The rankings completed by a major newsweekly,

---

9. David Riesman, *On Higher Education*, p. 112.

for instance, were notorious for allowing the colleges themselves leeway in reporting key data. For example, colleges could decide whether part-time faculty would count toward lowering their student-faculty ratio, a key component of the ratings. Another cottage industry, the informal and highly entertaining "insiders" guides to college campuses, offered an entirely different rating system. Most described a college's social life as a central element, including the best fraternities, athletic facilities, and whether drugs were readily available near the campus. Most mentioned, as part of the list, which professors were worth taking, which classes were "guts," or unde-manding courses that promised easy A's. With social life taking such an enormous role in how students chose where to go, universities frequently met the demand. In addition, by generating greater student interest, some college campuses could create an even greater sense of selectivity. As in the case of Brown University, which attracted the children of politicians, newsmakers, and celebrities, the concurrent rise in national prominence and popularity belied a disturbing loss of academic mission. And yet, be-cause selectivity implied excellence, many poseurs scrambled to set them-selves apart with specialized programs that fit into student interests. But these courses raised questions among supporters of traditional liberal arts that they taught lessons gleaned from reading the morning's headlines — environmental studies and medical ethics—or worse, taught students to trust only opinion and not truth—like semiotics and poststructuralism.

But while selectivity played a huge role in defining which colleges would retain prestige, the larger question of survival still faced every pri-vate college or university. The depression facing most private colleges in the early 1970s had faded in that decade, but the lessons went unlearned. That is, colleges viewed their strength in the size of their budgets. Swarthmore College, for example, was spending $40,000 per student, who was apt to pay only about $20,000 a year in tuition and board. Spending more on new and extravagant programs, especially when the national economy encouraged such growth, became quite fashionable—Yale Uni-versity, for example had to reconsider its relationship with Moscow State University because, in the end of the Cold War, academic diplomacy with Communist countries, once chic, no longer attracted interest or dollars. Lewis Perelman, one of academia's gadflies in the 1980s, suggested that colleges across the country were facing a self-made crisis: too many gradu-ates existed in the national economy, devaluing the diploma, which he called the "junk bond of the human capital economy."[10] Perelman noted that

10. Lewis Perelman, *School's Out*, p. 90.

the recession of the early 1990s struck the middle class hardest, with educated managers suffering the worst. Some universities felt the cuts immediately, with some schools, like Georgetown, cutting professional programs altogether. At the same time, a national cutback in defense spending hit several major universities hard, with billions cut from research allocations. Many of these trends led Perelman to argue that colleges no longer could claim to offer an exclusive privelege. Still, he said, there may be yet other forms of higher education. Looking at the distance learning movement, he predicted that colleges would face impossible financial pressure to release higher learning from the bounds of the classroom. Indeed, by the 1990s, it already had; in 1987, only ten states had distance learning programs and in 1989, all fifty did. A course given by satellite to video hook-ups anywhere in the country could cost one-fourth what it would cost to give the same class "live." Such a trend, Perelman noted, portended disaster for colleges and universities, which were bound to campuses.

Meanwhile, costs to students climbed at astronomical rates. Between 1975 and 1986, the cost for college went up 150 percent. That, Charles Sykes noted, was 25 percent faster than family income. For a family with just one wage earner, the difference was even greater: college costs went up 50 percent faster than family income. While keeping tuition low was never regarded as a serious goal by American colleges, this hyperinflation exacerbated the already-serious issue of access. For wealthy students, gaining a college education was not a problem, either because they had the talent to attend any school, or the money to attend those private colleges that needed their tuitions. Some students even bargained with colleges for better financial aid packages, a virtually unheard of practice a decade, or a lifetime, earlier. For needy students, access was a problem, but federal grants, scholarships, and financial aid could make up the difference, especially if a talented youth wanted to attend a prestigious private university (or, if the university desperately wanted such a student.) Still, black students, who tend to come from lower socioeconomic backgrounds, were attending college in lesser numbers in 1993 than they were in 1982. It is unclear, however, whether the cause of that downturn was strictly economically related.

IX. THE OTHER CHOICE

But for those students whose family income surpassed those requirements for scholarships, but could not support a $100,000 investment for a four-year degree, there remained only one clear choice: state universities. As a result, state campuses with less prestigious faculty enjoyed high student caliber, including campuses in the New York, California, Florida, and North Carolina state systems. These state colleges enjoyed subsidized budgets insured by fairly strong political connections and alumni loyalty, and most exploited this advantage throughout the 1980s. They attracted, with sheer wealth and promises of luxurious research facilities, faculty from tradition- ally more prestigious colleges. Such promise did not escape the wrath of some critics—Sykes chief among them—that such hired hands enobled the campus but did not really teach students, who were paying tuition rates that were going up faster than those of private colleges. The California system appears to have shown the first fissures. There, budget cuts forced classes to be cancelled in some cases, while overcrowding occurred in others. These developments not only prolonged the college careers of students, but also drove others away, to other state systems. Such a development could hardly have been imagined a generation earlier.

Among the students who benefited most from the new competition for tuition money were minorities, and in particular, black students. Special financial aid packages, paid visits to potential campuses, and intense re- cruiting were just some of the ways talented black high school students were wooed to the prestigious campuses. In one generation, artificially limited enrollments of such students were removed and replaced by a sys- tem of artificially inflated enrollments. Notwithstanding those students who clearly deserved a long-denied place in the academy, many black students were—and still are—given obvious assistance in gaining access to the nation's most prestigious universities. While one may argue that universi- ties simply sought to assuage their own liberal guilt over past discrimina- tion, the reality is that federal antidiscrimination laws required colleges to keep black enrollments strong. The results, unfortunately, were not at all what anyone could have expected. Besides applying separate standards of admissions for black students, many American colleges now adopt "race norming" as a way to put black students on an inflated scale of compari- son to their nonblack counterparts, especially on standardized tests. The same advantage is not normally accorded Asian-American students, who tend to excel on the tests.

But for some colleges, wooing black students may constitute an even more cynical approach to student consumerism. David Riesman suggested that at one of the West Coast's most sought-after schools, Reed College, the effort to placate black militant students in the 1970s was motivated by a desire to feel that the college was sufficiently open to earn a reputation of liberalism. Such a cynical approach served both the interests of black students and their white counterparts. Blacks said to whites "you need us more than we need you." In fact, they were right. Just as students at many colleges sought decent gyms, social life and so on, Riesman argued that diversity was a recruiting asset.

The legacy of student consumerism is just now exacting its toll. Grade inflation, where professors rarely give out grades lower than C's, particularly in the humanities and social sciences, is such a severe problem that several universities have promised to monitor professors whose standards appear lax. Stanford's professors recently voted to restore the failing grade, a signal of a national trend among colleges to lend credibility to grade point averages, to which many employers had ceased to pay attention. Recall, for a moment, what Theodore Gross's narrative on open admissions described: a college dominated by a demand for the commodity of a student sitting in a classroom. At CUNY, that trend portended the end of a meritocratic college. And at present, it is the reality at every campus.

X. A CAREER CONCLUDES, THE OSTRACISM COMMENCES

Readers can judge for themselves whether the op-ed piece at the head of this chapter made its point, but it certainly was the most influential thing I wrote in my life. It circled the globe, was reprinted (being brief) in hundreds of newspapers. It came back much magnified to Providence. *The Providence Journal-Bulletin* devoted a front-page story to the item, and one of its columnists wrote sympathetically about it. That was local. What made matters tougher for Brown—given its wrong-headed reading of what should have been a glorious moment for the university—was that I was called to put in an appearance on "The Donahue Show," NBC's morning news, and innumerable radio talk shows, and magazines sent reporters to interview me. I raised questions facing the academy at large, but the locals in Providence took everything personally. And they were right, for they stood for all that betrayed the educational ideals of generations past.

Brown's president called me in to say, "Now, don't embarrass us." I replied; "Don't embarrass yourself." The dean of the college called me in to tell me that "all the professors" found outrageous an article about my views in the *New England Yankee Magazine*. Intimidation by transients such as presidents and deans just confirmed my view that higher education required fundamental reform. So, when the New England Association of Schools and Colleges called me to give a plenary address at its autumn, 1981, meeting, I dealt with the presidents, provosts, deans, and others who stood in the way of change. My message was: "Deans, Provosts, Presidents, we professors don't want your jobs. So don't try to compete with us but respect us for our work." The assembled provosts, presidents, and deans got the message—and not a few wondered what was going on at Brown that one of its professors at the rank of university professor selected such a message as urgent for the world at large.

What I thought I was saying then, and now, is simply that it is time for universities to raise standards and repudiate the failed experiments of the 1970s. I imagined I was stating that the tough professors give generously to the students, but the easy ones exact a heavy price in students' self-respect and sense of achievement. I supposed that people would hear the message of someone who affirmed the established truths of American academic life: hard work and serious thought and deep reflection produced mature and educated citizens. And demanding less in the end betrays the country's future.

Perhaps some heard those—to me self-evident—propositions. Framed in a dramatic form, stated with a measure of irony and, I thought, wit, they should have made their way. But at Brown what was heard was a different message, which was, Brown is a silly, indulgent, trivial place, full of professors who offer the exchange, "I'm all right, you're all right." I had long since discovered that howls of indignation proclaim the presence of uncomfortable truth. Some years earlier, I had told the local Jewish community they were running out of effective leaders and should do something about it. At that point, the community leadership met to discuss what they could do to get me out of town, which turned out to be nothing.

So I knew from the response of the students and the disapproving silence of all my colleagues that I was more right than I had wanted to be, and that, alas, I was right on target about Brown. There I became fair game for all comers. By May, 1982, I was driven out of my department by the chairman, supported by the entire department and by the president and provost; I was denied the right to teach courses of my own choosing by the dean of the college, who treated the matter as a triviality ("so you'll teach something else") and did not explain her decision; I was even excluded from faculty meetings.

Within the months that followed the international uproar over the op-ed piece, an appointment in my field to my department was made without my being consulted—or even informed. I found out when I noticed a new name on the mail boxes and asked the secretary who it was. When I complained to the provost, he dismissed my complaint by saying, "The chairman has the right to do that." A tenure decision was reached from which my vote was excluded, contrary to the rules of the university. I was not even informed that the decision was at hand. No rules protected my rights as a citizen of the department and university—when the administration and faculty decided to abrogate them.

The chairman—Sumner B. Twiss—would not approve a new course I wished to create and persuaded the dean of the college and the relevant faculty committee to reject it. No one bothered even to tell me, and when I asked the dean—the same woman, Harriet Sheridan, who had told me everyone was mad at what I was saying—she denied it, saying only, "We put it on hold."

I: "Until when?"

She: "The future."

I: " You wouldn't do this to an assistant professor—censor the freedom to teach! Doesn't the university professor rank confer any rights at all?"

She: "No."

The upshot was, my professional judgment within my own field was dismissed; my freedom to teach what I thought best (a freedom my rank as university professor ought to have secured) was taken away; and my right as a citizen of the department to participate in decisions was denied me. Tenure affords only just so much protection: a paycheck for doing the job; no more, no less. Beginning to end, the provost did not answer my memos of complaint.

Not surprisingly, in my protest against the degradation of higher education and the dismissal of learning, I had left myself a tenured pariah, a well-compensated nonperson. And, everybody at Brown took for granted that I was unemployable elsewhere, so no indignity sufficed to pay me back for the monumental embarrassment that I had brought upon their heads. For a moment, I was more famous than God, and, for a long time afterward, I lived out the fate of the whistle-blower. For I had called into question the educational value of the previous decade's changes ("reforms") and pointed out that the kind of higher education offered at the more stylish universities and colleges not only did not benefit, but damaged the students. We professors—so I said, and kept saying—taught wrong and pernicious lessons of a social and emotional kind, but we taught little of intellectual worth or academic value.

XI. SCHOLARSHIP MAKES NO DIFFERENCE HERE

In the 1970s I had received by then honorary degrees or medals from Columbia University (the Medal for Excellence), the University of Chicago, and the University of Cologne, and a Von Humboldt Prize. More of the same were to follow in the 1980s, but that would made no difference at Brown. Later in the decade, the University of Bologna would confer its

Dottore ad Honorem in Scienze Politiche (indirizzo storico-politico), in the celebration of the 900th anniversary of the university; the University of Rochester the degree of Doctor of Humane Letters (L.H.D.); the Collège de France, its Medal of Collège de France on the occasion of my lecture there; and so on. None of this mattered; even routine congratulations were withheld. I ran an NEH Summer Seminar for College Teachers and organized for the same season an NEH Summer Institute for College Teachers, but the administration (which benefited financially from these activities) did not take note. When my term on the Council of the National Endowment for the Humanities (1978–84) came to an end, President Reagan appointed me to membership in the Council of the National Endowment for the Arts (1984–90), one of only a handful of people to serve on both councils. Brown took the overhead but did not take notice.

The reason was partly personal, but more a matter of policy. In fact, Brown's president, Howard Swearer, did not consider that scholarship made a difference, unless the scholarship came from favored professors. Most of them published very little, and only a few of whom achieved any sort of national distinction; he had a proclivity to favor the more Waspish ones, on the one side, and the blacks, on the other. No objective criterion pertained. He certainly did not want Brown to achieve the national recognition that it had gotten in Judaic studies. That would deliver a message about Brown he did not wish to circulate. Jewish money, yes; a formidable presence for Judaic learning within the ordinary curriculum, no. That is probably why he gave an honorary degree to Gore Vidal, notorious leftist and an anti-Semite. So he projected a well-defined image of what he wished to see, a college that not surprisingly resembled Princeton. That was not the only policy that that administration brought to realization. Another, more important one, corrupted the university at its very heart: its teaching function.

Under the Swearer administration, which spanned the late 1970s onward at Brown, solid scholarly achievement no longer would make a difference to careers or the conduct of universities. Instead, popularity among students took over to dictate who would enjoy priority and who would lose out. Spending time with students, not in education but in mere companionship, took on substance on its own. Professors who published came under the suspicion of neglecting not only teaching but also the new assignment of student-sitting. Professors who did not publish much became deans. Deans with dubious, if any, scholarly qualifications of distinction became provosts. But incompetence reaching its highest level presents no surprises. What made Brown special? It was that provosts lacking all academic

distinction presumed to dictate educational policy to accomplished professors—blowing cigar smoke in their faces, interrupting them when they tried
to explain their views, keeping them waiting for appointments, and abruptly
closing meetings. Professors in the Brown English Department told me they
would not meet with the then provost in his office, but only in some neutral setting, at lunch for example, because they found meetings in his office humiliating and demeaning.

Swearer carried no academic philosophy and found guidance in no
academic goals. He did not measure success in terms of scholarly greatness he might bring to the campus but only in crass terms, if possible,
fundraising, or, at all costs, popularity. Swearer took for his academic model
his fantasy of Princeton, his own college; including its snobbery and anti-
Semitism, not its remarkably high standards in several academic fields. He
forgot how much Princeton had gained from proximity to the world-class
research center, the Institute for Advanced Study, with its stratospheric
achievements in mathematics and theoretical physics in Einstein's time.
He brought to Brown, then a national research university, the uncomprehending educational standards of a college president, valuing the college's
power to attract large numbers of wealthy applicants (like Princeton and
Harvard), but by the end making the university a third-rate college.

Compared to the great men and women who had built the powerhouse
universities of the 1950s and 1960s, Swearer attained no stature at all.
Emerging from the Ford Foundation into his first presidency, at Carleton
College, Swearer found Brown a dead-end, for, as his presidency wound
down, he was not chosen for the presidencies of the major national foundations as they opened up. Nor did he gain the executive position in any
great museum or other institution of culture, although he pursued such jobs.
In one case, the chairman of the trustees simply told him he would not be
a serious candidate. When he left Brown's presidency, it was not for a still
more prestigious position, but merely to a professorship at Brown itself,
as though he were a publishing scholar who had earned himself a chair.
But the professorship was fabricated and empty, since he could not have
earned it by the ordinary academic criteria. So his disastrous presidency
left him with a booby prize. All he had done was raise a lot of money—
and then waste it.

His immediate predecessors, who had brought Brown from obscurity
to national prominence in a number of academic areas—mathematics being the greatest—would not have recognized the place Swearer left behind
at his death. Henry Wriston, president from 1937 to 1956, took a school
that belonged to the Ivy League only because it got to play football with

Harvard once a year and left a contender not in sports but in sciences. Wriston found superstars to staff each of his academic departments, supported them when they raised standards to their own level, and insisted on excellence in making future appointments. His successor, Barnaby Keeney, another benevolent dictator, built upon Wriston's success. In 1966 he went on to serve as founding chairman of the National Endowment for the Humanities, appointed by President Johnson. His successor lasted a brief spell, but Brown's final professional and academic president, Donald Hornig, coped brilliantly with the problems brought on by the end of the age of academic expansion and left Brown with a faculty of considerable and solid merit. Swearer would change all that.

One exemplary case shows the character of the change. My colleagues and I were formally instructed by the provost that our standards were too high, we demanded too much, and we would therefore be penalized. It came about in an odd, telling case. Specifically, in the mid 1980s, the program in Judaic studies declined to renew the contract of a first-term (three-year) assistant professor, on the grounds that (1) he had published nothing much since coming to Brown; (2) he had not even published the dissertation that he had completed for a degree conferred before his coming to Brown. Further, the writing he had done—the dissertation itself—we read and unanimously found wooden and dull, full of bad and obscure formulations and banal ideas. We took the view that in the tenure decision that would be made approximately a year and a half later, he was unlikely to meet our standards of achievement, and we preferred to renew our search in his field.

He appealed to various committees, characterizing criticism as mere personal abuse. The other professors who heard his gripe of course concurred—they too could not meet the standards we deemed ordinary. The provost sided with them. He wrote me a memorable letter, in which he stated: "You have imposed a standard higher than that prevailing in the university overall." When the provost of a university punishes a department for too-high standards, the university is finished. The punishment was to give the appellant a one-year terminal renewal, moving him to another department for that year. I resigned as codirector of the program; in reply to my letter of resignation I received a mere acknowledgement. Everyone was glad—I above all.

For the next three years, 1986–89, I taught only a handful of highly qualified students; never did Brown lack superb ones, even in its worst times.

XII. A TIME OF TROUBLES

With no harbor for refuge at home, in Brown, I found navigating a stormy world beyond equally parlous and uncertain. To explain: passing fifty in 1982, I had hoped Harry Wolfson's prediction a decade earlier would come true. In my conversations with him during his last months of life, I had asked him: When does the abuse stop? Do scholars ever debate scholarly issues, or is a scholarly career a sentence of death by gossip and innuendo? He told me two things. First, he said, if you don't want to be abused, don't write and don't publish; don't say anything new if you do; and above all, don't criticize other people. But, second, no matter what you do, people will finally get used to you, one way or the other, by the time you're fifty. I turned fifty in 1982 and detected not much change in the politics of scholarship. But just afterward, in 1983–84, I slogged through one confrontation after another.

The first came in a sequence of violently hostile, personally nasty reviews of a book of mine, *Judaism: The Evidence of the Mishnah*, which stirred up much discussion by insisting that all of the documents of ancient Judaism not be homogenized into a single Judaism but that each must be read in terms of its own system and structure. That routine approach to the ancient writings, commonplace in other fields, represented a considerable departure from the then-prevailing approach. One of the reviews, by Shaye J. D. Cohen, whom Brown later on would (predictably) choose as my successor when I left in 1990, condemned not only me but my graduate students of that period, whom in his review he called a bunch of ignoramuses. By appointing him later, Brown repudiated twenty years of its own educational work.

These reviews represented not debates on substantive issues, whether of results or method. They aimed at discrediting me as a scholar, denying my students valid credentials as well (one of my students, holding a Brown Ph.D., taught for some years at Haifa University, and found Israeli colleagues refused to call him "doctor"—titles matter there—but only "mister"). Not surprisingly, JTSA formed the main source. A few months after Cohen's review, and just before he died, Saul Lieberman of JTSA wrote a remarkably violent review of part of my translation of the Palestinian Talmud for the *Journal of the American Oriental Society* (a copy reached me on July 28, 1984, my fiftieth-second birthday), advising people to toss the book into the wastebasket—all on the basis of Lieberman's correction of the mistranslation of a few words here and there. At the end of this review, *JAOS* further announced that I had declined to reply. But what I had refused to do was *read* the review in advance, in the (stupid) theory that that would be undignified. The *JAOS* editor, Jack Sasson, quite misrepresented the facts. And afterward he refused to correct that misrepresentation. When, later on, I did wish to reply, he did not answer my letter asking for the right to reply, nor did any officer of the American Oriental Society respond either. When I reached the then president by phone, he apoplectically said, "No," and hung up on me. So much for the integrity of those in control of the media of scholarship.

When I actually read the review, I was greatly relieved. Knowing it was coming, wondering what sort of Parthian shot Lieberman might have fabricated, I was concerned that I not turn out to have misunderstood the document, its main lines of discourse, the structure of its arguments—its total character and message. Given the difficult character of the work—without an up-to-date dictionary, without a critical text, without a contemporary commentary or an exegetical guide of any modern standing—I wondered whether I might have misunderstood entire passages. What Lieberman did not say therefore brought considerable reassurance. And it was why the review missed its mark.

By specifically limiting his criticism to the trivialities of a handful of misconstrued words and phrases—none of them vastly changing the larger meaning or sense of the context—Lieberman had not mentioned what concerned me, nor had he given an overall analysis of the work. Instead he wanted Chicago to cancel the translation project and repudiate it. And what he did say proved unpersuasive. The publisher, Chicago, declined. Instead, they published an advertisement in the *Biblical Archaeology Review,* headed, "Proud to publish . . . " And they published all thirty-five volumes at a far more rapid pace than we had ever contemplated.

In fact, when we wade through the violent language he used, we find that Lieberman never alleged that I fundamentally misunderstood the context and meaning of a discussion, its purpose, and its structure. If he could have said so, he would have—with pleasure. He didn't because he couldn't. His review, which was published posthumously, made him famous outside of his small circle of admirers. When, before his death, he had showed it to Elie Wiesel, the latter advised him not to print it, because it would be the one thing that would define his memory. And so it came to pass.

But Lieberman's intent—to destroy me and discredit my *oeuvre*—was not his alone. In fact, the project was widely known long before it broke into public view. The plan was shared by a fair part of the sectarian and Israeli scholarly world, the rabbis and the seminary professors. I found that fact out when, a few weeks later, after the review was printed, an anonymous friend in New York City sent me a copy of a letter written by Morton Smith to William Braude, a Providence rabbi and self-styled scholar. In that letter, Smith forwarded Lieberman's review to Braude with instructions to do with it what he planned. This involved circulating the review hither and yon— throughout Brown and Rhode Island to begin with, and among the rabbis everywhere.

The many favorable reviews the translation was receiving (and would continue to receive) of course made no difference; these Smith and Braude and their cohorts did not circulate. At that same time the dean of the faculty of Hebrew Union College–Jewish Institute of Religion, Cincinnati, reprinted the review and sent a copy to every member of the faculty of that far-flung institution, in Los Angeles, Cincinnati, New York, and Jerusalem. Within a few weeks of that mailing, I got another anonymous letter, this one from Jerusalem which announced, "The entire scholarly community of Jerusalem rejoices that you have received your comeuppance from Saul Lieberman." I had no doubt that that was so. The fall of 1983 brought no respite.

We have now reached December of that same year. The Society of Biblical Literature had given me the accolade of presenting a named lecture at its national meeting, in Chicago, in the series, "How My Mind Has Changed (Or Stayed the Same)." It was a considerable occasion for me; I was to that point the youngest scholar asked to give that lecture. That evening, just before the lecture, Morton Smith came over to greet me and my No. 1 son, Samuel, then a student at the University of Chicago, who had come for the occasion. He showed great warmth toward us both, saying to my son; "Oh, I remember attending your bar mitzvah." When my lecture concluded and questions were invited from the floor, Smith proceeded to attempt a public assassination of the father of the bar mitzvah boy. For that, but not much else, Smith would be remembered.

The evening went along uneventfully until the end. Then, when my lecture was concluded and the respondent had finished, the chairman of the meeting, W. D. Davies, asked for questions from the floor. There was only one. All eyes settled on Morton Smith. Instead of asking his question where he stood, he ascended the podium, took the microphone, and opened and read his prepared address. What he did was simply denounce me, declaring that Lieberman's review had said what had to be said. His written-out remarks went on for some twenty minutes. I was called on to reply. I waited for a moment, for Smith to return to his chair.

But he never did. Rather, turning his back on me as I began to respond, he began to walk through the audience, passing out copies of the Lieberman review, which he had had printed in New York and carried with him in a plastic bag to Chicago. The audience was uneasy and embarrassed. I stopped talking and waited. The truth was, I couldn't think of anything to say anyhow. Then I noted something that I found disturbing. The people were laughing at Smith and throwing his handout onto the floor in his presence. I quieted the audience and drew a laugh by saying; "Well, things don't always turn out the way we expect them to." With Smith continuing his handout, the laughter went on. I then added, "But don't you laugh at Morton Smith. He has been a great scholar and he was my teacher. I will not repudiate him. And don't you laugh at him." Davies, silent to that point, immediately called it quits. For his part, he had nothing to say—not even a word of apology on behalf of the Society of Biblical Literature at the fiasco that their effort to honor me had produced.

Smith paid a heavy price for mounting this bizarre demonstration of his. From 1984 until his death some years later, he found himself isolated and ignored. Having embarrassed the Society of Biblical Literature, he was not again asked to present a plenary address, nor did he review books in the principal journals, present major papers, or otherwise receive the hearing of the scholarly world that he had formerly earned. He died a lonely, bitter man, lacking all influence beyond his narrow circle of believers. Setting out to destroy his student's career, he ruined his own.

If, by that point, any American or Canadian scholar had missed out on the circus, Hershel Shanks in the *Biblical Archaeological Review* printed Smith's speech verbatim, and reprinted most of Lieberman's now famous review in its next issue. In the editor's defense, I must say, he bore me no personal malice. It was simply his perception of the normal conduct of academic business in this field. Indeed, some years later, in 1993, after Shanks was convicted of plagiarism by a Jerusalem court and ordered to pay huge damages to an Israeli scholar whose work he had printed without permission in one of his books, I called attention to that fact in a Florida Jewish paper, whereupon he replied with the expected personal attack and described me as "a broken old man." Privately, though, at the same time he wrote me a quite friendly letter, sending me a copy of his reply in advance and also asking me to go out on the road with him and conduct insulting debates—whereby we could both make a lot of money. That struck me as a bit cynical, but also persuaded me that the man was not at all malicious, just venal.

As 1983 passed into 1984, the possibility of a chair at Harvard Divinity School came to me. That was because the chairman of the search committee, John Strugnell, called and asked me to apply, with the promise that I would get the chair. Commenting on the Chicago fiasco, he said; "Even the people who are not admirers of yours thought you carried yourself with dignity and honor." Expecting nothing, I did send in a resume and letter. When, in mid-January, on behalf of the search committee Strugnell brought my name to the Divinity School faculty and proposed that I be called to an interview—and I was the committee's first choice—the Harvard Divinity School faculty, most of whom I had never met personally (and the books of none of whom had I ever reviewed unfavorably, as a matter of fact), voted unanimously not even to invite me to come for an interview. Strugnell's despondent phone call that night informed me that the faculty would prefer to interview a more "irenic" candidate. They did not have to meet me personally to know I was not sufficiently "irenic" for their requirements—and who can disagree?

That result did not surprise me, since I had already received a letter from Yale's Department of Religious Studies, engaged in a similar search some years earlier, which announced, "Granted, you're the best in the world, but we have to choose what's best for Yale," which meant, I was told, absolutely anyone but Neusner. I replied saying, I doubt that the chairman of the search committee for a professor in surgery would have written such a disgraceful confession of academic bankruptcy. Yale ended up appointing a Brown alumnus whom I had taught as an undergraduate and had not wanted in my doctoral program.

The decision at Harvard came within a few weeks of yet another defining moment. In December, 1983, I had received an invitation from the Israel Historical Society to come to Jerusalem to deliver the keynote address at the meeting in celebration of the fiftieth anniversary of the journal, *Zion*. Would I send the manuscript off for translation into Hebrew, they asked. In January I wrote the lecture and sent it off. I took as my topic the Israeli tradition of scholarship on the history of the Jews and Judaism set forth in the pages of *Zion* over the past fifty years. It struck me as not only appropriate, but also as an elegant compliment. I was asked to talk about "methodology in Talmudic history." Well and good, how better to honor my audience than to review what they have published and identify the governing methodological principles and criticize them. I was surprised at the wit and maturity of the invitation—ask the critic to state his criticism, then argue. Maybe someone will learn something; perhaps someone's mind may be changed. It never entered my mind that all they really wanted me to do was come and tell them how great they were.

To prepare for the lecture, a student and I systematically reread them. I did not trust my own judgment; perhaps I would miss some element of critical thinking, expressed in a way I might not grasp. That is not how matters came out. What we found was simply a mass of uncritical and infantile paraphrases of rabbinic stories and fables. Every single author took for granted the literal historical facticity of all the Talmudic sources. In all of them, the writers took for granted that if a Talmudic passage said someone said something, he really said it, in exactly those words. If the story said he did something, he really did it, that day, in that way. In other words, much to my amusement, I found myself in an intellectually primitive world, which had yet to give up the medieval mode of reading holy books. In biblical studies this kind of historical writing finds no hearing; it is dismissed as fundamentalist and credulous. So, in my address, I explained with some care that, in accord with the prevailing principles of historical scholarship, nothing *Zion* had printed in the area of Talmudic history could find a hearing in critical scholarship. And I cited chapter and verse in explaining why what they had printed was worthless. I went on to lecture the Israeli scholars on the kind of historical work that I thought these documents can sustain and how to go about formulating worthwhile problems for investigation.

The topic was, "Methodology in Talmudic History." What I said was moderate and civil, but uncompromising. The following brief sample gives the flavor of the whole:

> When we speak of methodology, we may mean many things. To specify the very few things under discussion here, let us begin with the simplest possible definition. The method by which we work tells us the questions we choose to pose and the means we use to find the answers. Our method tells us what we want to know and how we can find it out. Method then testifies to the point at which we begin, the purpose for which we work. A sound method will guide us to questions both pertinent to the sources under study and also relevant to broader issues of the day. The one without the other is merely formal, on the one side, or impressionistic and journalistic, on the other. Proper method will tell us what sources we must read and how to interpret them. Above all, sound method will match the issues we raise to the information at hand, that is, will attend especially to questions of historical epistemology: what we know and how we know it.
>
> We cannot raise in the abstract the issues of historical methodology in Talmudic history. Talmudic history is a field that people practice. We cannot ignore what people actually do in favor of some preferred theory of what we think they should do. It furthermore would defy the honorable occasion at hand, to speak about Talmudic history without paying appropriate attention to the journal we celebrate here and now. Accordingly, let us first of all turn our attention to *Zion* itself and ask how Talmudic history is practiced in its pages: the methodology demonstrated here.
>
> The answer is in three parts. First, Talmudic history constitutes a

strikingly unimportant field in *Zion*. From 1935 (Vol. 1) to 1983 (Vol. 48), the journal published 476 articles, at the rate of approximately ten per volume. Of these, no more than twenty-eight in all fall into the category of Talmudic history, approximately one article for every two volumes. Talmudic history accounts, in all, for little more than 5 percent of all articles published in the fifty years we celebrate—a strikingly small proportion.

The second and third observations about the status and methodology of Talmudic history in *Zion* require less exposition.

The second is that when people practice Talmudic history in *Zion*, they limit their discussion to Talmudic history in particular. The field does not encompass its period, but only one set of sources emergent from its period. While many of the scholars represented in *Zion* draw upon sources outside the Talmud, none of the articles deals with a problem outside the Talmud. Accordingly, Talmudic history in the journal at hand finds definition as the study of historical problems pertinent to a given source, rather than to a chronological period to which that source attests.

The third observation is that the methodology of reading the literary sources, which define the problems and solutions of Talmudic history in *Zion*, begins in an assumption universally adopted by the scholars of the journal (and not only there). Whatever the Talmud says happened happened. If the Talmud attributes something to a rabbi, he really said it. If the Talmud maintains that a rabbi did something, he really did it. So among the twenty-one articles under discussion, I find not a single one that asks the basic critical questions with which historical study normally commences: How does the writer of this source know what he tells me? How do I know that he is right? On the contrary, the two Talmuds serve, in *Zion*, as encyclopedias of facts about rabbis and other Jews in the Land of Israel and Babylonia. The task of the historian is to mine the encyclopedias and come up with important observations on the basis of the facts at hand. The work of the historian then is the collection and arrangement of facts, the analysis of facts, the synthesis of facts. It is not in the inquiry into the source and character of the facts at hand. Just as, for the literary scholar, the text constitutes the starting point of inquiry, so for the historian, the text at hand defines the facts and dictates the character of inquiry upon them. This is the case, beginning and end. . . .

The formulation is civil, factual, reasoned. It was a constructive address, if not a very comforting one. So I got myself disinvited by return mail. When I wrote to the president, a man named Menahem Stern, whom I had received at Brown University and entertained in my home, he simply did not answer my letter, nor did anyone else. Thereafter, I never heard from Stern again before he was murdered, under mysterious circumstances, in a Jerusalem park some years later.

I turned in the winter of 1984 to a friend in Germany, Martin Hengel, who was also close to Stern. I asked him not to support my position but only to tell Stern that the action taken by the Israel Historical Society was a serious one, with weighty consequences. He declined to do so. He did not want to get involved. I did not think Hengel did Stern any favor by pretending nothing had happened. But I did not then call him "a good German," in the tradition of those who decades earlier had heard nothing and seen nothing and turned their back. All I did was write and say, "If you were in my place, and I in yours, I would have told him it was a serious matter." In reply—and writing in English, not in German, as he always had done—Hengel declared he would not attend the conference that I had organized in his honor at Brown University to be held a few months later, in late July, 1984. That conference moreover was to produce the volume of scholarly essays ("*festschrift*") in his honor. So he did not come, but we did hold the conference and we did publish the volume as planned.

Naturally, I published the article elsewhere, so the Israel Historical Society accomplished nothing in trying to suppress its critic. And I published it again on two anniversaries of the disinvitation, first the fifth, then the tenth. So the 1980s unfolded. But worse was to come later on.

XIII. GETTING FIRED—AGAIN

As soon as I could leave Brown, having accomplished my goals, I did. But, along the way, I also got myself fired once more. This time, it was as editor of a scholarly monograph series that I had created and sustained at Brown. When I went off as university professor emeritus, I discovered through a third party that I had been fired from that job. Let me explain.

I had come to Brown to raise my children in Providence. As our fourth and youngest child, our only daughter, worked her way through her high school years, I realized I had accomplished my goal in Providence. The children had grown up in a stable, lovely community, in a city we all loved, among neighbors on Vassar Avenue who formed an intimate family. Opportunities to move on now presented themselves, and faced with fresh opportunities, I took one of them. It came about through my service on the National Council on the Arts, the citizens' advisory council of the National Endowment for the Arts. There I had met and grown to admire and like a Florida state senator, Bob Johnson of Sarasota, whom President Reagan had placed on the council in 1986. Senator Johnson and I shared a basic philosophy of how we thought public programs in the arts should be conducted, and from an alliance, a friendship developed. A man of gruff demeanor, I called him a pseudo-redneck, because he wore a veneer of tough hide over a core of sentiment, sensibility, and wit. He had the gift, also, of perspicacity, in council discussions seeing to the heart of matters more quickly and more accurately than I ever could. In the Florida senate at that time he served on the committee on higher education. In that context, in 1988 he asked me, "Why in the world don't you come down and join the Florida system?"

Why not indeed? For years nothing had held me to Brown except my wife's and my premier commitment to our children's upbringing. Now, there was no need to stay in Providence either. A year later, in the spring of 1989, I told Senator Johnson that I would indeed like to move into a huge state university system, where there were rules and standards that did not require negotiation every morning. Within the system, I wanted to live on the west coast of Florida, which, I had heard and soon found out, preserved much of the state's natural beauty. At the same time I approached Brown's provost and asked whether I might get the benefit of early retirement; I was then fifty-seven and eligibility began at sixty. But the program was to be phased out before that time, so I would never become eligible. For the first time in fifteen years, I got a prompt and favorable reply—indeed, a cordial one: of course. Brown would pay me for another five years, whatever I chose to do. The conditions placed no restrictions on what I might do later on. I took the deal and then decided on the next step in my career.

Within days I had a chat with the president of the University of South Florida, went down for a lecture and a visit some weeks later, and, considering other offers and possibilities that came my way at that time, chose the University of South Florida as the next chapter in my life. After I completed my research year at the Institute for Advanced Study, my wife and I moved to St. Petersburg. My original intent was to teach only one semester, supported as I was by Brown's funds as well, but I quickly came to like and trust my colleagues and to respect the professionalism of that unpretentious campus. A year later, I agreed to teach full-time through the academic year, as I have ever since. Driving out of Providence en route to Princeton, I determined that I would never retrace the road back.

My leaving Brown produced two unanticipated consequences, one trivial, the other important. The trivial one is quickly told. It came about a year after I left, in 1991, when my former colleagues chose as my successor Shaye J. D. Cohen—not a doctoral alumnus of Brown's, whom they had taught, but the man who had declared Brown's doctoral alumni a bunch of ignoramuses. In that way, Ernest Frerichs, Wendell Dietrich, and their colleagues repudiated twenty years of their own work, since more than a few of the doctoral alumni of Brown had to their credit far more substantial accomplishments in scholarship and publication than Cohen did.

But the important consequence took place during the year in Princeton. When I left Brown for the Institute for Advanced Study in August, 1989, I thought I left behind some co-workers, colleagues, and friends. I soon discovered that I had been much lonelier at Brown than I had ever imagined. Toward the end of that year, I got myself fired as the editor-in-chief of Brown Judaic Studies, the scholarly monograph series that I founded in 1976.

To understand the story of that series, which my colleagues stole—without ever confronting me with their decision—we have to begin with my intent in founding it. Brown Judaic Studies was not a sectarian series. I had to begin it to provide an outlet for my doctoral students' dissertations and some overflow of my own monograph probes, which my publisher, E. J. Brill, could not cope with; they were then publishing my forty-three volume Mishnah-Tosefta translation and commentary. I opened the series to all comers and provided a medium of scholarly exchange for a wide variety of viewpoints and authors; I printed not a few books that I thought methodologically in error. In doing so, I gave to others the opportunity for a fair hearing that had been denied me for twenty years, from 1960 to 1980, by those in charge of the media of scholarly publication in the United States. During those two decades I could not publish a scholarly book in the United States. Fortunately, the late Frits C. Wieder, Jr., of E. J. Brill, gave me a lavish, international hearing, and the locals could not stop it.

Not only were publishing opportunities severely restricted to "our crowd," but such monograph series as then existed were managed on a very narrow basis. I wanted to make mine an expression of the scholarly judgment of a variety of colleagues. So, when I created Brown Judaic Studies, therefore, I determined to make certain everyone had his or her say in a reputable monograph series. And that is precisely how I ran the various monograph series I conducted elsewhere, at E. J. Brill, for instance, during that period and since then as well. Anyone who examines the titles I have published in this and my Brill series, including work by Israeli scholars I never thought well conceived, knows how I have opened doors, even to people who closed doors to me.

As it happens, I also financed the series, book by book (excluding my own, which made their own way on ample sales), and I wrote the majority of the volumes. I donated the copyrights to the trusteeship of Brown University, with instructions to allow free use of everything. For the whole of this series' history until June 30, 1990, I solicited, arranged for critical reading, and saw through press the rest of the approximately 225 volumes published between the time I founded the series and the time I left Brown University, in 1990.

Now, when I woke up on July 1, 1990, I had no reason to imagine that there would be any change in my editorship of the series, since, as I left Brown University in 1990, by vote of the Brown Corporation (equivalent to its board of trustees), I held the title of professor emeritus. That meant I was a continuing member of the Brown faculty, and naturally I took for granted I would continue as editor-in-chief of the series and its manager. So, when I organized South Florida Studies in the History of Judaism, at the request of the Scholars Press board, I carefully differentiated the established series from the new one, so that there would be no overlap or duplication in the future. The new South Florida series was approved by the Scholars Press board only after they, and I, were entirely satisfied that each series under my direction would serve a distinctive purpose.

That is how matters stood in June, 1990. No one else at Brown had the qualifications or competence or the scholarly standing to solicit and evaluate manuscripts in the history of Judaism. None could hope to keep the series going. When I had founded the monograph series, I did so on my own. No one at Brown University then assisted in any way, although as I said, many were perfectly happy to attach themselves to my work, and I let them. Once the series got under way, I invited some colleagues from Brown and elsewhere to join in the editorial direction of the series. None of them did much; none of them solicited a manuscript for the series or otherwise advanced its interests or its work. I never believed that they could, but I wanted to give them a share in my work.

But, when, in early July, 1990, I moved from my position as university professor and The Ungerleider Distinguished Scholar of Judaism Studies at Brown to emeritus status at Brown and also to my new professorship as Distinguished Research Professor of Religious Studies at University of South Florida, these other editors took over the series. Without consulting me, without discussing with me, or without even informing me of their decisions, the persons in charge of Judaic Studies at Brown, in consultation with the then administration of that university, simply took over the series. They so informed Scholars Press, without indicating to Scholars Press that their actions were taken unilaterally and without consulting me or winning my approval (which I should never have given, having no confidence whatever that those I left behind could sustain this series in a competent manner. Time proved me right). One day I was the editor-in-chief, in charge of all business of the series. The next day, Scholars Press informed me through its production manager that someone else was in charge and I had no more say in the series. It was that simple. So—appropriately indeed—ended my career of twenty-two years at Brown, and my fourteen years as founder and editor-in-chief of that series.

Because of this, I resigned from my position as university professor emeritus and The Ungerleider Distinguished Scholar of Judaic Studies Emeritus, thus declining to maintain a relationship with my chair at Brown. So far as anyone knows, this is the first time in the more than two centuries of the history of Brown University that an emeritus professor rejected that title and severed all relationship to that university. I insisted that the Brown Corporation publicly rescind the titles that it had wanted to confer upon me when I was awarded early retirement. And I required the *Brown Alumni Monthly* to inform the several generations of Brown alumni whom I had taught that I no longer had any relationship of any kind with the university that they and I had long valued. This the magazine did, in its predictably ungracious manner. Of course, there was no point in my resigning as editor-in-chief, since that office had simply been taken away from me. There was nothing from which to resign. None of the letters that I wrote in protest was ever answered by any of the parties to whom I addressed them, not one: not President Vartan Gregorian, not Provost Maurice Glicksman or Provost Frank Rothman, not Professor Ernest S. Frerichs, not Professor Calvin Goldscheider—none of them. It is a sorry story, one that disgraces the responsible parties and their university.

For a brief moment I supposed that the reason Frerichs did not call me to discuss, or even to announce, his action was that he was then hospitalized with hip surgery. But during the summer I learned otherwise. A long-time co-worker and friend, Herbert Basser, at Queens University in Canada, had sent me a book for Brown Judaic Studies, which I had accepted. Now, I asked him to move the book into the new series, South Florida Studies in the History of Judaism, because it would fit better with the special interests I planned to emphasize there. When he agreed, he got a phone call from Frerichs, threatening that if he published in the South Florida series, he would lose all scholarly respectability and would never again publish a scholarly book. Basser stuck by his decision. When I learned of the exchange, in late summer, 1990, I realized that Frerichs was able to communicate from his hospital bed—with anybody but me.

My sometime colleagues at Brown gained nothing in their odd conduct. Their series collapsed and from 1990 forward had to go begging for projects, while mine has flourished. Since it was founded, the South Florida Studies series has taken over the major part of the monographic publication in Judaic Studies in the discipline of religious studies, with Brown Judaic Studies now a remote second and declining fast. In our first four years, from 1990, we published more than one hundred titles – approximately one book every two weeks for forty-eight months. A comparison of the number and quality of our new titles with the new titles published by Brown Judaic Studies in the same period tells the entire tale. Apart from my own titles in my Talmud translation, which Scholars Press asked me to leave in the old series, their list is negligible and lightweight.

So the upshot is simple: No one gained in the way in which the editorial direction of the series was taken from me, but Brown University lost what it ought to have prized and treated with respect and honor. I mean, not this series, but their own *dignitas et gravitas*. But that is how it was meant to be: neither persons nor universities can be better than they are. The only surprise comes in finding out just what they are. And, anyhow, I was used to getting fired—and I was used to Brown. The one thing I ought not to have been was surprised. But I was.

XIV. RESTORING REASON, RENEWING RATIONALITY

In the past twenty years, not a single important step in defining the tasks of universities has been taken. We professors go through the motions of curricula that have yet to prove their value. Our policy on the campus is simple: Do whatever you want. Take this or that or nothing very much. In these pages I take as my source of bad examples the university I have known longest and best, which is Brown. But while that university defines the extreme in requiring no particular courses but only a major, Brown does signal the failure of purpose and the absence of goals that characterize higher education in the two decades beyond the deluge that inundated the academy in the late 1960s and early 1970s. But where to start?

Higher education still finds its definition in the answers to three questions: (1) who teaches (2) what (3) to whom? Twenty years of dismantling the received programs and familiar purposes of colleges and universities focused on politics and personalities, that is, answering who should teach whom. Curiously, the sorts of people who have been in control of universities for twenty or thirty years, Roger Kimball's "tenured radicals," have had slight interest in *what* is taught. That, then, is their weak point; they know full well whom they want to teach and who is to do the teaching. They spell out in detail what is not to be taught, which is, in general, the curriculum of dead white males So they cannot explain what is to be taught, therefore also why it is to be taught.

In a strategy of sustained assault upon the pointless mélange of topics and purposeless information that today stands behind the baccalaureate degree, we begin the work of reconstruction that is not only urgent, but also timely. For twenty years after the revolutions of the late 1960s have yielded not a single important educational idea, not a single well-crafted curriculum. The curriculum debate at Stanford found contending parties unable to appeal to shared conceptions of education; the whole focused around issues of politics, not learning. The universities have simply gone through the motions of a received pattern barely grasped and scarcely understood. We who wish to restore and renew the traditions of learning that made universities important to society have the curriculum pretty much to ourselves.

Why has it happened that a country once proud of its academy turns away in a disgust that even within the academy many find entirely justified. What formerly was beyond price has now become too expensive. What marks the end of the golden age? It is the end of the wish to excel, resulting in the leveling of the academy. When the universities gave up their own standards, then, for the public beyond, academic achievement—research, sifting of received truths, renewal of intellect in age succeeding age through the processes of reasoned criticism—no longer finds self-evident appreciation. And, it goes without saying, no one knows or cares how to order the excellence of universities. Since the substance of learning does not count, age, wealth, and marks of class status (the children of famous people in attendance) mark one college as preferable to another. Brown University in the 1970s would present only the most extreme case of exploiting the presence of the children of the famous: Presidents' children in the freshman class made a rather ordinary and unimportant university into a hot school—for a while.

By our own word, we in universities allege that in the maturing of young people what we teach plays a considerable role, one so critical that parents and society should devote scarce resources to our work with students. But if we cannot explain what we teach and why, provide an account of a well-crafted education, then our word is worthless. But if we claim that we have a solid message to impart, where do we start? It is with a sustained attack on the anti-intellectual view that any opinion is as good as every other one, and that we cannot make judgments as to what is true and what is not true, let alone what is right and what is wrong. In the two decades when no one cared about what is taught—but only about who taught whom—the universities have surrendered to relativism, first moral, then intellectual. That is the view that everything is right for someone, depending on context, and nothing is ever wrong everywhere and all the time. Accordingly, one subject is as good as the next, one opinion as valid as the next, one act as honorable as the next. That has meant universities could not lay claim to reason as arbiter of truth, experiment as test of knowledge, sustained critical inquiry as purposeful in finding out what is so, and what is not. And that accounts for the utter incapacity of the leadership of twenty years to deal with the curriculum. If you don't know what is true and what is untrue, then what difference does it make whether you teach this, that, or the other thing. Everything is equally worthwhile (or worthless). And all that for $25,000 a year.

Indeed, on the campus as we know it, just as the universities cannot tell you what is true and what is false, so they cannot tell you who is sane and who is having emotional problems. When professors are the target, they are at fault. Just as all beliefs are equally valid, so all behavior is equally acceptable. Then the campus in its appeal to reason and rationality (in the form just now portrayed) is unable to say: "You are behaving in an inappropriate way," "This is wrong," "This falls outside the range of correct behavior," or simply, "No." As I found at Brown, psychotic breakdowns, in the classroom and seminar and elsewhere, are not treated as psychotic breakdowns, but as normal behavior. And that brings us to the dirty little secret of the campus—its toleration of lunatics, its inability to protect itself from acted-out insanity. That accounts for the failure not only of intellectual standards, but even of rules of routine civility.

And it explains why, when the students disrupt classes or interrupt lectures with personal attacks on professors, the professors are put on trial, not the students. And, when they are tried, professors do not receive the ordinary protections of due process. On the campus, people do what they want, when they want to; all considerations of fairness, probity, and equity lose currency when professors say what those in charge find intolerable or invoke standards that those in charge (whether students, deans, or other professors) find intimidating. If students fail, it is presumed the professor is at fault, and other professors gladly jump in to impose judgment upon him. When I was at Brown, the then head of the faculty "senate" alleged that by accepting employment at Brown, we professors had voluntarily relinquished the protection of the Bill of Rights and therefore could not claim due process. When I pointed out to him that a case in New Hampshire had explicitly rejected that bizarre opinion, he went on to other business. I found he was just making things up as he went along.

XV. IT'S THE FACULTY, STUPID!

Then who should teach? The right teacher for the university is an active, publishing scholar who also loves to share what he or she is learning, cares that students learn and pays attention to how they progress. The academy in America from the beginning joined two activities—learning and teaching—

in the premise that these ordinarily quite distinct matters form a union that is natural and necessary, because they impart upon one another a character that each on its own must lack. We Americans aver that the best setting for learning is that laboratory and classroom where everybody learns and also teaches, in community and in partnership, if not—in the nature of knowledge—in equality of knowledge. Research that leads to publication but not conversation in a classroom awaits the test of argument, critical hearing, dialectical response. Teaching that does not flow from and toward publication lacks purpose, authority, and conviction. In the former case, the human component is missing from the equation of intellect. In the latter case, the intellectual constituent of the life of learning is lacking. Elsewhere in our own day, as in other times, people do not take for granted that research scholarship is best conducted in dialogue with students, or that learning is best undertaken with scholars. But in our view—a view broadly affirmed as official truth in the golden age of our universities—without the verb *teach*—an active, transitive verb—the object, *what*, loses all context. Without the *who*, the verb dangles. And once we speak of teaching, then the definitions of how the teaching takes place and the goal for which teaching aims also lose all consequence.

Let me make this point concrete. In my experience in research institutes and professorships, particularly at the Institute for Advanced Study in Princeton, 1989–90, and at Clare Hall, Cambridge, University, in the summer semester of 1992, I was struck by the arid and self-absorbed life of those who remained on the permanent staff of research institutes. At IAS I found the permanent "professors" disdainful of the work of others and uninterested in learning from others; but also, I noticed, they did not find themselves driven to share what they knew with others. The social scientists and historians at IAS had all done their best work before they got there, and, palpably and measurably, their own work over time can be shown to have faded into triviality. Reading the writings of permanent staff as these unfolded over the years, both before joining the institute and after arriving, I noticed a decline in vitality and originality—and even in sheer volume. So a life of research divorced from teaching in the social sciences and humanities exacts heavy costs.

True, students take time and often cause worry, but they also lend consequence to the enterprise and impart vitality; they not only ask questions, they force researchers back upon the fundamentals of their work and require that they spell out—for others, therefore also for themselves—the explicit logical steps that have carried them to their conclusions. That is an astringent, if wearing, task, and one that sustains research scholarship. The Institute for Advanced Study, in the area in which I worked, retreated into that same hierarchical snobbery that characterized the declining Ivy League universities in my time, as though self-importance replaced self-criticism, such as research requires. At Clare Hall, much to my surprise, I found equally remote and indeed quite off-putting the resident corps of graduate students who were welcomed into the community of scholars; like the permanent members of IAS, they banded together to the exclusion of the outsiders who had come for a semester; they wanted nothing to do with mature, working scholars. This was particularly striking in the case of young graduate students in English literature who did not wish to pursue conversations with visiting overseas professors expert in the very field of their doctoral dissertations. But the senior members of the Cambridge institute proved remarkably welcoming, not only socially but—more to the point—intellectually. My advice to Clare Hall was to get rid of the graduate students or admit only those with the maturity to benefit from the exceptional opportunities at hand.[11] After a year at the one and a semester at the other, I concluded I should never consider appointment in a research institute; a research professorship is quite a different matter, with none of the disadvantages of appointments solely for research or principally for teaching, but only the advantages of both.

That personal observation may now be stated in more general terms. Were we to frame matters of learning and culture in other terms altogether—assigning priority to the *what* of the academy's mantra, (1) who, (2) what, and (3) to whom, for instance—we should find ourselves analyzing an institution of a completely different character, purpose, and social utility, from the university. Research without teaching takes place in institutes organized for that purpose; teaching without research serves in primary and secondary schools, but not—so we conceive—in universities. And that conviction of ours forms the basis for the indictments of the campuses where research scholars do not teach and teachers do not pursue research, and where the classroom does not define the venue for active learning but for the mere organization and transmission of information to whom it may concern.

Why concentrate on the university's unique union of research and teaching? Severe and legitimate indictments leveled against universities—

---

11. The neighboring universities—Princeton University, Cambridge University—in both cases struck me as quite isolated from the research centers in their midst, with the connections more formal and hierarchical than substantive. I hasten to add that my impressions pertain to the fields of history and social science at IAS and of theology and Oriental languages at Clare Hall; other fields in both places may exhibit different qualities of mind and attitude.

tenure protects sloth, teachers bore, scholarship in the humanities and social sciences masks dissemination of merely personal and self-celebratory opinions—have forced universities to face two tasks in the coming century. The first is to explain to the political community why universities in their present form—places that link scholarship to research and to teaching—should continue to occupy the critical position in the processes of learning, education, and culture that they presently retain. Second, the academy has to make the case for professors' teaching in classrooms, talking to students whom they can know and with whom they can work from day to day—that is, teaching joined to the labor of research scholarship. Television, interactive computers, self-teaching in correspondence courses—these serve up education at a per-unit-cost with which the university in its present definition (education principally through the professor in the classroom) cannot compete. So if cheaper and more effective media for transmitting information serve, then why undertake the costly process of placing a professor in front of students? The answer to that question will settle the fate of the American university as we have known it—and have defined it up to the present time.

In the renewal of higher education, the curriculum demands attention—but only in the context of scholarship, in both publication and teaching. And that means sustained and serious rethinking of what we think and teach, and why it is worthwhile to think and teach what we do, rather than something else. Pioneering in the renewal of what was good, leaders in the renovation and in the innovation in higher learning will win for some universities that paramount position in the intellectual life of this country. These stand as the relics of a discredited age. Where are the leaders of learning in the twenty-first century? The country waits for its future Harvards and Yales and Stanfords (Brown never belonged among them), which led but now lead no more. We do not now know which universities will make themselves great in the coming century, although we anticipate the greatest opportunity awaits the state university systems, not because they have money, but because they follow rules and respond to the public interest. Nothing focuses the mind so well as having to explain one's work to a state legislature or board of regents. Clearly, the now established intellectual bankruptcy at the once prestigious universities represents a great opportunity for a new entrepreneurship in sustained learning, initiatives of the intellect in the free market of ideas. For the opportunity for greatness tomorrow is contained in today's challenge: regain for universities access to intellect, return high ideals of authentic learning to the life of colleges and universities. To teach is to empower students to join in the adventure of discovery—but that is another story, which we plan to tell.

BIBLIOGRAPHY

Baker, Liva. 1976. *I'm Radcliffe! Fly Me!: The Seven Sisters and the Failure of Women's Education*. New York: Macmillan Publishing Co., Inc.

Barzun, Jacques. 1968. *The American University*. New York: Harper & Row.

Bloom, Allan D. 1987. *The Closing of the American Mind: How Higher Education Has Failed Democracy and Impoverished the Souls of Today's Students*. New York: Simon and Schuster.

Bowles, Frank and Frank A. DeCosta. 1971. *Between Two Worlds: A Profile of Negro Higher Education*. New York: McGraw Hill Book Company.

Brint, Steven and Jerome Karabel. 1989. *The Diverted Dream.: Community Colleges and the Promise of Educational Opportunity in America, 1900–1985*. New York: Oxford University Press.

Brubacher, John S. and Willis Rudy. 1976. *Higher Education In Transition*. New York: Harper & Row Publishers.

Carnochan, W.B. 1993. *The Battleground of the Curriculum: Liberal Education and American Experience*. Stanford, Calif.: Stanford University Press.

Cheit, Earl F. 1971. *The New Depression in Higher Education*. The Carnegie Commission on Higher Education. New York: McGraw-Hill Book Company.

———. 1973. *The New Depression in Higher Education—Two Years Later*. The Carnegie Commission on Higher Education.

Clark, Burton R., ed. 1984. *Perspectives on Higher Education*. Berkeley, Calif.: University of California Press.

Conant, James B. 1948. *Education In A Divided World*. Cambridge, Ma.: Harvard University Press.

Coyne, John R. Jr. 1970. *The Kumquat Statement*. New York: College Notes & Texts, Inc.

Curran, Charles E. 1990. *Catholic Higher Education, Theology, and Academic Freedom*. Notre Dame, Ind.: University of Notre Dame Press.

Digest of Education Statistics. 1993. National Center for Educational Statistics. U.S. Department of Education.

D'Souza, Dinesh. 1991. *Illiberal Education: The Politics of Race and Sex on Campus*. New York: Vintage Books.

Freeland, Richard M. 1992. *Academia's Golden Age: Universities in Massachusetts 1945–1970*. New York: Oxford University Press.

Greeley, Andrew M. 1969. *From Backwater to Mainstream: A Profile of Catholic Higher Education*. New York: McGraw Hill Book Company.

Gross, Theodore L. 1980. *Academic Turmoil: The Reality and Promise of Open Education*. Garden City, N.Y.: Anchor Press/Doubleday.

Hall, James W., ed. With Barbara L. Kevles. 1982. *In Opposition to Core Curriculum: Alternative Models for Undergraduate Education*. Westport, Conn.: Greenwood Press.

Hirsch, E.D. Jr. 1987. *Cultural Literacy: What Every American Needs to Know*. Boston: Houghton Mifflin Co.

Jencks, Christopher and David Riesman. 1968. *The Academic Revolution*. Garden City, N.Y.: Doubleday & Co., Inc.

Kaiser, Charles. 1988. *1968 In America: Music, Politics, Chaos, Counterculture, and the Shaping of a Generation*. New York: Weidenfeld & Nicolson.

Kaysen, Carl, ed. 1973. *Content and Context: Essays on College Education*. New York: McGraw Hill Book Company.

Kerr, Clark. 1991. *The Great Transformation in Higher Education 1960–1980*. Albany, N.Y.: State University of New York Press.

Kimball, Roger. 1990. *Tenured Radicals: How Politics Has Corrupted Our Higher Education*. New York: Harper & Row.

Lagemann, Ellen Condliffe. 1989. *The Politics of Knowledge*. Middletown, Conn.: Wesleyan University Press.

Lavin, David E., Richard D. Alba and Richard A. Silberstein. 1981. *Right Versus Privilege: The Open-Admissions Experiment at the City University of New York*. New York: The Free Press.

Magat, Richard. 1979. *The Ford Foundation At Work*. New York: Plenum Press.

Marsden, George M. 1994. *The Soul of the American University: From Protestant Establishment to Established Non-Belief*. New York: Oxford University Press.

McGill, William J. 1982. *The Year of the Monkey: Revolt on Campus, 1968–1969*. New York: McGraw-Hill Book Company.

Morison, Robert S., ed. 1966. *The Contemporary University: U.S.A.* Boston: Houghton Mifflin Co.

Penick, James. L., Carroll W. Pursell, Jr., Morgan B. Sherwood and Donald C. Swain, eds. 1972. *The Politics of American Science, 1939 to the Present.* Cambridge, Ma.: The MIT Press.

Perelman, Lewis J. 1992. *School's Out: Hyperlearning, the New Technology, and the End of Education.* New York: William Morrow and Company, Inc.

Riesman, David. 1980. *On Higher Education.* San Francisco: Jossey-Bass Inc.

Roebuck, Julian B. and Komanduri S. Murty. 1993. *Historically Black Colleges and Universities: Their Place in American Higher Education.* Westport, Conn.: Praeger.

Smith, G. Kerry, ed. 1970. *1945–1970: Twenty-five Years.* San Francisco: Jossey-Bass Inc.

Steinberg, Stephen. 1974. *The Academic Melting Pot.* New York: McGraw-Hill Book Company.

Sykes, Charles J. 1988 *ProfScam: Professors and the Demise of Higher Education.* Washington D.C.: Regnery Gateway

———. 1990. *The Hollow Men: Politics and Corruption in Higher Education.* Washington D.C.: Regnery Gateway.

Wallerstein, Immanuel and Paul Starr, eds.1971. *The University Crisis Reader: The Liberal University Under Attack, Volume One.* New York: Random House.

Wechsler, Harold S. 1977. *The Qualified Student: A History of Selective College Admission in America.* New York: John Wiley & Sons.

NEWSPAPER ARTICLES

New York Times, February 28, 1993. "Colleges Luring Black Students with Incentives."

———, September 1, 1993. "More Young Californians Spurn Their Strained University System."

———, September 18, 1993. "Court Gives M.I.T. Another Chance in a Federal Price-Fixing Case."

———, September 22, 1993. "College for Commuters: Last Car on Early Train."

———, September 25, 1993. "Combating Rape on Campus in a Class on Sexual Consent."

————, October 6, 1993. "California's Budget Cuts Prolong College Careers."

————, December 1, 1993. "Luring Faculty Stars to Teach More."

————, December 12, 1993. "Amid Joblessness, the Joys of Tenure."

————, January 9, 1994. "New Pressures on the University."

————, January 9, 1994. "The Russians and the Poles Are Coming."

————, January 15, 1994. "Women's Colleges Find a New Popularity."

————, March 23, 1994. "Academic Disciplines Increasingly Entwine, Recasting Scholarship."

————, May 1, 1994. "College Seniors Find More Jobs but Modest Pay."

————, May 4, 1994. "College Fund Is Threatened over Speeches."

————, July 6, 1994. "Colleges Caught in Middle as Parents Seek Best Deal."

————, October 2, 1994. "New SAT Sets Students Cramming."

Philadelphia Inquirer, September 4, 1994. "All-female Colleges Staging a Comeback."

St. Petersburg Times, April 15, 1991. "Taking Advantage of the System."

Tampa Tribune, October 2-4, 1994. "2+2: Florida's Failure."

Washington Post, March 13, 1994. "Separatist Movement Spreads to College Dorms."

INDEX